Eleni Gage is the daughter of Nicholas Gage, whose international bestseller *Eleni* told the story of his mother's imprisonment and eventual execution during the Greek Civil War. This is her first book.

www.booksattransworld.co.uk

NORTH OF ITHAKA

One woman's odyssey into her
family's extraordinary past

Eleni Gage

BANTAM BOOKS

LONDON • TORONTO • SYDNEY • AUCKLAND • JOHANNESBURG

NORTH OF ITHAKA
A BANTAM BOOK: 0 553 81596 2

Originally published in Great Britain by Bantam Press,
a division of Transworld Publishers

PRINTING HISTORY
Bantam Press edition published 2004
Bantam edition published 2005

1 3 5 7 9 10 8 6 4 2

Set in Perpetua by
Falcon Oast Graphic Art Ltd.

Bantam Books are published by Transworld Publishers,
61–63 Uxbridge Road, London W5 5SA,
a division of The Random House Group Ltd,
in Australia by Random House Australia (Pty) Ltd,
20 Alfred Street, Milsons Point, Sydney, NSW 2061, Australia,
in New Zealand by Random House New Zealand Ltd,
18 Poland Road, Glenfield, Auckland 10, New Zealand
and in South Africa by Random House (Pty) Ltd,
Endulini, 5a Jubilee Road, Parktown 2193, South Africa.

Printed and bound in Great Britain by
Cox & Wyman Ltd, Reading, Berkshire.

Papers used by Transworld Publishers are natural, recyclable
products made from wood grown in sustainable forests. The
manufacturing processes conform to the environmental
regulations of the country of origin.

To the people of Lia,
past, present and future.

Other countries may offer you discoveries in manners or lore or landscape. Greece offers you something harder – the discovery of yourself.

Lawrence Durrell

CONTENTS

ACKNOWLEDGEMENTS

Thank you to everyone who made my life in Greece full of adventure, full of knowledge, especially my friends and family in Lia, Ioannina, Corfu, Athens, and all over Epiros. And to everyone in the US who shared in my experience, whether they visited, listened to my stories, read my emails, or offered their unsolicited opinions on my stay: my incredibly involved parents, NickGage and Joanie, my fearless sister Marina, the tantalizing trio Katherine, Kay and Arlene, the peripatetic duo Elsa and Anna, the larger-than-life-sized thitsas and their husbands, and the unfailingly supportive Eleni, Efrosini and Themis Nikolaides.

Many thanks to the people who wanted to hear the story of my idyll in Epiros in the first place: Andy McNicol and Joni Evans; and to those who helped share it, including Tracy Fisher and Eugenie Furniss. To Katherine Fausset, Nathan Lump, Natasha Wimmer and my parents for reading early drafts and making invaluable suggestions with as much diligence as if it had been their jobs to do so. And to Doug Young and

Kate Samano for editing the book with as much care and affection as if it had been a friendly favour and not another day at work.

To everyone who offered their support with such generosity, I wish I could give you all a place as exciting and welcoming as Lia to call home.

6 December

I'm trying to crucify three oranges. But I can't work out how to attach the slippery, swollen fruit to the wooden cross without impaling them, which would make juice and pulp spurt everywhere – all over my carefully chosen skirt and on to the stone courtyard, where it would lie in sticky trails and be tracked into the house by my guests.

The thing is, I've never decorated a rooftop cross before. It wouldn't have occurred to me to do so now if Foti hadn't told me, just a few days ago, that in Greece, once the roof of a new house is complete, the chimneys built and the shutters and other finishing touches in place, the owner adorns a wooden cross with oranges and money-filled handkerchiefs, then plants it like a flag on top of her new roof. The workers then complete the ritual by scrambling on to the roof to retrieve their booty, signifying that the house is finished and ready to receive its happy inhabitants.

I had thought a simple housewarming party would do the trick. (That's how I inaugurated my New York apartment, after all, to celebrate my new status as the proud owner of a thirty-year mortgage and a home slightly larger than a restaurant's walk-in freezer.) So I asked Father Prokopi to make an announcement in church last Sunday, inviting everyone in the village to the Gatzoyiannis house for the blessing of the home. Then I heard about this cross. And in the year that I've lived on this mountain top, I've learned that if a ritual exists, it's wise to observe it — otherwise you risk provoking the wrath of fate, the saints, or, worst of all, your fellow villagers.

So yesterday I drove down the mountain to the nearest city in search of handkerchiefs, filled them with twenty Euros each and knotted them on to the cross, which is now leaning against the stone pillar that holds up the verandah's slate roof. Crisp white linen with subtle blue borders, the money-filled handkerchiefs are now waving in the breeze like sails. That was the easy part.

Wire! There's a tangle of wire under the mulberry tree, where the builders must have tossed it. It's going to have to do. I grab the wire and twist it around the cross's arms, then around and around the oranges themselves. No mess, no pulp. Perfect.

Of course, I'm probably doing it all wrong. For all I know, the rusty wire counteracts the good luck of the ritual, for reasons too ancient for me to guess. It's not just a question of a perfectly decorated cross, I think, as I sit on the stone steps to the front door, staring down at the mountain peaks rising like waves in the distance. Maybe renovating this house was wrong in the first place. And the party — a potential disaster! I've been running around to find just the right foil-wrapped sweets for the event, and I never stopped to wonder if the villagers even want to come here, to a place where their friends and relatives were imprisoned, tortured and killed. Thirty-seven of them were buried right here in the yard outside the house.

Legally, I had every right to rebuild this home, which now looks cosy and benign, like the stone cottage of a woodcutter in a fairy tale. Before the Greek Civil War in the late 1940s, my family's house stood on this land, so it's mine to do what I will with. But during the conflict, the Communist guerrillas occupied the village and took over the house as their headquarters. The basement stable, where my family kept sheep and goats, became a jail where the soldiers confined prisoners. Our garden was turned into a makeshift burial ground. The thirty-seven bodies were removed from their shallow graves after the war; neighbours who knew the victims still remember the stench that filled the air.

My grandmother was among the last prisoners kept in the basement, but by the time of her execution the yard was full of corpses, so the condemned were marched to a ravine on the next mountain top to be shot. After the war, the building was abandoned; its roof rotted and the house collapsed in on itself, as if to bury the memories of all it had witnessed. The ruins scared me when I visited the village as a child and haunted me once I left — crumbling piles of rocks that formed visible signs of my family's tragedy. None of my relatives wanted to see the house stand again. My aunts begged me not to move here to reconstruct it, then warned that I'd be threatened by wild animals, homicidal intruders and dark curses if I defied them. Still, I was determined to rebuild the house, both as a monument to my grandmother, and, for myself, as a tangible link to my family's past and our village. I wanted to transform my relationship with our shadowy, sorrowful history from ignorance and fear to something I could understand, or even control.

But in all my planning, I had never envisioned the day when I'd welcome to the house dozens of people who have a much longer history with it than I do — and perhaps an even deeper emotional tie. My guests were children during the war. How will they feel when they see the house that they remember as a prison resurrected as a home? Will they burst into tears, as my aunt did upon seeing it? Or maybe it will inflame old hatreds, jealousies and political schisms, and turn my housewarming party into a screaming fight like the shouting matches I've witnessed over Greek coffee in the kafenion.

I'm probably a fool to be having this party. I wanted to thank the villagers, who have tolerated and fed me all year and taught me their skills, from rolling out filo pastry to picking oregano, from reading the future in coffee grounds to placating angry sheepdogs. But although they welcomed me as an outsider, perhaps they'll resent the way I — a hopelessly citified, twenty-eight-year-old American journalist — have built a home here, reviving a past that belongs more to them than to me, and re-creating a place that symbolizes the village's tragic history. The land may belong to my family, but perhaps this ruin wasn't mine to rebuild.

The cross is ready now. But am I? An old woman hobbles through the gate and towards me, up the stone path leading to the house. She is one of the wizened, fragile widows who live at the other end of the village and only leave their homes for church services and feast days. With her almost translucent skin and halo of white hair, she looks like a cotton puff stuffed into a black dress and kerchief.

'Oh, my child,' she sighs, a tear trickling from one of her turquoise eyes, 'I have memories here, and not just a few.'

1

RESTORATION

«Κάθε αρχή και δύσκολη.»
'Every beginning is difficult.'

My aunts said I'd be killed by Albanians and eaten by
wolves. Of course, that only made me more determined
to go. Determined, but a little wary. Maybe more
than a little. It all started the day after Thanksgiving,
2001.

'Lenitsa, you put on weight?' Thitsa Lilia asked.
Three of my four aunts were sitting at the kitchen table
of my parents' house in Worcester, Massachusetts, eating the leftovers of yesterday's Thanksgiving pies and
scrutinizing me.

'I don't think so,' I shrugged. 'It might be the
sweater.'

'Of course it's the sweater. You got a beautiful
figure, just like your aunt,' said Thitsa Kanta, referring
to herself. She sighed. 'I don't know why you not
married yet – twenty-seven years old and single.'

'Maybe you join the church group when you go back to New York,' Thitsa Olga suggested. 'They got lots of Greek boys there.'

'Maybe,' I answered. There was no point in telling my aunts I hadn't asked for their dating advice. Most people use the term 'Greek chorus' figuratively. Well, I have the real thing, live and in person, a supporting cast made up of my four aunts, Thitsa Olga, Thitsa Kanta, Thitsa Lilia, and Thitsa Tina. None of them is over five feet tall – in fact, they resemble Flora, Fauna, and Merriweather, the fairy godmothers in *Sleeping Beauty*, more than any chorus in a Greek tragedy. But they fulfil the same function: commenting on any action taking place in my life, interpreting oracles, explaining the past, and making predictions for the future.

As I started boiling my Greek coffee in its copper *briki*, my father burst through the kitchen door. 'Look at this,' he gloated, brandishing a black and white photo. In it, my father is thirty-eight years younger and twenty pounds slimmer, standing in front of his parents' house, which has not yet fallen into ruin.

Every year, on my summer trip to Greece, I have faithfully visited the shell of this house, which I thought of as the Gatzoyiannis house, after our original last name. But when the wind blew over the stones, rustling the branches of my grandmother's prized mulberry tree, I wasn't sure if the house wanted me there. The ruins were forbidding, especially when seen through the arched frame of the *exoporta*, the outer door to the courtyard in front of the house. The wood of the door had rotted away, so I could step through the stone frame and on to a path towards nothing, where the house once stood. All that remained was a collection of grim piles of grey stones swallowed by moss, and a

16

rusted metal window frame smothered in swells of ivy.

But in my father's old photo, the house still looked like a home. Rain had damaged the roof in some places, but the outer door was still sturdy, and he leaned against it, smiling, wearing an open-collared shirt and excessive sideburns.

'Wow,' I said, looking up from that tanned young man to my father's face, now covered in a bushy grey beard. 'You look girly. You're so skinny! And that shirt!'

'Not girly,' he insisted. 'Byronic – that's the word you're looking for.'

'Lenitsa, bring that here so your old thitsa can see,' Thitsa Olga demanded.

Staring at the photo, I felt as if a spotlight had been directed on to a dark corner of my mind, revealing the outline of an idea that had been hovering there, indistinctly, for years. I could move to Greece and rebuild the house in the photo, transforming the ruins into a home again, so that if my grandparents' ghosts ever wandered back, they would recognize it as their own. After all, there was nothing to keep me here. As my aunts pointed out, I wasn't married. And I was growing increasingly bored with my little job, my even tinier apartment, and the slow parade of would-be soulmates who marched proudly into my view to the fanfare of trumpets, but turned out to be sweaty and silly when I saw them up close. Lost in my thoughts, I slowly made my way to the table – too slowly for Thitsa Kanta, who grabbed the photo by one of its serrated edges before I sat down.

'Look at NickGage's hair!' crowed Thitsa Kanta, differentiating her brother from her other significant Nick, her son, NickStratis. 'He looks like a drug dealer.

But so handsome!' She sighed. 'Lenitsa, we all old now. Your father, your thitsas.'

'You can see part of the house behind him,' I said, pointing to a small room sticking out to the right of the front door, a little L-shaped addition to the square frame of the grey stone house. 'What's that?'

'That was the *plistario*,' Thitsa Olga said. 'Where we wash ourselves. We fill a water barrel and it had a pipe and a thing at the end where water comes out.'

'A spigot?'

'Yeah, that,' she continued. 'And there was a *fourno* where we cook, roast lamb at Easter. One side of that room was open, with a tin wall for the rain.' I tried to imagine a teenaged Thitsa Olga loading a pan into the beehive oven, her long braids swinging.

'And next to that room?'

'That was the *mageirio*, where we cook in winter,' Thitsa Lilia answered. 'It had a fireplace, where our mother make the cornbread in the *gastra*, that covered tin pot you put coals on top. We had pallets next to the fireplace, to sleep on in spring and autumn. We sleep outside in summer, in the Good Room in winter.'

I knew the house only had four rooms, not counting the basement where the goats and sheep were kept, but my aunts had managed to turn it into a whole country that they journeyed around seasonally, just like their flocks, who had spent summers up on the mountainside and winters down in the valleys. 'And next to the *mageirio*?' I prodded.

'Oh, that was the *palia kamera*, the old, old room,' Thitsa Kanta explained. 'That was the first room, built when my grandparents get married long time ago – 150 years. It was small, just a cabinet and a door to the hallway.'

'So the hallway ran all the way from the front door to the back door?' I asked.

'Oh, yes,' Thitsa Lilia replied. 'Outside the back door was a tree that made so many apricots. Further on we had the chicken coop, past that the outhouse. On one trip from America, Patera brought a toilet seat up the mountain.'

'But we wouldn't sit on it!' Thitsa Kanta giggled. 'We weren't used to it, so we just stand on the seat.'

'When visitors come, we drink coffee in the Good Room,' Thitsa Lilia said. 'It was on the other side of the hallway, opposite the *palia kamera*. On one wall was the fireplace and on the other wall Mana had the iron bed Patera brought set next to the window. You can jump from the bed out the window on to the verandah.'

'Beyond that was the courtyard?' I asked.

'Oh, yeah, it was nice and flat, Patera had it covered in concrete,' Thitsa Olga recalled. 'In summer we bring our pallets and sleep outside, and we hear the shepherds playing their pipes. It was so beautiful! When I think of those times, I cry.'

All three thitsas were misty-eyed, recalling the fragrant apricot tree, the haunting music of summer nights. This was the moment to spring an early Christmas present on them, to turn my hazy idea into an actual plan.

'Guess what! I'm going to quit my job, move to Lia and rebuild the house,' I announced.

'What? You crazy?' Three voices shrieked in unison.

'You gonna get killed by Albanians and eaten by wolves!' Thitsa Lilia wailed.

'Scorpions, they gonna hide on your pillow to bite you!' Thitsa Olga keened.

Thitsa Kanta rose from the table. 'I'm going home

now. I can't listen to this or I get sick – you know I have the acid reflux,' she declared. 'You go back to New York, back to your good job, and when you come home for Christmas, you tell us you changed your mind and you gonna stay right here and find a nice husband.' She strode out of the door, with Thitsa Lilia and Thitsa Olga marching behind her.

I was shocked. The thitsas were always urging me to do Greek things – to date Greek boys, go to the Greek church, then sit around our kitchen table with them, drinking Greek coffee and eating Greek sweets (but not so many that I get fat and repel the aforementioned Greek boys). So when I told them I was leaving my job and apartment in New York and moving to Greece to live in the village where they grew up, I thought they would be delighted. Now I realize I had been as blind as Oedipus.

Over the next month, they continued to raise objections in the shrill, piercing voices they had cultivated shouting to each other across mountain tops back in Greece. Thitsa Olga phoned me to wail, 'Aren't you scared of ghosts? How can you go to that house?' Each time Thitsa Lilia came to my parents' house to watch the Greek TV channels they get via satellite, she casually mentioned the mountain wolves or the desperate Albanian refugees walking across the border and into the village, no doubt in search of Greek–American girls to kidnap for ransom or shoot out of bloodlust. My father was more supportive – he offered to buy me a gun to combat the wolves and Albanians. My mother, who isn't Greek but is easily terrified, worried that as I lay in bed I'd be smothered by falling ceiling plaster, caused by goats jumping off the mountainside on to the street-level roof of my great-grandparents' house, where I planned to live while the renovation took place. Thitsa Tina didn't say anything – as usual, she wasn't speaking to the others as the result of some sisterly squabble – but hers was a disapproving silence. As for Thitsa Kanta, she simply appealed to a higher power: 'I'm praying to God that you'll meet a Greek boy, get engaged and stay here.'

I shouldn't have been shocked by their reaction. The house I wanted to rebuild had been the scene of musical summer nights, but it was also the site of the violence that had shattered their family for ever. My aunts remembered suffering in Lia during the German and Italian invasions of the Second World War, the years of starvation and conflict culminating in the arrival of Greek Communist guerrillas, who occupied the village during the Civil War. The guerrillas sent local women on gruelling work details, trained the girls for combat, and, finally, began to take all the children from their parents to deport them behind the Iron Curtain. The guerrillas were losing the war, but they hoped that if they resettled and indoctrinated the children, and trained them to be soldiers, they might win a larger victory.

After hearing about the deportation plan, my grand-mother and namesake, Eleni, plotted her family's escape. But she was forced to stay behind for a work detail on the June night in 1948 when my aunts and my father, who was then nine years old, fled Lia. They walked down their mountain and across the minefields of no man's land until they reached the Nationalist soldiers' camp up on the next ridge. From there, the children were sent to live in a refugee camp and ultimately sailed to join their father, who had gone to work in America before the start of the Second World War. My grandmother, alone back in Lia, was arrested, imprisoned, tortured, and ultimately executed for planning her children's escape. Along with thirteen others, she was shot by a firing squad in the mountains high above her house; their bodies were thrown into a ravine.

With four of her children in a refugee camp, and one, fifteen-year-old Thitsa Lilia, threshing wheat for the guerrillas in a distant village, my grandmother's final weeks were spent without her family, but in their home. The Communist guerrillas had taken over my grandparents' house, for both practical and political reasons, to use as their headquarters shortly after they arrived. With its four rooms, the house was the largest in the village. But the guerrillas also wanted to punish my grandmother for having a husband who worked in America, so they evicted her and her family. The Good Room became the guerrillas' office and the basement a makeshift jail, where the soldiers corralled prisoners accused of disloyalty, as many as thirty-one at once, crammed in so tightly that they were forced to sleep sitting up, their hands bound in front of them.

It was in the basement of her own home that my grandmother spent her last days, wondering if she would be the next to be called up into the *palia kamera*, the Old Room built for her in-laws' wedding, to be tortured, or taken into the yard to be shot and buried, like dozens of others, under her apricot tree. The entire house bore witness to the inmates' suffering. A teenaged girl escaped from the *palia kamera* by knocking the rusted metal bars out of its old window. The soldiers watched the captives in the basement by looking through a trapdoor in the floor of the Good Room. It was the basement where the prisoners lived in terror and pain, and the basement ruins that frightened me most, even though I swore to my aunts that I wasn't scared. Each time I visited the ruins, I would approach the gaping hole of the foundations, now choked with vines, nettles and scrub pine, and stare through the hollow window casements into the 12-by-15-foot space. I never climbed down into the basement area – it was too overgrown. But when the wind blew down the mountain through the cypress trees around the church of St Demetrios, the moaning sound made me think of the prisoners' cries. I wasn't frightened of wolves or Albanians, but Thitsa Olga was right: I was scared of ghosts.

By now, the house had been empty for fifty years. After the guerrillas retreated behind the Iron Curtain, taking all the surviving villagers with them, the Gatzoyiannis house stood deserted. For a few years after the war it was used by Greek Nationalist soldiers assigned to patrol the Albanian border at the top of the mountain, in case the guerrillas who had kidnapped Lia's children should mobilize forces and return. But by 1953 the fear of invasion had diminished, and the Nationalist soldiers, too, abandoned the house. When my father first returned to visit in 1963, the roof had sprouted leaks. Rain dripped between the slate roof tiles, rotting the wood below so that the roof finally caved in. By the time I saw it as a child, the house had tumbled down.

I knew that my aunts resented their home for turning on them. Their happy memories there were so eclipsed by the tragedy which followed that each insisted, 'I never want to see that house again.' Although the ruins scared me, too, I also felt it wasn't the house's fault. Each time I stood at its shell, surrounded by piles of stones, I sensed that the house had been as much of a prisoner as the people crammed inside. My family's tragedy was compounded by the fact that the home my grandparents had loved was now nothing more than the ruins of a prison. But there was something I could do to make amends. My aunts and father could not be turned back into the children who had jumped on beds and fallen asleep to shepherds' lullabies, but the house could be rebuilt as it was before the war.

My aunts' feelings weren't a factor when I made my impulsive decision; it hadn't occurred to me that they would get so upset. But now, seeing their reaction, I realized I was still determined to go. My father had restored his grandparents' home – the Haidis house – and organized the building of a village inn. But although he'd had an architect draw up plans to rebuild the Gatzoyiannis house of his childhood, he could never bring himself to start construction. I understood my aunts' violent opposition and my father's reluctance – they remembered the site as their mother's prison. But I was convinced that the house needed to be restored to a home.

When it became clear that nothing could stop me, the thitsas became resigned to my leaving. They didn't like it. But since I am as intractable as anyone else from Epiros, our native province, there was nothing they could do. (In Greek, when you want to say someone is stubborn, you call him or her an Epirote-head.) So my worried friends and family tried to take control. They started offering advice. My room-mate in New York suggested that I fill a tin can with coins and shake it at any attacking goats, to scare them away. My mother gave me a keyring which also functioned as a rape whistle and high-powered flashlight. Thitsa Kanta, as concerned with my standing in the villagers' eyes as with my physical safety, said, 'Just dress nicely, and close your windows when you change clothes.'

I nodded at everyone with a smile that meant, 'I'm too nice a person to tell you that you're being ridiculous.' I was sure I'd be safe living in the renovated pink-stone house that had belonged to my great-grandfather, Kicho Haidis. Lia is home to only 140 families, and although there really are both wolves and Albanian refugees, the crime rate is practically zero. This compares quite favourably to Manhattan, even post-Giuliani. And Lia is perhaps the most enchanting place I've ever seen, with a natural beauty so lush and over-ripe that it's almost embarrassing. The steep mountainsides explode with green overgrowth and riots of wildflowers, and in spring enthusiastic mountain streams gush right over the road. It's enough to make you want to tell Mother Nature to rein it in a little; she doesn't need to try quite so hard.

But Lia's dramatic beauty masks a history of turmoil. The village has always been a scene of oppositions. Even geographically, it narrowly missed being split in two. When the borders of Albania were ratified in 1913, the province of Epiros was cut in half. Today one half is in Greece and the other section, Northern Epiros, is Albanian. Lia is on the Greek side, but only just, and when Communism first fell in Albania in 1991, illegal immigrants started escaping over the mountain-top border into Lia, only a kilometre below it, in a constant stream.

My aunts don't care much about borders, treaties or politics. They remember Lia as a place of violent hostility between villagers during the Civil War of 1946–9. The locals were sharply divided in their political loyalties; at my grandmother's trial, some of the villagers testified against her. After growing up and becoming a journalist, my father wrote a book about those years. Like me, the book is named after his mother, Eleni. I had never read it or seen the film based on the book. When my friends discovered that fact, they were always incredulous. 'You're kidding,' they would say. I always answered, 'It just hits too close to home.'

From my childhood, I knew I wasn't prepared to read the story. My family lived in Athens when I was three to seven years old, as my father investigated the events of my grandmother's life and death. I still remember the time a middle-aged man from Babouri, the village next to Lia, stopped by our house, gave me a bar of Ion chocolate, then went into the living room and told my father how he had watched his own parents be tied to a tree and shot during the Civil War. I sat on the stairs, eating the silky chocolate in its red, white and pink wrapper and listening, unnoticed but horrified. I decided then to avoid sad-looking old Greeks and their traumatic memories as much as I possibly could.

After four years in Athens, we moved back to Worcester, Massachusetts, where my father and his sisters had come to join their father, and where they all still lived. By then I had decided that my parents weren't doing a very good job of sheltering me from life's harsher side, and that it was up to me to shield myself from unpleasant realities. I became obsessed with Technicolor movie musicals (and was shocked, shocked! when they didn't have a happy ending – why did no one warn me that the King dies at the end of *The King and I*?). I read all the *Anne of Green Gables* books. And I imagined that when I grew up I would look just like Marcia on *The Brady Bunch*.

But I was also fascinated by the transplanted-Greek-village culture that surrounded me in Worcester. Since my mother isn't Greek, she pointed out that my aunts' quirky habits and superstitions were actually folklore that was passed on through generations and had survived the long boat ride across the ocean. This was my inheritance. I shouldn't hand my aunts soap, scissors or a knife, because that would cause an argument. Occasionally I'd find a putrid garlic clove tucked into the pocket of my good coat, where Thitsa Olga slipped it during church to protect me from the evil eye. And when Thitsa Lilia opened my bedroom door to wave incense around as I studied for my January exams, I knew she wasn't doing it for ambience, but to exorcize evil spirits on St Basil's day.

Always eager to have luck on my side and evil spirits out of my bedroom, I became more intrigued by Greek folklore as I grew older, and often felt torn between two equally compelling realms. I loved the sitcom-safe American pop culture and yearned to be like the blond, well-adjusted icons I admired. But a part of me was irresistibly drawn to the darker mysticism of my aunts' beliefs and customs. Although I never understood the motives behind their machinations, I was intrigued by the rituals themselves. So when I got to college, I put my cultural confusion towards class credits, studying Folklore and Mythology, with an emphasis on Modern Greece. After graduation, I moved to New York and started a career that combined my interest in rituals with my relentlessly optimistic desire to focus on the lighter side of life, writing about celebrities, weddings and beauty products for women's magazines. After five years in New York, I had an apartment, a career, and all the free make-up a girl could ever want. But I knew that, as much as I was steeped in my family's hybrid culture,

I was neglecting a part of our past, a history I had spent years trying to ignore.

So as 2001 ended, I began preparing for my move to Lia. When my friends asked why I was leaving Manhattan for the mountains of Northern Greece, I told them I was doing it for my family, to transform the ruins of past generations into a home for future ones. But the real reason was more selfish. Having spent my girlhood living among my family's ghosts, and my adulthood trying to avoid them, I felt driven to return to the site of my ancestors' home to seek out the ghosts of my past and turn them into protective spirits for my future. I wanted control over a past I couldn't change. And I hoped to integrate the American and the Greek sides of my self into one well-adjusted whole. Of course, I didn't tell anyone that – it all seemed too pathetically earnest, too 1970s-divorcee: 'Yeah, it's real important that I go live on a mountain and find myself.' So I wrapped my earnestness in irony, referring to my plans as 'my little odyssey'. Odysseus had spent ten years after the Trojan War trying to get home to Ithaka, a small island southwest of Epiros; I could take ten months to journey through my family's homeland. My catchphrase worked; most of my friends just assumed I was getting back to my more scholarly roots. And I half-believed it, too.

Still, it was obvious that I had a split personality – at least to anyone who looked at my official documents. My American self, Eleni N. Gage, had a blue US passport that would permit me to live in Greece for only three months without registering as a foreign alien at a police station every so often. But because I had a father born in Greece, I was entitled to a maroon and gold passport as 'Eleni Gatzoyiannis', which would permit me to stay indefinitely. So throughout January, February and March of 2002, I spent at least one morning a week at the Greek Consulate in New York, sighing dramatically as the passport officer informed me of yet more documents that Mr Natsis, the all-powerful official in charge back in Ioannina, required. I had hoped to reconcile both sides of my personality into a well-integrated whole, but I couldn't even get them official identification. 'I'll take my papers and deal with this when I get there,' I huffed to the clerk. Clearly, if Eleni Gatzoyiannis was going to be found, it wouldn't be at the Consulate in New York.

I wasn't surprised by this setback; Greek bureaucracy is notoriously, well, Byzantine. But it forced me to acknowledge that my odyssey might not be all smooth sailing. Walking away from the Consulate, I remembered something from one of my Greek literature classes. In Homer's *Odyssey*, Odysseus gets to Ithaka and is delighted to have reached home. But in Nikos Kazantzakis' retelling, Odysseus finds Ithaka disappointing and feels trapped, wishing he were still at sea. As the weeks sped on, I began to worry that my odyssey would end up a letdown. What if I went to reclaim my Greek past and, after a year of loneliness, didn't like what I found? But it was too late for second thoughts; I had already rented out my room and quit my job, stubbornly eradicating my life in New York.

Then, in the round of medical check-ups I conscientiously scheduled before setting off to the remote mountain village, my doctor found a tennis-ball-sized cyst on my right ovary. This was nothing to worry about, she assured me. Women get cysts all the time. But after my laparoscopic surgery and a biopsy, it turned out that my cyst wasn't a friendly garden-variety growth. It was a low-malignant potential cyst, a rather rare type of tumour that wasn't cancerous, but wasn't completely benign either. A follow-up CT scan showed that I had two small cysts remaining on my ovary. These might just be normal cysts that would clear up on their own, the doctor explained. But if blood tests indicated elevated levels of cancer hormones, that meant they could be low-malignant potential tumours as well, and would have to be removed, delaying my trip even longer.

I was so wrapped up in planning my departure that my medical troubles just seemed like a hassle, an unfair delay. My initial departure date had been 21 March, the fifty-second anniversary of the day my father and aunts had arrived in America. It had all seemed so perfect, so circular, and now my odyssey had been put on hold.

As I waited for the results of my blood tests, I started to grow apprehensive. Trained by my aunts to look for omens, I wondered if this was a sign that they were right, and Lia was somehow inherently evil, a place that brought misfortune to all who lived there – or even contemplated living there. But I could not really believe that the brightly coloured landscape of my childhood holidays, whose electric-blue dragonflies and neon-green chameleons still skittered around in my memory, could be the cause of sorrow.

The Eleni N. Gage who smiled back from my blue American passport knew it was a coincidence that this health problem was revealed just as I was due to leave for my trip – and a lucky one, too, since I was able to take care of it before setting off. If I hadn't caught it, the doctor said, my ovary might have twisted around the cyst and exploded when I was on a mountain top miles from medical care. But the Greek side of me whispered that there are no coincidences. This was the hand of fate trying to keep me away from Lia, from reclaiming my past. It might even be divine irony; the obstacle God sent in response to Thitsa Kanta's prayers for something that would make me stay.

I called my parents to float my theory that if one prays for a man to keep one's niece from going to Greece, God thinks it's hubris and sends a cyst instead. But they found that unlikely. My father explained that the thitsas didn't really want to sabotage my trip, they were just worried about me because of the horrible experiences they associated with Lia. 'We all go to the village in our nightmares,' he said. I knew that. Even I sometimes visited the village in anxious dreams, discovering it as a world I had never belonged to. This was part of the reason I was so determined to see Lia in the stark light of day, to incorporate it into my everyday life, instead of relegating it to vivid memories, hazy dreams, or stopovers between island hopping, short visits that were protected by the unreal enthusiasm of holidays.

The next morning, my doctor called. The tests were good. I was free to go to Greece, as long as I had ultrasounds every few months to make sure that the remaining cysts weren't growing; if they disappeared or stayed small, they were most likely harmless.

I boarded a flight that afternoon. The people around me on the plane shifted their legs over their under-the-seat bags, and complained to the surly stewardess about the lack of blankets. I just sat there grinning. Not my oncologist, not the Greek Consulate, not even the all-powerful alliance of my aunts could keep me from moving to Lia. I was the captain of this ship, and I was about to embark on my odyssey, to become a native in the village of my family's past, and perhaps even change my future.

2

FORWARDS BACK

«Πρέπει να βρέξεις κωλο για να φας ψάρι.»
'You have to get your ass wet to eat fish.'

1 April

I've finally made it to Greece, but what with acquiring a rental car, a Greek cell phone, and a few signed documents from the US Consulate here in Athens, it will be at least a week before I get to Lia and see the ruins that will, I hope, become a house. So I'm forced to settle for the next-best thing: a meeting with the man with the plan, the architect, George Zervas.

He had a set of drawings waiting for me at the hotel when I arrived, with a note saying that after all this time, he was excited about beginning the house's renovation. Actually, it didn't say exactly that. In Greek, there is one word for renovation, and another, αναπαλαίοση, for re-oldation — making something old again. I suppose that's what we're doing — since I can't go back in time, we're bringing the past into the future.

Of course, I've never seen the house standing, so to me it's all new. And Zervas has it all there in the drawing: windows framed by wooden shutters stare out from the second floor, under a sloping slate roof. The old grey stones that once formed the original house are stacked on top of each other again, a freeform puzzle of random shapes. It looks as cosy as a gingerbread house, as strong as the Great Wall. And about as implausible as any other April Fool's Day joke. Maybe if I could get in touch with Zervas, I'd actually believe that re-oldation is possible.

'It's so beautiful!' I exclaimed, as George Zervas unrolled his plans across the lacquered coffee table in the lobby of the Athens Plaza hotel, and made a sweeping gesture with his small, elegant hand. 'I can't wait until it's finished. How long do you think it will take?'

Zervas shrugged, his grey moustache twitching. 'The sooner we get started, the sooner it will be finished,' he replied. 'Beyond that, I couldn't say. Time is just a construct.' He leaned back, the better to expound on his philosophy. 'I've been able to break the boundary of time, like scientists are always trying to do. It's easy – just don't wear a watch!' He added that he also didn't believe in cell phones, computers, or answering machines – anything that allowed the outside world to intrude on his thoughts.

I smiled weakly. If you're about to start a re-oldation project, I suppose you want an architect who doesn't believe in linear time. But I'd budgeted just ten months to oversee the rebuilding of my grandparents' home. A birth only takes nine months; why should a rebirth take much longer? Now that I knew my ethereal architect had broken the boundary of time, I was starting to get nervous.

'The design is so rustic, just like the original house,' I said. 'It can't take that long to stack the stones that way, can it?'

'When you're my age, you realize "long" is a relative term,' the seventy-something Zervas responded in his elegant, reedy voice. 'Not everything is as simple as it seems. Did you know there's not one straight line on the Acropolis? It's all ellipses, parabolas. There were four or five great architects when Pericles commissioned the Parthenon. He chose the design most based on mathematics.'

I'd been to the Parthenon many, many times, and never noticed any parabolas. But I was already finding the rebuilding of our own house to be less than straight-forward. In theory, we shouldn't be planning to rebuild the house at all — like my citizenship, the project was not yet officially recognized by the Greek bureaucracy. First, the plot of land on which the ruins stood had to be legally confirmed as being neither forest land nor an archaeological site. This shouldn't have been difficult to resolve; there are houses above, next to and below the land, and a house had stood on this spot from at least 1870 to 1953. But both the Greek forestry and archaeological services make their own rules. Getting the OK to build a house is like getting into the college of your choice; you need a great application. An engineer has to arrange the required papers into a packet, sign it off; then pass it on to the forestry and archaeological services. These august bodies can then take months, or even years, to approve the plans. Or not. I could only cross my fingers that it would all work out in the hands of an engineer Zervas had recommended.

Zervas, an elfin man whose eyes darted around the room as though looking for a wider audience, could not be bothered to discuss the approval process. He was busy uniting entire planes of thought. 'Architecture is the practical and the spiritual coming together,' he opined, inspired at the thought of the Parthenon. 'It is poetry.'

Knowing more about folklore than architecture, I tried to steer the conversation towards more familiar terrain. 'Do you think we'll find the lost treasure of Ali Pasha when we dig up the ruins of the house?' I asked.

Ali Pasha was the Albanian vizier who ruled Epiros for the Turks from 1778 to 1822. A tyrannical despot, he partied with visitors such as Lord Byron, built mosques, harems and seraglios, and generally menaced the Greek population until he rose up against the Sultan, who, understandably angered, had him shot, then, just for good measure, beheaded. Ali Pasha is said to have buried his ill-gotten gains somewhere in the area he governed – why not my basement?

'Oh, I know where his treasure is already,' Zervas replied, sipping his coffee. 'It's in Ioannina, in the old city, but not at his palace. I used a divining rod to detect it.'

I was only slightly surprised that Zervas, who lived in his own surreal world, had treasure-dowsing powers that matched his skill at outwitting time. 'Then what?' I asked. 'Did you dig it up?'

'Oh, no. If I had wanted to dig it up, I would never have found it,' he explained patiently. 'So many others have tried to find it, to profit from it, and failed.'

This logic sounded as circular as the walls of the Parthenon. If he'd found the treasure of Ali Pasha, shouldn't the government be notified? 'Don't you want to be sure you're right?' I asked.

Zervas shrugged. 'Ali Pasha cursed the treasure so it moves when you try to unearth it,' he explained. 'That's the legend, anyway. Some men dreamt that they had found the treasure, so they went to the place they saw in their dreams and dug until they came upon a large chest. They slid ropes under the trunk, then climbed out of the pit to pull it up. But as they tugged, the rope snapped. "No matter," said one man. "We'll come back tomorrow night." But when they did, there was no trunk, no pit, no ropes. It was all gone.'

Zervas hugged me goodbye and started strolling towards the thick glass of the lobby door, about to pull his own disappearing act.

'Wait,' I called after him. 'When are you coming to Lia?'

He pivoted. 'You find the workers, sign a contract for the house, then I'll come. Just call when you need me. Who knows what buried treasure we'll find?'

His smile was so encouraging, it wasn't until he was gone that I realized I couldn't call him once I'd assembled a team; he never answers his phone. I was raring to go and my architect was as elusive as Ali Pasha's legendary treasure. But at least he was excited about the rebuilding, which was more than I could say for the seventy-something crowd in America. In fact, all over Athens, I was getting kudos from strangers who were as astonished as my thitsas at my plans, but much more encouraging. 'Bravo! An Athenian girl would never go and live for a year in a village,' a taxi driver commended me when I told him my plans. 'I wish I could return to my village on Zakynthos, but I made a mistake I'll pay for for the rest of my life. I married the wrong woman. Now we're divorced, I can no longer fish with my father. I drive this stupid cab to pay her alimony.'

During the rest of the ride to the car-rental office, the cabbie proved to be as chatty as he was bitter. He was typical of his countrymen in his longing for his lost home. The concept of a natal village occupies a major place in the Greek psyche. It is the alpha and the omega, the beginning and the end, both in theory and in practice, because the village is where many Greeks were born before they moved to a big city, and also the place they hope to retire to, eventually to die and be buried there. This is a Greek's cherished goal, to lead a life that ends up where it began, that is not a straight line but more of an ellipse.

Since wars and industrialization drove Greeks into cities in the middle of the last century, fewer and fewer people are born in a village. But even those who have been born in a city return to their families' villages for holidays, hence the huge traffic jams at Easter, when everyone streams out of Athens. Of the almost 11 million people living in Greece, 4.5 million of them live in Athens. But their natal village is one key to their identity, something that distinguishes them from the other tenants in their high-rise apartment building. Are they Epirotes, stubborn, fair-haired people who cook pitas (filo-pastry-covered pies)? Are they Corfiotes, musical and easy-going? Or are they dark-haired and adept at fortune-telling like the Anatolian Greeks from Asia Minor?

Geography isn't destiny in Greece any more than anywhere else, but people seem to find comfort in these stereotypes, to want to celebrate regional individuality even as they live in the European Union. Everyone wants a place to consider home, somewhere that represents a romanticized past. According to a Greek song about *xeniteia* – life in a foreign place – 'The bread of exile is bitter.' But as villages today are depopulated, most Greeks live in a kind of exile from their village. Although they may really prefer the comforts of their city apartment, they pay homage to their village as having the purest air, the cleanest water, even a key to their own personality. This is why urban Greeks return to their villages in summer, or leave their children there on holiday with grandparents. And it is why I was moving to Lia.

By the time the cabbie dropped me off at the car-rental office, it wasn't my village I was concerned about, but the car that would bring me home. There she was, a silver Hyundai Accent, the only automatic the company had. (I can't drive a manual car, a major handicap in Greece.) I named her 'Asymina' – Silver One – because of her colouring. I should have named her 'Asyminoula', because she was compact and adorable and I knew the intense Greek passion for cuteness. Everybody and everything that is good in the world gets a nickname formed by adding a diminutive ending to the existing word. At a petrol station, the attendant confided he had trouble with the 'Roulas. 'The what?' I asked, thinking perhaps he was dating twins, say, Stavroula and Dimitroula. 'You know, the Evroulas? The new currency?' Of course! The petite and personable Euro!

I drove Asymina past the urban sprawl of Athens to Rion, where I backed her on to the ferry to go across to Antirion as twenty Greek men shouted advice. It was too early in the year for tourists, so sailing with me were a rowdy soccer team, a gypsy playing a guitar and an old woman sitting under a poster showing the Euro denominations and the slogan, 'The Euro: Currency of a United Europe – Get to Know It!'

Back on dry land, I drove through mountains and

fields, past fish farms and tavernas covered in wisteria. As the seven-hour trip stretched on, I began to have some doubts about my mission. What if Zervas never showed up in Lia? What if the car broke down and I had no idea what to do with it? And where was I supposed to find workers for the house?

I found myself desperately looking for omens, but all I saw were dramatic road signs, which had no words, just pictographs that could be understood by any citizen of a United Europe. They were yellow triangles bordered in red with a black image in the middle showing, say, a black sheep, a curve, a skidding car, a cow, or a silhouette of a man walking across the highway with his arms akimbo, signifying, perhaps: 'Disoriented old people cross at random here.' In extreme circumstances the highway patrol lined several signs up in a row, with one exclamation point at the top and another at the end, as if to say, 'Careful! You might skid around this curve and send a black sheep flying into a disoriented old person crossing the highway at random. So watch it!'

As the shadows lengthened across the road, I realized it was too late to worry about my future. I was already there, at the bridge over the Kalamas River, the turning-off point for Lia. I was entering deepest Epiros. After the Iron Curtain closed, its proximity to Albania made Greek Epiros a political hotspot. When my mother first visited Lia in the sixties, it was in an area known as 'the Forbidden Zone', and as a non-Greek she had to get special permission to cross the Kalamas after passing through a military checkpoint. I was born in 1974, the year they dissolved the Forbidden Zone, so to me it all sounds very sexy, like the lambada, the Forbidden Dance. And the area still has a bit of an off-limits, Forbidden Zone feel. Border guards sometimes wait at the foot of the bridge, scouting for cars ferrying illegal immigrants from Albania, and camouflaged sentry posts flank the river. When I turn on to the road that winds up the mountains to Lia, I have the sense I'm going where not many people have gone before, to search out new worlds.

Lia sits on a remote mountain in Epiros, the most remote province of Greece. The name comes from the word *apeiron*, 'infinity', which may be a reference to the seemingly endless rows of mountains reaching to the sky. Lord Byron, who visited in 1809, wrote that other regions of Greece were 'eminently beautiful', but were 'nothing to Epiros, where places without a name, and rivers not laid down in maps, may one day when more known be justly esteemed superior subjects for the pencil, and the pen'.

The admiration is mutual; Lord Byron is beloved by all Greeks. But while history proved him to be a great Philhellene, it has shown him to be a lousy soothsayer in predicting Epiros's tourist boom. Epiros is still the least urbanized, least-touristed region of Greece. It was also the last province to win independence from the Ottoman Empire – in 1913, after 460 years of Turkish domination. When my grandfather set sail for America in 1910, he threw his hated Turkish fez into the ocean. He was inspired to go abroad for work as a teenager, after meeting an Epirote in a three-piece suit that the well-dressed man said he'd bought in a place called 'Ameriki'. My grandfather had left Lia itself at the age of nine, to work as a travelling tinker's apprentice, in 1902.

Now, one hundred years later, I was staring at a sign that read 'Lia, 24 km', feeling as if I was almost home.

Most foreigners imagine Greece as a scattered chain of islands, with whitewashed houses rising like opals from volcanic cliffsides. But for me, Greece will forever be this tiny village of waterfalls gushing over mountain paths, and grey stone houses balancing on sloping hill-sides against a background of ever-shifting shades of green. I drove up the winding road, flanked by waves of hunter-green mountains occasionally punctuated by clusters of houses, bright lavender Judas trees, and herds of rowdy sheep so woolly they looked as though they might bounce down the mountain if pushed. When I drove through a village, the sound of my car lured curious children out of doorways, and old men in coffee shops turned to look up from their backgammon. I noticed the crushed carcass of a truck that had rolled off the road, sticking out of the mountainside like the gnarled trunk of an olive tree, and I zoomed past a shepherd woman chatting away on a cell phone.

Finally, after endless hairpin turns, I spotted the sign that says 'Entering Lia. Welcome to our hospitable village.' I drove through the village as the sun began to set, softening the sharp contrast between the blue of the sky, the dark green of the mountains and the early, lime-green leaves of the trees. As I passed the playground and the Xenona inn, which had not yet opened for the season, I rolled down the window in order to smell the village air, a scent I associated with woodsmoke, fragrant earth, and herbs we didn't have back in the US.

I continued on to the town square, bordered by the *kafenion*, the church of the Agia Triada (Holy Trinity) and the stone building where my father went to school, which now holds offices for the village and the border police. During the Civil War, a man had been tortured to death in that building, I remembered, and I sped on, through the heavy mist, turning past the Goura, a spring covered by a plane tree so old it has been declared a national monument.

Then I arrived, stopping on the road above the roof of the Haidis house, where my great-grandfather, Kicho Haidis, had lived, and where I would stay while rebuilding the Gatzoyiannis house. I parked under a walnut tree, behind an old white van used by the neighbours, Dina and Andreas, who are travelling fabric salesmen. Είδη προικός, it said in block letters on the back door. 'Dowry supplies': everything a woman needs to get set up in her new life. A good omen, I told myself, trying to forget about the haunted schoolhouse and the fact that I'd be living in the house below all alone.

The van was parked on the main road. You could drive along this road for miles without seeing another car, but in Lia it was the equivalent of a major highway, and the first horizontal road in town. When my father left in 1949, he had never seen a wheeled vehicle; people didn't use them, because they climbed up footpaths dug into the mountainside like scars. A vertical village, Lia grew from the top down. Sitting in the centre of the Mourgana range, it wraps itself around the necks of two grey and green mountains. From the abandoned border-guard station above town, you can scale footpaths up to either peak. At the top of the shorter path is the church of Prophet Elias, the patron saint of the village. Near the peak of the other is Kastri, where the walls of a *kastro*, a castle dating from the third century BC, rise in massive blocks of crumbled majesty.

The Greek archaeologist Sotirios Dakaris suggested that the *kastro* and the civilization that surrounded it linked a chain of Hellenistic cities; a signal fire lit at one *kastro* would be visible to the soldiers in the next. This early telegraph system probably worked until the city was destroyed in AD 167 by the armies of the Roman general Aemilius Paulus. Like so many generals, Aemilius Paulus had serious anger-management issues. In one day of his rampage, Plutarch writes, 150,000 Epirotes were enslaved and seventy cities were levelled. I hoped my stay in Lia would be less action-packed.

According to some historians, Lia was founded in its current location in the mid eighteenth century, when villagers from a settlement known as Maleshovo moved up the mountain and joined disheartened refugees moving down it to form a community. At the time, all of Epiros was part of the Ottoman Empire. In the mid 1700s, local Turkish officials notified villagers in the town of Agios Panteleimon that they would have to convert to Islam to retain their property. They fled, and those non-converts were the first immigrants to Lia. A hundred years later, emigration from Lia became the norm. Men left the rocky village to work as travelling tinkers, going from village to village to repair pots and pans, or found jobs abroad, returning once a year or once a decade to father children. Their wives and families awaited them, sometimes too trustingly; one woman waited for her husband for seventy years, until her death. In the meantime, he had started another family in America.

As an American of Liotan descent moving back to Lia, mine was the only case of reverse immigration I could think of – a person who had never lived in Lia moving to the village instead of away from it – as I unloaded my oversized wheeled suitcases from Asymina. I dragged them down the main road, which bisected our neighbourhood into two sections I liked to call uptown and downtown. The entire neighbourhood was known as

Motsala, after the spring which gurgles out of the mountain just outside the outer door to the Haidis house. My grandmother, then Eleni Haidis, grew up in this house. At nineteen, she was working in the garden by the spring when a thirty-two-year-old visitor strolled up the path and noticed her. A fruitseller from Worcester, Massachusetts, he was wearing a really great-looking suit. He would soon become her husband, continuing to work in the US and visiting her in Lia every few years.

The Haidis house was where I was planning to live while rebuilding the uptown Gatzoyiannis home. A two-storey building with a courtyard made of pink stone, the Haidis house still had its original grey keystone over the door. It read «Κόπιασε, φίλε,» 'Rest, friend,' and it must have had magical powers of attraction, because by the time I'd lugged my bags down the steep path, I already had my first guest. Dusk was falling and the house was rapidly veering from cosy to gloomy, so I was delighted to see Foti Tsandinis at the door. He once owned a pizza place outside Worcester, and I recognized his shiny pate and tiny blue eyes. When Foti's wife was diagnosed with cancer, she quit chemotherapy and came to Lia with her husband to live out her remaining two years. Now a widower, Foti was president of the group of Liotes who ran the Xenona inn. As if to advertise that he had lived in America, Foti was wearing an all-denim ensemble – jeans, denim shirt stretched over his ample paunch, and denim jacket, accessorized by a leather cap, as it was still chilly.

'I thought I'd see how you're doing,' he said, kissing me hello. 'I promised your aunt I'd keep an eye on you.'

That explained how he had found me like a heat-seeking missile the minute I arrived. This was the work of my Thitsa Kanta. Her husband, Thio Angelo, was the brother of Foti's deceased wife, so they were related by marriage. Furthermore, when these senior citizens were children and Thitsa Kanta and Thitsa Lilia were too tired to herd their sheep up the mountain, Foti, a shepherd boy who was even poorer than they were, would do so in exchange for bread. Now, seventy years after watching over Thitsa Kanta's sheep, Foti felt responsible for herding her misguided niece.

'Great!' I exclaimed, although I was annoyed – not so much that Thitsa Kanta was checking up on me, but because I was so pathetically glad to have company, even though I had no idea what to say to this man. So, like a good Greek hostess, I quickly offered to make him some coffee.

Unfortunately, the stove had other ideas. Although the lights went on, the burners did not heat up. Glad to see that his presence really was needed, Foti looked at the fusebox and flipped a switch. Suddenly we were enveloped by the same darkness that shrouded the two empty houses in the neighbourhood.

I soon realized that although the house had a large decorative candle, I had no matches. Then I heard footsteps on the road above. My uphill neighbour, the elderly church cantor Spiro Karapanos, was enjoying his evening stroll. I called out to him and he threw down a lighter. With his white hair, round glasses and sports jacket, Spiro looked like a university professor, but he was actually a retired railway worker and knew a thing or two about fuses.

He ambled down, handed me a bouquet of purple wildflowers, flipped the fusebox back on, then moved on to the stove. Spiro seemed on the verge of identifying the problem when Foti invited me into the courtyard to admire the stars. Obediently I followed, but I manoeuvred us back inside just as Spiro was wrapping up the stove's shredded electrical cable, chewed through by a greedy mouse. Apparently, Foti had been trying to distract me from seeing a roasted mouse carcass. Although my aunts were oceans away, it seemed I now had some overprotective new uncles. I tried to let that thought comfort me as Spiro and Foti ambled away into the darkness and I plugged in my electric radiator, and settled down to bed.

That's when it started – a scrabbling noise like the rolling of hundreds of dice. It must be the goats on the roof that my mother had warned me about, I decided. Why hadn't I taken Foti up on his-invitation to stay in his spare room? I rose from the bed, my flashlight/rape whistle in hand, and opened the door to the outside. There was no one in my courtyard, no goat on the roof, and the street above the house was still and dark. I felt as though I was the only person in the world, which would explain why the blinding moon was so intent on shining down on me. Then I heard it again: a cavalcade of scraping and thumping. The noise was coming from inside the ceiling. Anything that could fit in there was too small to hurt me, I reasoned. And maybe the noise would keep away ghosts.

The next morning, the sky was the clear, bright blue of the ceilings of some Greek churches, and as the clouds rolled off the road in smoky wisps and settled into the valley below, I felt full of energy, relieved to be alive. So I drove up to the neighbourhood of Perivoli, where my grandparents, aunts and father once lived.

The term 'high-rise' takes on an entirely new meaning in Lia. The area of Perivoli – 'the Orchard' – is a literal embodiment of the phrase, at the halfway point between the neighbourhood of Mesochori – 'Middle Village' – which is a measly 675 metres above sea level, and the *kastro* at the top of the mountain. Perivoli's landmark is Agios Demetrios, a grey stone church ringed by towering cypress trees. A few metres up from Agios Demetrios are the remains of my family's home. Although it was eerie and abandoned, the ruined building had an overgrown cragginess I'd always liked. But today, staring at the gorgeous decrepitude, my early-morning confidence crumbled too and I wondered if I should let sleeping shells of houses lie. Maybe it was naive to reconstruct a house where so many had suffered and died, to try to wrap our family history up into a Technicolor happy ending. In the clear light of morning in Lia, my plan to reclaim my Greek past seemed presumptuous. So American.

I was still questioning the wisdom of my odyssey when I arrived back at the Haidis house to find that my neighbours, Dina and Andreas, had returned from a dowry-selling trip and visiting their grandkids. It was a second marriage for both of them; each had two children from their first marriages. Several years ago, Dina's son died in a car crash, and last summer, in a coincidence that shows fate's cruel lack of imagination, Andreas's son was also killed in a car accident. Today, the couple still wore black mourning clothes. Dina, a handsome, middle-aged woman with chestnut hair pulled tautly into a ponytail, brought some pita – savoury stuffed pie – over for me. She told me that Marianthe, a friendly old lady who lived near the Xenona, recently lost her son to a heart attack, and that her husband died of cancer and grief fifteen days later. Dina's grandson had played with Marianthe's granddaughter last summer. Dina had told her eleven-year-old grandson that his friend had lost her dad, too, and he replied, 'She has the same black fate I do.'

When I was eleven none of my fellow sixth-graders worried about fate. But the belief in fate is so prevalent in Greece that it has even shaped the language: τύχη, which means 'luck' or 'fortune', is the root of many words, including 'success' (επιτυχία), 'failure' (αποτυχία), 'happiness' (ευτυχία) and 'misery' (δυστυχία). The word τύχη itself comes from the goddess Tyche, who had the power to determine men's fortunes. According to Robert Graves's The Greek Myths, 'Tyche is altogether irresponsible in her awards, and runs about juggling with a ball to exemplify the uncertainty of chance: sometimes up, sometimes down.'

Dina's examples of unfair, tragic fates in the village filled me with apprehension. I could have been drinking with my friends at the wine bar near my apartment in New York instead of listening to a catalogue of recently deceased Liotes and their bereaved loved ones. Was it possible that the villagers shared an unlucky fate, and if they did, was I making myself part of that dark future? As for my present, it was looking increasingly bleak. I didn't even have a working stove.

But Dina invited me to dinner that night and I soon learned that if the people of Lia were overly cursed with tragedy, they were also blessed with an acute ability to enjoy life's small pleasures: everyday blessings such as savoury food, strong wine and the company of friends. Dina and Andreas lived across the path from me, in a whitewashed house that Andreas had expanded from a one-room shack into a village compound. It had a complex irrigation system to water the garden and feed two pools: one for a fish hatchery and the other for their grandchildren to swim in when they visited. It also had a greenhouse, a grape arbour, a man-made waterfall, a tin roof (because Andreas liked the sound it made when the rain hit it) and, that night, a fire in the fireplace.

Crowded around the table with us were Dina and Andreas's yapping Pekinese, Ruda, and two strangers with faces that were almost as round and well scrubbed as our dinner plates. Dina introduced us. Also new immigrants to Lia, the men were Albanians, a father-and-son team who lived in Dina and Andreas's freestanding extra room next door. They were working around Lia in the hope of earning enough money to bring over the rest of their family: the mother, Xalime, and single youngest daughter, Dorina. Vladimiros, the father, was in his forties, with elegant mannerisms and a good command of Greek, although he tended to mix up genders, much to everyone's amusement. Netvil, the son, was fifteen, and was known as Net.

'I'm going to baptize Net this summer,' Dina announced. The boy blushed. He and Vladimir were Muslim Albanians, unlike the ethnic Greeks living in Albania, who are called Northern Epirotes and are Orthodox Christians. 'He insisted only I could do it,' she confided. The only problem, Dina said as she pivoted between the stove and the table on which our plates were set, was that Net didn't want to change his name, but you need the name of a saint to be baptized in the Orthodox Church.

I was so pleased to be eating with people instead of sitting hungry and alone across the street that I was determined to help. 'What about Nectarios?' I asked, digging the obscure saint from deep in my memory bank.

'Great!' said Andreas, who, despite a certain lack of teeth, retained the wiry, tobacco-riddled good looks of a retired Marlboro Man. 'Net – ladies love that name.'

Net seemed pleased with his new Christian name, and I was feeling optimistic, too. The neighbourhood was more populated than I had thought, offering some protection from wolves, refugees and loneliness. And maybe fate sent these men my way on purpose. Zervas had told me to find workers for the house, and Vlad and Net needed jobs – I could hire them, at least to dismantle the ruins so we could recycle the stones.

As we drank vast quantities of wine and *tsipouro* (the homemade moonshine favoured by Vlad and Andreas), and ate roast chicken, I asked Dina how she had met Andreas.

'At thirteen I married a man my parents chose, then I had two kids, and got divorced,' Dina began, tossing her ponytail. 'By seventeen, I was single and living with my parents and children in Lamia. Andreas sold fabric and he kept coming around to the spring where we women would wash our clothes.'

'I gave her some material for a dress, you know, to make an impression,' Andreas interjected.

'He kept hanging around me, and I got embarrassed and worried about what people might think.' Dina shrugged. 'So I married him.'

Thirty-three years later, the match seemed to be working out. Dina and Andreas formed the social hub of the neighbourhood, being among the youngest of the few families who live in Lia year round. Over dinner, we made plans: trips to take, festivals to attend, meals to cook, schemes that got more outlandish as the moonshine diminished.

Finally I walked back across the way, only to discover that whatever lived in my ceiling was having a dinner party just as raucous as the one I'd left. The next day Net crawled into the attic to evict my uninvited guests. He pulled himself through the trapdoor in time to see several squirrels scurry out – just as an electrician from Ioannina arrived to fix the stove.

Those first few weeks, when I wasn't fighting vermin or unpacking, I hung out at the *kafenion*, the unofficial head-quarters of any Greek village. A *kafenion* always contains a TV tuned to the news, sports, or a beauty pageant, a freezer full of ice cream, and lots of old men playing cards and debating loudly. Ours also had some groceries for sale, a potbellied stove in the middle of the room, a potbellied owner married to a petite Northern Epirote sylph named Stella, and their dervish of an eight-year-old son, Costa. It was frequented by a gang of regulars, including a friendly, kerchiefed, toothless lady who had had a daughter thirty-odd years ago but never had a husband. Self-propagating, like Zeus from whose head Athena sprang, she had crossed the gender divide and spent her days sitting in the *kafenion* with the men, while the rest of the women worked.

The *kafenion* was Lia's business and commercial centre. On Mondays, Wednesdays and Fridays, at about ten a.m., the postman came to have a coffee and pass out the mail. Although the population of Lia swelled to about three hundred in summer, in winter there were only about fifty full-time residents, and Liotes who were in the *kafenion* collected mail for their missing neighbours; in any case, the village was too small to have street names, so home delivery was not an option.

The postman was in his late thirties, dark-haired, handsome and well liked, but overshadowed by the blonde doctor who came on Tuesdays and Fridays.

Greek medical residents are required to spend a year doing an agricultural rotation, and this was hers. She managed to fill prescriptions, listen to complaints and look sexy in her tight jeans all at the same time, and was therefore justly revered. I imagined that she and the postman, who overlapped on Fridays, were involved in a passionate affair, because he always smiled shyly as he handed her rolled-up copies of *Agricultural Doctor* magazine as if they were long-stemmed roses. But this could just have been a figment of my scandal-starved imagination as I went through gossip-column withdrawal.

On Sundays there was church, of course, but since the village has four churches and just one priest, who was also responsible for two other towns in the tri-village area, we waited to hear the church bells ring to learn where the service would be held. On Thursdays and Saturdays there were no scheduled activities, but Lia had plenty of unplanned visitors, like the gypsies who drove through town in their trucks, hawking everything from live chickens to plastic tables, blasting Greek tunes over loudspeakers.

Slowly I adjusted to the daily rhythm of the village. There was so much to do getting settled that my mood swung constantly between excitement and frustration, pride and anxiety. During the day, I tried to wrest control of the house from squirrels and ants, or worked in the garden I was planting, with Dina's help, on the four small terraces that climbed up the courtyard wall. A hopeless city girl, I would ask questions like, 'So, tomatoes grow above ground, not underground?' But Dina didn't laugh; she just showed me how to place seeds deep into holes in the soil, then surround them with *kopria*, goat dung she buys from a shepherdess named Iphigenia. She was so confident that the garden would be a success that she suggested that we plant a clove of garlic, just in case, to ward off the evil eye attracted by the admiration and jealousy of passers-by on the road above.

I also spent time entertaining unexpected visitors who arrived in a steady stream, bearing gifts of homemade pita or bread. I don't know whether they assumed that, as an American, I was inherently unable to cook, were glad to see a young person in the village, or were just curious about the newcomer. But my aunts had taught me my duty as a hostess, so I kept a doily-covered tray at the ready, and on it I would serve coffee, water or juice, and spoon sweets that a kind neighbour had given me. Spoon sweets are candied fruits or fruit rinds preserved in their own gelatinous juices. They must be difficult to make, because homemade ones are always served with great pride, so although I find them cloying, I always force myself to eat a few bites.

Once the kind, gossipy, bread-bearing ladies had gone home to cook dinner, I would sit on the verandah watching the sunset. As dusk fell I would stare at the horizon, missing my aunts and even the grandmother I never knew, wishing they were here to enjoy the beauty of a place that to them was steeped in trauma. With mountains all around, the sunset wasn't a ball of fire flaming out on the horizon, just long, slow, quiet shifts of light and expanses of pink in the distance. In New York, surrounded by high-rises, I never saw the sunset. On my verandah in Lia, with a view that stretched for miles in all directions, I could almost convince myself I belonged here.

After dark, I would go out in search of dinner, usually to Dina and Andreas's, where every meal was a masterpiece. A few times a week I would join Foti and a gang of garrulous local men to drive along the hazardous mountain roads to tavernas in neighbouring villages. My favourite nightspot was Louie's Grill in the diplomatically named village of Agii Pantoi – All Saints. Another reverse immigrant, Louie had spent eleven years in Australia before returning to open a taverna, where he served his own wine, squirted into carafes from a Poland Spring water dispenser. His taverna was decorated with wall plaques, each bearing the face of a philosopher and a couplet about the great thinker's relationship to wine, such as, 'They all had lots of ladyfriends,/ten or twenty-five/But Plato who didn't drink at all,/He had only . . . five.'

On these nights of booze and lamb chops I realized that in the winter and early spring, the village is a cross between a gentlemen's club and a retirement home. Every night, men between the age of fifty and – well, I don't know, but my great-uncle lived to be 107 – pile into cars and go to a taverna, where they eat fried cheese, drink moonshine and insult each other happily. Their wives are either dead, in Athens babysitting the grandkids until term finishes, divorced (in one rare case) or at home doing something useful. It is an exact reversal of Lia's pre-war situation, when the village was filled with women raising children, and the men were all off working in Athens or America.

Two weeks after I arrived, Foti called with a late-breaking bulletin: the Xenona was open. I drove over and introduced myself to Nikki and Fanis, the new innkeepers. Nikki told me she was born in Lia, but left as a teenager, moving to Germany to live with her sister. In Germany she met and married Fanis, another Greek immigrant, a truck driver turned businessman, and together they had lived all over Africa before moving to Athens when their children were ready for high school. Now their children were married, Nikki and Fanis had come back to her village and rented the inn. With their smattering of German and English, they were determined to turn a profit by increasing visitors to Lia, which normally attracts outsiders only on major holidays and in the hunting season.

'Africa – how exciting!' I exclaimed.

'It was,' answered Fanis, who was tall and debonair, with impeccable posture. 'I'll tell you a secret if you promise not to tell anyone else – they'll never believe me.' I nodded and he leaned forward. 'Once, in South Africa, I danced with Elizabeth Taylor. It was a fancy dinner party and she grabbed my hand and pulled me to the dance floor, saying, "Come here, Zorba."' He sat back and smiled.

'Is that why you came back?' I asked Nikki, a no-nonsense woman with short, reddish hair and toffee-coloured eyes. 'So Fanis wouldn't run off with Elizabeth Taylor?'

'No,' Nikki laughed, looking up from the sink. 'We moved to Athens so our children could grow up in Greece. And we came here because – well, this is home. My brother lived in South Africa too, but when he was dying of cancer, he asked to be brought back to Lia. As soon as the ambulance crossed the border from the next village, he died.' She nodded, proud of her brother's stubbornness and excellent timing. 'There's a shrine erected to him right on that spot.'

Now I understood why no one here seemed surprised that I, too, had made my way back to Lia. My friends thought I was quixotic, adventurous to move to this tiny village; my family thought I was crazy. But not one villager had asked what I was doing here, and I loved no longer having to explain myself. The Liotes simply took it for granted that I would want to be here, where my family began.

After a few weeks, I had to trek to Ioannina, the nearest city and the capital of the province. Built on a lakefront at the foot of several mountains, Ioannina seemed partly caught in a time warp still inhabited by Lord Byron and Ali Pasha. The old section of town, known as the *kastro*, contains Turkish houses and mosques-cum-museums whose minarets rise above the Byzantine city walls. Outside the *kastro* are streets of wooden buildings filled with silversmiths and stores selling *bougatsa* – cream- or cheese-filled pita – and beyond that is a tangle of modern apartment buildings, cafés and shops. An hour from Lia, Ioannina was my urban centre, and home to our family friends George and Kaity. My father is their son's godfather, so we are related in the eyes of the Church. They were ecclesiastically bound to help me with the annoying tasks of relocating.

Shortly after I arrived, George took me to see Mr Natsis, the passport official/puppetmaster who had made me run all over Manhattan to gratify his bureaucratic whims. Natsis had recently decided that I had to sign, in front of him, a statement expressing my desire to become a Greek citizen – those that had been faxed from the Consulate in New York were irrelevant. So George and I typed one up and arrived to find Natsis stooped over coffee in a tiny room littered with folders. It was like seeing the Wizard of Oz behind the curtain. This little bald man had made me, and all five marble floors of the Greek Consulate in New York, tremble?

Natsis glanced up from his folder. He looked like a typical Greek civil servant: miserable. In a country where the average worker is lively to ebullient, I couldn't help but notice that every government clerk was ashen-faced and unsmiling. In Greece, the waiters are amused, the soldiers are raucous, the priests, jubilant. But the civil servants are grim, harried, worn out by the pressures of shuffling papers until two p.m. five days a week (except for strikes and holidays). They're exhausted by the endless toil of creating hoops for the fearful public to jump through in order to achieve their unrealistic goals of building a house, obtaining a visa or mailing a package.

George put my paper in front of Natsis. I signed it with a flourish.

'You should have had this from the start, from the *proxenio* in New York,' Natsis spat, stamping the document.

'I did! They faxed it to you!' I insisted, wanting credit for my wasted mornings. But George hustled me out of there before Natsis could take an even stronger dislike to me.

Led by George, who seemed to be on first-name terms with everyone in the city, I moved on to a computer store to make history. I was ordering a computer, which we all believed would be the first in the entire Mourgana range. It would connect me on my mountain top with the outside world. For such a trail-blazing machine, the salesman explained, it made sense to get the most expensive model, with a low-radiation flat screen.

'I'll get the Internet, way up in my village?' I asked.

He assured me it would work and that he'd deliver it once the components arrived from Athens. No, he didn't take credit cards or cheques. Cash only. I could pay the 1,600 Euros upon delivery.

The main task I wanted to accomplish in Ioannina would be far less expensive but much more difficult. Although he hadn't been able to bring himself to start the project, my father longed to see his childhood home rise again, so he had offered to pay for the reconstruction. But the rebuilding was up to me, and I felt that before I could start, I needed to read *Eleni*. I knew I wouldn't be able to do it in Lia, alone in the house where my grandmother was born, a house which might be full of ghosts if a few noisy squirrels didn't scare them away each night. So I told George and Kaity that I planned to stay with them for a few days. I wanted company, but I also needed the distractions of a city, to put some distance between myself and the story I could no longer avoid. I needed to walk outside and be a stranger, not a neighbour, and I couldn't do that in Lia. I had grown up hearing my family's story from my aunts' tearful reminiscences or overheard laments. But I had tried to spare myself from too many painful details. Now that I was about to reconstruct my grandmother's home, it was time to learn about the life she spent there.

I felt I couldn't start rebuilding the house until I had a sense of its past. So I began to read *Eleni*. The first section was fun, learning about my aunts as children. But as the story intensified, I could only read for an hour at a time, with the promise of one of Ioannina's many distractions at the end. I read up to the part where Eleni says goodbye to her children, knowing they will escape while she has to remain behind. Then I went to Diethnes, a sweetshop my grandfather used to frequent, and treated myself to *kaimaki* ice cream, vanilla with rosewater sauce. I returned to Kaity's house, and went to bed early to read some more. The escape chapters were easy, because of the suspense, but I trembled as I turned the pages. I stopped before the section called 'Retribution', because I knew I couldn't handle it in the dark. Instead I flipped through a Greek *Vogue* I had bought at the local bookshop.

The next morning, I finished reading *Eleni* to the reassuring noise of Kaity bustling around preparing breakfast – rinsing plates, squeezing fresh orange juice and lifting hardboiled eggs out of a pot with a clinking spoon. It was difficult to read about my grandmother's capture, imprisonment, trial, torture, and execution by firing squad, but once I had done it, knowing exactly what took place helped me separate the story from myself. The shadowy, incomplete childhood vision I had had of my family's history had been replaced by a reality – a horrific reality, but something concrete and contained. I realized these were things that had happened once, not a cycle that would continue, even if you put people with the same names in the same place. Now I was glad to be reclaiming the home, transforming it from the ruins of a prison to a place where people could be happy again. I realized that I couldn't change my family's past, but at least I could reshape my relationship to the village where it had taken place.

A week later, back in Lia, the computer guy arrived as promised.

'Wow, you live really high up,' he noted.

'Yup.' I didn't want to chitchat – I wanted to check my email.

'Well, I bet it's nice and quiet here,' he said, starting to put the machine together.

'Yeah, that's why I really need the Internet for work.'

I was not at my friendliest. My brave face began to crumble as he kept trying, and failing, to make an Internet connection. While he typed futilely, I panicked quietly, pacing around the living room and swearing softly in English. I could tell he wondered if it was the altitude or the isolation that had got to the crazy American woman.

When the boy gave up, shrugged and asked to be paid for his time, I explained that I didn't want a doorstop, or even a typewriter, that cost 1,600 Euros. If he couldn't hook it up to the Internet, he'd have to take it back.

He looked confused – return policies are as popular as credit cards in Ioannina. And he was just an attractive nineteen-year-old, who didn't want to deal with a hysterical American on a remote mountain top when he could be back in Ioannina, drinking a café frappé on the harbour and calling his friends masturbators, that most cherished of Greek insults.

After consulting his boss via cell phone, we decided I would keep both the cash and the computer, and he'd come back the next week to try again. He took off, leaving me quivering with frustration.

I had no ties to the outside world. Luckily, my neighbours were starting to seem less like a Greek spin-off of *The Golden Girls* and more like potential friends, fascinating companions with decades' worth of stories to tell. One night, Dina invited me for dinner, tempting me with the promise of *lachanopita*, a vegetable pie containing ten different kinds of greens, including nettles. I arrived to find Andreas and the elderly raconteur Vangeli Panagiotou drinking wine mixed with Coca Cola, the libation of choice for male Liotes. A dashing widower with an impossibly high forehead that I came to recognize as Epirote-pattern baldness, Vangeli made up in stage presence what he lacked in teeth.

The conversation at Dina and Andreas's was always as exciting as the cocktails; a few nights earlier they had been polling guests for names of women who might be interested in marrying the son of some clients of theirs in Arta; the son was rich and handsome, but had been a little, well, nervous, ever since a cabinet fell on his head during an earthquake over twenty years ago. But tonight, the main topic was the house I was about to start building – the men remembered it when it had belonged to my grandmother, Eleni Gatzoyiannis. Vangeli called her Kichina Gadzoyanova, a village nickname created by feminizing my grandfather's nickname, Kicho, and their last name. (This was fine by me; having cleverly avoided getting married, so far I get to keep my own name.)

'Kichina had a great house,' Vangeli said, dipping a kiwi slice into his wine and Coke. 'Kicho sent money from America to make a cement courtyard, so it was straight and flat, like no other yard in Lia.' He even remembered attending my father's lavish baptism as a six-year-old boy. 'It was the first time I saw cement and the first time I ate white bread. Everyone ate *bobota*, corn bread, but Kichina paid for white bread to keep us kids satisfied while the grown-ups ate inside.'

Vangeli also recalled the Haidis house, which I now lived in, as it was originally, before it was burned by the Germans, who tossed an old woman, a distant relative of mine, into the flames because she refused to leave her goats. Later, when George told me they had unearthed her skeleton while renovating the place, it became harder to convince myself that the sounds I still heard in the night were squirrels.

'Where have the years gone?' wondered Vangeli,

shaking his head at me. 'I remember your grandmother, Kichina Gadzoyanova, standing in her yard as clear as day. She looked just like you – blonde, blue-eyed.'

Andreas choked up, recalling how he had seen the guerrillas lead her, battered, unable to walk and tied on to a donkey, to the yard of the Haidis house to point out where she had buried some 'treasure', a few by-then-rotted blankets she had saved for Thitsa Olga's dowry. 'Those were ugly times,' he said. 'Towards the end of the Civil War, we kids joined my father in Ioannina, but my mother stayed behind to take care of the house. When the retreat orders came, the Communists took everyone to Hungary, and it was six years before my mother could return. We all met her boat in Igoumenitsa.'

'But she was always afraid, my mother-in-law,' Dina added. 'She lived in fear until the end of her days.'

To a small degree, I knew how Andreas's mother must have felt. I was happy to be talking to people who remembered my grandmother. But although I now knew the details of her life, I still got nervous when villagers talked about the war, as if the past could creep into the present and envelop us. So I was glad when Andreas brightened as he began to reminisce about my great-grandfather, Kicho Haidis.

'He was sneaky,' Andreas laughed. 'When they dismantled the Motsala spring to rebuild it, they found a hose he had installed to irrigate his fields. "It just drew a little water," he said when they caught him.'

'All the old-timers were sneaky,' added Vangeli. 'They had to be cunning to survive under the Turks.'

Years ago, they told me, sneakiness was the mother of invention in Lia, where most men were itinerant tinkers, who travelled around mending pots. They developed a dialect called *alafiatika*, so that they could talk to one another without customers understanding. The *kalantzides* – tinkers – had names for all the important things in life: *tsakta* is bread, *shoro* wine, *tchukali* meat.

Full of wine, nettles and new vocabulary, I staggered home past the spring my great-grandfather had tapped illegally.

As glad as I was to be learning Lia's secret language, I still longed to be able to communicate with the world at large. But it had been hubris, I reasoned, to think that I could be a one-woman technology centre here in the Mourgana mountain range. So when the computer boy returned, I greeted him sullenly and read, with my back towards him, as he worked. I couldn't bear to watch.

He interrupted me. 'Could you come here a minute?' I got up, slowly. 'I want to show you how to connect to the Internet.'

'It works?' I gasped.

He wagged his finger at me. 'You should have more faith.'

He took off, still chuckling at the foreigner who lived so high up that new modems couldn't recognize her slow Internet connection; he'd had to come back with an outdated model.

I'd never been so happy to see a handsome man leave. He was right; I needed a more positive attitude. Now that my computer worked, I was ready to take care of more important business. I ran to the phone and called Thomas – the only local contractor and the man I planned to hire to build the Gatzoyiannis house. I told him I was ready to negotiate prices.

As he strutted up to the house, I was glad to see that Thomas was only about fifty – young for Lia – and muscular. Short and sturdy with black curly hair and ice-blue eyes, one of which wandered a bit, Thomas looked like he would have wrestled in high school, if he hadn't quit school as a teenager to work.

Our summit meeting took place on the porch of the Haidis house. Thomas said the house could cost as much as thirty million drachmas, but he would do it for twenty-five. (It was clear that he hadn't got to know the Euro.) I insisted that that was several million more than the prices I had been quoted in Athens. (Of course, Thomas, as the only contractor for miles around, had a certain home-field advantage over an Athenian import.) Our referee, Foti, who was Thomas's godfather but my Thitsa-Kanta-appointed protector, kicked at the stairs of the porch and removed his leather cap.

'Those guys in Athens would hire Albanians under the table, then do it for less because they don't pay taxes or health insurance and all the profit goes tsak! right in their pocket,' Thomas objected. 'I live here, so I need to run an honest site – I can't have investigators coming up to check on me all the time.'

'I want it to be a good deal for us both,' I insisted. 'But I don't want you to take advantage of me because I'm an American – or a woman. This is a small house you're building, not a villa!'

'Can I make a suggestion?' Foti interrupted, putting his cap back on. 'Why don't you both draw up a budget, think about it for a few days, and decide after Easter – building won't start until after that, anyway.' He had a point. It was mid April, Easter was just a few weeks away, and we would all be busy with church services until then. I was new here; I needed to make friends, not enemies. We agreed and shook hands.

Having triumphed over technology and avoided an

ugly confrontation, I was proud of conquering the Mourgana range. This triumph lasted until, after an orgy of email-checking, I went downstairs and stepped ankle-deep into water that had flooded my basement kitchen. I was wet, but not surprised; I knew by now that my odyssey would have its share of obstacles. Squirrels and kitchen floods may not be as dramatic as an angry Cyclops or duplicitous nymphs, but they were just as troublesome to my progress. Odysseus had his crew to help him. By now I had mine. I rounded up the usual experts to battle the lake in the kitchen. Foti thought it had flooded because of the rain. Spiro said there was a leak. Finally Fanis arrived from the Xenona and, proving to be as nimble a plumber as he had been a dancer, replaced the rubber joints that held the pipes together; they had frozen during the winter then burst when I ran the water, causing leaks.

After my advisors left, I started setting things in order. I pulled back my quilt to put new pillowcases on the bed, and there it was: a large black scorpion, curled up on my pillow like a mint at a fancy hotel. On closer inspection I realized it was dead, and threw it in the bin. But I worried about the implications. If Thitsa Olga was right about scorpions, were my other aunts right about Albanians, wolves and ghosts? I took my blanket and slept on the banquette in the living room, leaving the light on.

I was still lying there the next day when Vladimir knocked on the door. I had told him I wanted to see anything he found while tearing down the old walls, no matter how useless it seemed. Even a shard of pottery would be of interest, because it had belonged to my family. And I was still hoping, just a bit, that he might find the treasure of Ali Pasha. But what he had in his hand was far more exciting. When he'd lifted up the rock above the house's original cornerstone, he had uncovered a Turkish coin. I turned it over in my hand — it was bronze and concave, with Arabic-looking writing and a curlicue design that resembled a flower. I had learned that back when the house was built, masons would place a coin on the cornerstones of a house to make it *siderenio*, strong as metal. I knew our house existed when my grandfather's older brother was born in it in 1870, during the Turkish occupation. If I could decipher the coin's date, which was not written in modern Arabic numerals, I would have a better idea of the date of construction. It seemed that putting up with a few sleepless nights during my odyssey could be worth while. The coin was a clue that would lead me back in time, and also a sign that I was finally moving forward, starting to round the bend that would close my ellipse.

3

DIVINE INTERVENTION

«Αφού μπήκες στο χορό, θα χορέψεις.»
'Since you're standing on the dance floor, you're
going to have to dance.'

23 April

*I'm sitting on a boulder watching Net stack the stones
that cover the courtyard of the Gatzoyiannis house in neat
piles, ready for re-use. Heaving a pick and a spade, Vlad
and Thomas are digging trenches about three feet deep.
They're really just deepening the original foundations of
the house, so that we can pour in concrete. I'd join in,
but when it comes to lifting rocks, I'd be comic relief
rather than any real help. So I'm writing in my journal,
taking pictures, and patting the stray dog that followed
me up here. All of which I can do while eavesdropping.*

*'Net, you should be in school, jackass,' Thomas yells.
'You don't want to be my age and working with your
hands, ruining your back.'*

'School expensive,' Net shrugs. 'I like work, to make money.'

'All money gone in the pyramids,' Vlad explains to Thomas. He's told me this before — like so many Albanians, he lost all his savings by investing them in crooked pyramid schemes, whose collapse led to rioting in Albania in the late 1990s.

'School's free — the government pays,' answers Thomas, who has no children of his own, but several devoted godchildren in villages throughout the Mourgana. 'They'll even pay for a cab to take Net back and forth to school in Filiates.' He turns to the boy. 'You're shy, because you make mistakes in Greek. But by September, you'll have muscles and money from working all summer, and speak Greek better than I do. Eleni, what do you think?'

Finally, a situation where I can help. I put down my pen and look up. 'I think he'd be the most popular boy in the class.'

Greece is not for spectators. It's as if the entire nation was raised to believe that in the University of Life, participation counts for 90 per cent of your grade. I learned this the first time I tried to parallel park in Ioannina. It soon turned into a group effort, with coaching from local shopkeepers, who shouted directions and pantomimed jerking the steering wheel in the hope that I wouldn't crash into their window displays. I welcomed the help — I'm a team player. It was the critical commentary that stung. First, a jowly truck driver rolled down his window to say, 'You don't know how to drive, my girl,' to which I replied, 'I sure don't,' in my best clueless-foreigner voice. Then several girls in halter-tops honked at me, convinced I was giving women drivers a bad name. Finally, a man in a BMW spat, not at me, but at the wheel of my car as I blocked the one-way street.

But even when I wasn't starring in the slapstick comedy that is driving in Ioannina, I was often sucked into audience participation. Once, as I circled the block looking for a parking spot, I witnessed an argument in front of the ATM machine. It started out between two guys, but soon involved a screaming woman, a priest and the police. As I backed into a makeshift spot, wedged between a Mercedes, a Fiat and a large blue fruit truck stopped in the middle of the street, a matron in a passing car rolled down her window and asked, 'What's going on?' I thought she was commenting on my driving until she added, 'Over at the bank – what's happening?'

All I could say was, 'I don't know.' In New York I had carefully honed my avoidance reflex, learning to turn away from any unpleasantness in the street, no matter how loud or foul. Collision between two taxis? Not my problem. Hirsute college student selling pot? At least he's showing some initiative. Homeless man defecating in the middle of Saint Mark's Place? I can't see you; I am suddenly engrossed in the body-piercing options on display at the end of the street.

Once I arrived in Greece, I quickly realized that there were no sidelines for me to stand on any more. Each time I heard church bells in the morning, I'd bound out of bed, determined to find whatever service I might be missing. (Church in Lia is never boring – children spend the liturgy chasing each other around the nave, the occasional snake slithers in to be stomped on by a vigilant church council member, and parishioners interrupt the service with theological debates; one Sunday a visiting Liote got into a screaming fight with Sofia the cantor, sixty inches of religious fervour with curly grey hair and a Minnie Mouse voice, debating when it was appropriate to take Communion.) I even feigned interest in soccer, and boned up on national politics in case I needed to take part in a heated debate. With so many of my days devoted to excavating my family's past, I sought out any distraction that didn't have to do with my history. Luckily, the most important events required no preparation; I just got swept up in them, like the rest of the country.

The spectacle that demanded the most audience participation of all was Easter. I arrived in Greece shortly after Lent started. My family observes Lent in America following Greek Orthodox customs: not eating meat, dairy products or anything higher on the food chain than shellfish. To be honest, we usually shorten our fasting period from the full forty days to Holy Week itself, and then outdo ourselves trying to find delicious combinations that are kosher, so to speak, like shrimp in lobster sauce. Now, that's exactly what all theologians say you shouldn't do, turn Lent into a forty-day shellfish banquet. But I felt OK about this bending of the rules. After all, the main point of fasting is not to approximate Jesus's suffering, which would be impossible, a Sunday School teacher once taught me, but to de-emphasize the physical and nurture the spiritual side of life, to act as a constant reminder that this is a special, sombre time of year. This is also why weddings, baptisms and other celebrations aren't held during Lent.

Apparently, my family wasn't alone in trying to turn Lent into a culinary adventure. En route from Athens to Lia, I stopped at a roadside McDonald's to use the bathroom and spotted two huge posters advertising the specials that were available to help us celebrate McLent.

That's right, not Lent at McDonald's, nor Easter at McDonald's, but McΣαρακοστή, 'McLent'. I stole a place mat that commemorated this happy marriage of the commercial and the spiritual. On a bright-green background were printed the words 'Everybody ready?', and then in different colours and fonts, 'fAstIng'. 'Fasting is an old tradition and an opportunity to try something new,' explained a paragraph under this eye-catching header. 'Now old and young alike can avidly follow the custom and enjoy the renowned McLent!' I managed to spill a little coffee on this gem, but it didn't obscure the photos of the delicacies in question: spring rolls, fried shrimp, seafood salad, a McVeggieburger and apple pie. At the bottom of the paragraph was the slogan 'Surrender to McDonald's!' I, for one, had already been conquered.

I hadn't spent Lent in Greece since I was seven years old, so to me McLent was a new and exciting endeavour. I soon realized that even more Greeks were following the build-up to Easter than the wind-up to the World Cup that obsesses the nation every fourth summer. Approximately 95 per cent of Greece's population is Greek Orthodox, and since the religion is so widespread, it has become commonplace, fitting easily into everyday life without requiring too much soul-searching. For me, in America, Greek Orthodox Easter meant a weekend of celebration, capped off by a huge feast at my parents' house, to which I invited interested non-Greek friends who had nothing else to do that weekend. But in Greece, right from the start of Lent, Easter fever was everywhere; even on TV, which was clogged with ads for various types of lambades, the decorated Easter candles that godparents buy for their godchildren to take to church on Sunday. I hadn't known lambades were such a big deal, but I was glad to learn, because it provided me with a conversation-starter for chatting up kids: 'What does your lambada look like?' The smallest children, whose parents still had control over them, were carrying traditional versions, decorated with ribbons, flowers or wooden boats. The ones with purchasing power, four-year-olds and upwards, lobbied for lambades decorated with the colours of a favourite football team for boys, and, for girls, the internationally adored Barbie.

By the middle of Lent, I had acquired my fair share of Easter décor, including candles in the shape of red eggs (red to symbolize the blood of Christ), and a table runner embroidered with red eggs and yellow chicks. But I still needed some more prosaic household items, like a garden hose and small dessert plates on which to serve spoon sweets. So I headed to Filiates, an old Turkish city that had aged, quietly, into a provincial Greek town. At forty-five minutes away, it was the nearest commercial centre to Lia. I parked in front of a fountain on the main square, and went straight to the παντοπωλείο, the Everything Store. It was aptly named. The garrulous old man behind the counter said he had anything I could ever want – but since it was all massed in dusty piles, I had to tell him what that was, and he would search for it. The old man's body was as frail as his personality was robust. Thin, tall and stooped, he was as speedy as one would expect a seventy-four-year-old man with an intravenous drip in his arm to be. As he shuffled around lifting up toasters and placemats in search of my dessert plates, he told me about himself and his recent illness. But he also wanted to learn about me. Was I married?

I wasn't. In New York, this response often invited a crinkly-eyed smile of reassurance: 'A good man is hard to find in this city!' But the wise Everything Man saw the decision to marry as a unilateral one on my part. 'Find someone to share your bread with,' he advised.

At that moment, my cell phone rang; Kaity's number lit up.

'Hello, girlfriend,' I trilled. (Kaity and I called each other 'girlfriend' despite our twenty-five-year age difference; I did the same with my best friend in Lia, a six-year-old named Popi.)

'Where are you?' Kaity asked from her third-floor apartment in bustling Ioannina.

'In Filiates, at the Everything Store.'

'Find a church and go to it,' she said, issuing an emergency bulletin. 'It's the holiday of the *Hairetismous*, the Greetings to the Virgin Mary.'

'Oh.' I paused, racking my brain. 'Is this a major holiday?'

'Not really,' Kaity said. 'But I'm not calling because of the service. See, if you take a flower off the garland that surrounds the icon of the Virgin Mary and sleep with it under your pillow, you'll dream the name of the man you're going to marry.'

I knew that this kind of practice is not sanctioned, or even condoned, by the Church. But with a belief in fate and a belief in God both being so fundamental in Greece, it was only natural that the two would intertwine like the vines that were beginning to grow on the grape arbour in my yard. I told myself I was only interested in this ritual as a folklorist. But the truth was, sleeping on the banquettes of the Haidis living room had me wishing there was someone to share my bread with in the kitchen. In New York, with so many distractions,

I liked being single. On good days, I thought of myself as a shorter, blonder version of Mary Tyler Moore, tossing her ill-advised beret into the air. But in Lia, I wished, just a little, that I was rebuilding the house along with a partner. So I packed up my purchases, paid the Everything Man, and asked directions to the nearest house of worship, in order to find out if the Virgin Mary planned on sending Mr Right my way.

I found the large, newish church just past the main square. The priest was intoning in front of the altar, behind the flower-framed icon of the *Panagia*, the All-Holy One. All of Filiates was there – harried mothers and dutiful fathers with toddlers in tow, toothless crones and clusters of tough-looking teenaged girls wearing denim. I stepped in line with a row of older women heading towards the altar. Each kissed the icon, although none took a flower. But why would they? These women were grandmothers, they knew whom they'd ended up sharing their bread with, and were probably sick of him by now.

It was finally my turn. I kissed the icon, grasped a white carnation and was about to escape. Then I felt the eyes of the faithful boring into my back. Here I was, a stranger in a pleather raincoat – I couldn't be seen stealing flowers from the Virgin Mary! I dropped my carnation back on to the icon, trying to make it seem as if I had picked it up accidentally, due to a strange tic of the hand. Then I crept back to the church entrance and hid behind a carved wooden iconostasis, sullenly watching a gang of teenage boys in tracksuit bottoms come and kiss another silver-covered icon of the Mother and Child. Following one buzz-cut head as it dipped down, I noticed that two flowers had been placed behind the icon – a white carnation and a deep-pink, almost red rose. A second chance! As I stood there, debating whether the Virgin Mary wanted me to take the rose or not, a young mother lifted her chubby four-year-old up towards the icon.

'Aren't you going to kiss it?' she asked.

He reached up enthusiastically, took the icon in both of his meaty little hands, tipped it towards himself and gave it a big, loud smack – knocking the rose on to the table right in front of me. It was divine intervention. I snatched up the rose, my heart pounding so loudly I could hear it through my sweater, through the pleather and over the priest's chanting. Then I sauntered out, clutching the flower, expecting to be stopped by the men who were standing behind the candle booth. But no one made a move. My rose and I were home free.

It wasn't until I was back in the car and safely on my way to Lia that I noticed how intensely fragrant the rose was, a heady combination of incense and rose essence. I did put it under my pillow that night, but I didn't hear any names in my sleep; at least not any that I remembered.

The tomato plants in my garden were now so tall that Dina had had to show me how to stake them. But my popularity with non-vegetable inhabitants of Lia wasn't growing quite so rapidly. Dina had started the staking project while I was in Filiates, and she told me that Net had strolled by on the road above and laughed at her for struggling with the long sticks.

'Eleni doesn't have real stakes,' she had explained.

'If she doesn't know how to tend her own tomatoes, maybe you should let them rot,' he'd replied.

'I told him, "That's a fine thing to say about someone

who is employing your whole family!"' Dina scowled. 'And he said, "I was just kidding."'

Net was always nice to me, but so awkward that I felt uncomfortable myself. Did the boy really want to curse my tomatoes, and, by association, me? Like me, he was a newcomer here. But his comment made me wonder about the native Liotes. How did they feel about my bumbling presence, an ignorant New Yorker always in need of advice and agricultural instruction?

However, with Easter coming, I was too busy to stew about Net's remark. The Saturday before Holy Week started, I went to Ioannina to stock up for the holiday. I was sitting on Kaity's balcony, eating a *tiropita* while she smoked her morning cigarette, when I heard bells ringing. I looked down to see groups of children, all under ten, ringing doorbells and asking, «Να τα πούμε», 'Should we say them?' 'Them' turned out to be a type of *moirologia*, literally 'fate words', mourning songs that people improvize about a dead friend or relative. It was the Saturday of Lazarus, Kaity explained, when kids go from door to door to sing for the people inside, who then give them a few coins or sweets. The song starts by describing Martha and Mary's tears for their departed brother, Lazarus. Then, because Lazarus was resurrected by Jesus, he has the unprecedented opportunity to participate in his own *moirologia*. 'What did you see?' his sisters ask him about the afterlife. 'I saw fear and I saw terror, I saw passion and I saw suffering,' he reports back.

This sounded like a scary image of the afterlife for kids to sing about, but the ones I saw seemed perfectly happy, counting their shiny Evroulas. Maybe they figured that Lazarus must be happy as he got to come back, and now they had cash to buy ice cream on Holy Saturday, their last chance to eat dairy products for a whole week. Perhaps there was even a Lenten message for me in the song of Lazarus: resurrection is possible, even if it's of a fallen house and not a beloved brother.

On Palm Sunday, I woke up to the kind of cataclysmic storm that makes me understand why the Ancient Greeks called the Mourgana range and its surroundings the *Keraunon Oroi*, Thunder Mountains. This Sunday's storm was way scarier than the Disneyworld roller-coaster of the same name. But Palm Sunday is the kick-off for Holy Week, and, as a newly minted Liote, I was not going to be rained out. Religion was a major component of everyone's daily life here, not just a convenient end to a Sunday drive. And I wanted to be a part of the action. I was determined to start Holy Week off right, by going to church and receiving palm fronds in memory of those that were showered on Jesus on his return to Jerusalem. Most people place the palms behind the icons on their mantel, where they are said to bring good luck the entire year. I was not about to let a little rain – or even the gushing torrents that were pelting Lia – jeopardize a year's worth of luck. Since moving to the village, I had somehow become superstitious. In New York, I didn't bend down to pick up lucky pennies on the pavement. But in Lia, alone in the Haidis house, I felt I needed any divine help I could get.

I ran up the slick path and squished, sopping wet, into my car to drive through the thick, wet fog towards Agia Paraskevi, the church at the end of the village, next to the Xenona. I had barely set out when I saw the village president, Nikolas Skevis, hobbling towards me with his cane, water coursing off his raincoat. I pulled over to offer him a lift. That's when he broke the news. 'There's no church,' he said, shaking his head as drops of water hit me through the open window. 'Father Prokopi is sick. He went to the hospital yesterday.'

I was stunned. The storm was bad enough, but a sick priest during Holy Week is like the Grinch who stole Christmas. 'What about Easter?' I asked.

'We'll see how he feels,' Nikolas replied, puttering onwards.

As the dice-sized drops turned to hail and started bouncing off the windscreen, I assessed the situation. If Father Prokopi did not get better, we would never get a substitute priest during this, their busiest time of year. There are forty-two villages in Epiros that have no priest at all, Father Prokopi told me once when he was bemoaning the fact that young men don't want to become priests. ('It's their girlfriends,' he confided; Orthodox priests can marry and most, like him, do. 'Girls today don't want the pressure of being a priest's wife.') I was going to have to take Easter week into my own hands. My only option was to continue on to the village of Lista, six kilometres away, and get palms there.

I inched on through opaque fog, and by the time I got to Lista, church was over. Father Vangelis, a little priest with a white beard and bright blue eyes, was enjoying coffee with his flock in the *kafenion* across the street. As I walked in, every head turned to assess the sodden newcomer.

'Are there any palms left?' I asked, breaking the silence.

'There are always palms on Palm Sunday,' Father Vangelis replied, rising from his chair with ecclesiastical elegance. 'Let's get some.'

I followed him up a slippery ramp to the Church of the Dormition, which he unlocked. As I stared at the sky-blue ceiling, Father Vangelis seized a huge bunch of palms that had been adorning an icon. 'Take these back to everyone in Lia,' he said beatifically.

Back in Lista's *kafenion*, the proprietress served coffees and tried to stir up discontent. 'Pappoulis,' she asked Father Vangelis, 'is a priest even allowed to be sick during Holy Week?' It was clear that news of Father Prokopi's illness had raged through the tri-village area.

Clutching my coffee cup for warmth, I leaned in to hear Father Vangelis's reply. He raised his hands as if in benediction. 'Father Prokopi has an intestinal problem; that's what the hospital told him,' he reported. 'Now, you can perform a service with a forty-degree fever, but if you've got an intestinal problem, and you have to keep running back and forth to the bathroom, it can't be done.'

Toula, a well-coiffed, middle-aged blonde who was president of the brotherhood of the nearby village of Glousta, sprang out of her chair and stalked over to our table. Glousta was the third village in Father Prokopi's roster. The priest didn't have a car, so he had to walk from church to church or depend on his parishioners to give him a lift. But since Glousta was located some way down the mountain off the main paved road from Lia, and even further from Father Prokopi's home in the village of Babouri, it was his least-favourite location. A former teacher, Toula was used to being in charge – and she was not about to let Easter bypass her village. She sat next to Father Vangelis, pulled out a pen and notepad, and started pressurizing him to perform Glousta's Holy Week services.

'Father Prokopi will be fine by then,' he assured her.

But Toula would not be moved. 'Even so,' she

argued, 'if he's not feeling well, it's too far for him to come.'

Father Vangelis knew there was no escape. He began to barter. 'Well, you people from Glousta will have to drive the *gerontakia* (little old people) from here in Lista over to Glousta for the Resurrection – I'm not doing another one here,' he commanded.

This was fine by Toula, as long as the service was in her hometown.

'And the congregation can't leave after the Resurrection on Saturday night,' Father Vangelis continued, sensing he had the upper hand. 'Everyone has to stay to the end of the liturgy.' This was a major demand, as all over the world Greeks rush home immediately after the Resurrection at midnight in their desperation to end the seven-week Lenten fast, leaving their lonely priest chanting to an empty church.

Toula agreed to his terms – what else could she do? A deal was struck. It meant that Father Vangelis would be driving all over the mountain range, but the people of Glousta would have Easter after all. As I left, I wondered how old he was, and how he could move so quickly in his long gown. But mostly I wondered about our own Holy Week. In some towns, there were two services a day during Holy Week. But with a priest shortage and the intestinal problem that had smitten Father Prokopi, we Liotes were in serious trouble.

On Holy Monday, I drove to Filiates, which was teeming with women carrying huge trays of *koulouria*, braided Easter cookies, to be cooked in the massive ovens at the bakeries. I was on a less culinary mission, heading to the municipal registry, where I picked up the ID number required for my Greek passport. After five months, I now had all the materials necessary to become a Greek citizen. It was a minor Holy Week miracle. I took my hard-won ID number and drove over treacherous mountain passes to the town of Metsovo. There I could find both a fax machine to send my ID number to the Consulate in New York, which would issue my passport and post it to me, and Holy Week services, which I'd be unable to attend in spiritually underprivileged Lia.

Metsovo is to Lia as Elizabeth Taylor was to Joan Collins circa 1960: a larger, more glamorous role model. A mountain village full of grey stone mansions, it has a history of being favoured by fate. Despite the gut-wrenching curved roads that lead to and from the town, it has always been central for travellers, lying on the most logical route from Epiros to Thessaly and Macedonia. Most Metsovites speak Vlachika, an unwritten language of Latinate origin, as well as Greek. Some historians theorize that the Vlachs are descendants of Roman soldiers who were stationed in Metsovo, and others think they developed Vlachika to trade with the Romans who travelled the route. Today Metsovo is a thriving tourist town with a ski lift, cheese factory and vineyard. But I was here to visit some old family friends, loyal Metsovites who had a fax in their home and promised they could find a liturgy or two for me to hit.

'The Holy Tuesday service used to be my favourite,' my host, Ioanni, told me. 'The gospel reading refers to Mary Magdalene washing Jesus's feet, so prostitutes feel they have to attend. This makes it a very popular service with teenaged boys.'

'Are there prostitutes in Metsovo?' I asked, shocked. I certainly hadn't seen any scantily clad ladies on street corners. In fact, the streets were filled with older women in traditional Metsovite costume: heavy black skirt, breast-hugging black top with bell sleeves embroidered in scroll-like designs, embroidered apron nestled just under the bust, and headscarf. The outfit is adorable, but tends to make the wearer look squat and pyramid-shaped.

'Oh, no!' Ioanni replied. 'I lived in Athens when I was a teenager.'

Deciding to see the service for myself, I slid along the cobblestone roads to the church. It was packed, but none of the pyramid-shaped ladies looked guilty enough to be leading double lives.

The next morning, I took advantage of my proximity to healthy priests yet again, attending church to have holy oil dabbed on my forehead. This time, the church-going ladies were walking around clutching bouquets of leafy green branches. Elena, my hostess, explained that the plant is called *mai*, and that you pick it on 1 May to 'catch the May' and gain control over the month. *Mai* is thought to have dangerous magical properties, perhaps because its name resembles the word for magic, *maghia*.

'They say you shouldn't get married in May,' Elena continued.

'Because it's bad luck?' I asked.

'No – because you might be driven mad by lust and make a hasty decision.'

Surrounded by nothing but toothless old men in Lia, I didn't want to be driven mad by lust in a Maenad-like frenzy. And I wanted to celebrate Easter like the Epirotes around me, to really be a part of the event. So I asked around and determined that the source of the *mai* was just outside Metsovo, on a hill that slopes up from a crossroads.

Approaching the hillside, I noticed a shepherd lying on the grass, and decided I'd ask him to point out the magic plant. But when I got closer, I realized he was fast asleep. I was on my own. I picked the green stuff that looked most like the branches the crones had been carrying.

When I arrived in Lia triumphant, my arms full of *mai* to craft into a May wreath for our door, Vladimiros came up to greet me.

'Your tooth hurt?' he asked.

'No,' I said. 'Why?'

'Oh, because in Albania that plant is very strong for cure toothaches. But it also makes rash,' he said, rubbing his forearms as if they itched.

He had brought his wife Xalime to meet me, having just got the cash and papers together to bring her over the border from Albania. She didn't speak a word of Greek and had been very car sick on the mountainous roads. But at the sight of my wreath, hung proudly on the verandah, a huge smile spread over Xalime's face, and she pointed at it, rattling away to Vlad. I couldn't tell if she was admiring the wreath or mocking it. I had tried to fit in with my fellow worshippers, but it seemed that I'd failed. At least, I hoped, I might get points for effort. I left my imperfect wreath on the verandah, where, in true Easter spirit, my kindly neighbours admired it politely.

The next day I awoke to another minor miracle: church bells. Father Prokopi's health had improved enough for him to perform the morning service for Holy Thursday, when the souls of the dead are said to rise and walk among us for the next fifty days. I followed the sound of the bells to Agia Triada, where he read the names of Lia's departed – who at this point seriously outnumber the living Liotes – and gave communion to those who were present in the flesh as well as in spirit.

As I left church, I noticed that quite apart from any dead villagers who might have been walking among us, the village was full of Liotes who had moved away and were back to celebrate Easter. The empty houses in uptown Motsala were now full, and outside one of them stood a four-year-old boy. «Να σου πω,» he would call out to passers-by, 'Let me tell you.' It's a useful phrase for starting a conversation, as it builds suspense. I took the bait. 'What?'

'There was a scorpion in the house!' he exclaimed.

'No!' I gasped.

Sensing a responsive audience, he continued to wax poetic. 'Yes! And Daddy killed it. He stomped on it like this, Paf! Paf! Paf!' The Pafs were accompanied by frenzied hopping. 'And then I stomped on it. Paf! Paf! . . .'

I could have watched the scorpion slaughter re-enacted all morning, but the boy got called inside by a harried-sounding mother. All mothers were harried, as the entire village was busy with Easter preparations. Some people had gone to clean relatives' gravestones. Others were baking more Easter cookies, or, like me, dyeing eggs. I collected leaves, wildflowers and stalks of grass, arranged them artistically on white eggs, wrapped the eggs in squares of cut-up tights, tied the fabric with dental floss, and dropped the shrouded eggs into a pot of red dye. Once they have been boiled and the tights and leaves removed, the eggs are entirely red except for a white pattern where the foliage used to be, and a white star where the fabric was gathered and tied up. (The tights and dental floss are recent innovations; cheesecloth and string were the norm in pre-Hanes Lia.) I finished polishing my eggs with olive oil just in time for more church.

Holy Thursday's evening service features the reading of the Twelve Gospels, twelve sections of the Bible that recount Christ's passion. In Father Prokopi's case, it was the Twenty-Four Gospels, because he performed the service in Babouri first, before being driven over to Lia to repeat the Gospels to us – it would have been a gruelling task even when he was a recently ordained, strapping young priest in the best of health.

Now just a few years off retirement, Father Prokopi read the Gospels seated in front of the altar. A slim man with a white beard, white hair, and the sorrowful blue eyes of a saint about to be martyred, Father Prokopi looked even more holy than usual as he sat upright in his wooden chair. He had dark circles under his eyes and a raspy voice due to his illness, but he fulfilled his duty – and Lia's spiritual longing – beautifully, chanting through all Twelve Gospels for the second time that evening, never once sneaking in a condensed version of a scripture.

The service's high point is the description of Jesus's crucifixion, when a two-dimensional wooden statue of Christ on a cross bearing three candles is carried around the church three times and hammered into a stand on the middle aisle. We all held our breath as Antonis, the Church Council president, disentangled the candles from the chandelier, then a huge taper fell on to the stone floor. It lay there sputtering until several old ladies pointed it out and Antonis retrieved it. Unfortunately, this climax takes place in the middle of the service; after it, you've still got six Gospels to go. I have to admit that most of us left ailing Father Prokopi alone to finish reading the Gospels to a few faithful old ladies, including one who was kneeling on the stone floor knitting away.

I thought the knitting lady should be paying a little

more attention to the service, but I was in no position to judge, as I went across the street to the Xenona for some après-church booze (another Lenten no-no). There I found two scholars from the National Archaeological Offices, who were doing research on the area and had just climbed down from Lia's *kastro*. It would take lots of work to uncover, they said, but there was definitely something important there. An ancient coin from the far-off island kingdom of Thassos had been found near the *kastro* a few years ago, indicating that ancient Lia was once a prominent trading community.

Finally, I had official confirmation of what the locals had been telling me – that Lia had a long, illustrious history. I hoped the archaeologists would find more artefacts of historical importance, but not in the yard of the Gatzoyiannis house, because then we would be forced to stop building and turn the property over to the Archaeological Services. A few years ago a man in Glousta stumbled upon a royal tomb from the Hellenistic era while trying to build a garage. Now the golden crown and earrings that were unearthed are in the Archaeological Museum on Corfu, and the poor man still doesn't have anywhere to park.

All the archaeology talk was starting to make me nervous when Father Prokopi strolled in, exhausted. He had finally finished the Twelve Gospels times two, and I told him he deserved some refreshment. He pulled up a chair and ordered some tea. It being Holy Thursday, Father Prokopi was thinking of his beloved deceased parishioners, who are much more easily satisfied than the living Liotes.

'Human beings, we need meat, milk,' he said, gesturing to the table in front of us. (It contained neither, this being Holy Week and all, but he was speaking figuratively.) 'The dead, may their memory be eternal, all they ask for is a Trisagion service in their memory and that we light a candle to them once in a while.'

Dead saints, apparently, can be somewhat more demanding. Father Prokopi told me that Agios Athanassios had once visited him in a dream, moaning 'They've abandoned me. Help.' So now Father Prokopi was busy renovating the monastery of Agios Athanassios, on a hilltop below Babouri and Lia, in order to prepare it for a monk from the Peloponnese to take up residence. The monastery had been abandoned since its last inhabitant, a toothless, hundred-year-old nun, died twenty years ago.

'She was a simple old nun,' Father Prokopi told me. 'One day her herd of cows was missing. So she prayed to Agios Athanassios, "Effendi, either you bring me my cows or I burn you to the ground." In half an hour the cows were back. It was a miracle.'

This story fascinated me. First, because the nun called her patron saint 'Effendi', which means 'master' in Turkish and is the way village women addressed their husbands during the Turkish occupation. Second, it didn't seem super-holy to threaten to burn a monastery. Perhaps our friend the nun was a pyromaniac?

'I guess even saints feel fear,' I said.

'No, the saint was rewarding the nun,' Father Prokopi explained patiently. 'The story shows how much faith she had in him.'

This wasn't Agios Athanassios' only miracle. 'When my father was sick and couldn't walk, I let him spend the night in Agios Athanassios,' Father Prokopi continued. 'The next day he walked all the way back to Babouri himself.'

I could write off the cows as bovine practical jokers, or, at best, a coincidence. But Father Prokopi wouldn't lie, so his father's recovery represented a bona fide miracle to me, a testament to the power of faith. I headed home, ready to face the rebuilding of the Gatzoyiannis house and happy to be living in a village where miracles still took place.

In larger villages, the women and girls spend all Holy Thursday night decorating the Epitaphion, singing the Virgin's Lament as they tie flowers to a carved wooden bier that represents Christ's coffin. But in Lia there weren't enough ladies young and strong enough to stay up all night singing and arranging flowers. So Good Friday morning found me and a few other women in the clifftop church of Agia Paraskevi, preparing blooms to decorate the Epitaphion, as Father Prokopi read from the Bible and an energetic twelve-year-old boy tugged on the rope in the tall stone bell tower, sending chimes ringing out over the sloping fields below. His sister begged the bell-ringer to stop the cacophony, but Antonis, as church president, said the boy didn't have to stop until he felt tired, which seemed unlikely to happen this Easter.

We women were under the supervision of Spiridoula, Lia's honorary chairperson. The wife of the contractor Thomas, and the village's youngest full-time female resident, Spiridoula was a born leader, with a sturdy figure, sensibly short blond haircut, and the ready smile of a woman who always knows what she wants to happen, and is confident that it will. She merrily shouldered many major civic responsibilities, including overseeing the Epitaphion décor. Several men were in attendance too, listening to the service, and when the priest got to an important part, Spiridoula would signal to us to put down our knives and carnations and listen for a few minutes. Then she'd start cutting again, and we would follow suit.

At the end of the service, as Father Prokopi read about Jesus's descent from the cross, Antonis removed the statue of Jesus from the cross in the middle of the church. Then Father Prokopi stepped away from the altar with his shoulders wrapped in the pall, a gold-embroidered purple cloth that represents Jesus's body, which he placed on the Epitaphion, where Spiridoula strewed flower petals on top of it.

'Make a beautiful Epitaphion, ladies,' he said. 'I'll see you tonight.'

Before leaving, Father Prokopi surprised me by dropping to his elderly knees and scooting under the Epitaphion three times. A few men followed suit, then Spiridoula shooed them out of the church so that the older, skirt-wearing ladies could crawl laboriously under it as well without inviting voyeurism, then kiss the pall, now covered in rose petals. The book *Calendar Customs of Greece* explains that people crawl under the Epitaphion 'in order that its Grace may touch them', but the women told me that it brought good luck in the coming year.

With the men gone we could now decorate freely. Spiridoula had even brought a lantern to put inside the crown on top of the Epitaphion so that light would shine through during the evening procession. She had bought pink, white and red carnations; other people donated voluptuous roses from their gardens, and the red and pink flowers along with the orange centres of the daisy chains made the Epitaphion look vaguely Indian, like an adorned litter from a maharajah's palace. But we weren't done yet. Some men shyly offered white wild-flowers as a filler, which met with the Spiridoula seal of approval, and I had brought blue irises from Dina, who wasn't participating in the Easter festivities because she was still in mourning for Andreas's son. 'They always use my irises on the Epitaphion,' she said. 'Since I can't bring them this year, you will.'

Visitors kept dropping by, following the custom of seeing as many Epitaphoi as possible; the more you hit, the better your luck for the coming year. I crawled under the Epitaphion too, and Spiridoula tipped me off that people take flowers from the Epitaphion home with them after the evening service to save as *filakta* — protective amulets. 'In five minutes it will be naked again,' she said, smiling. She didn't care that all her hard work was ephemeral; after the procession, the Epitaphion has fulfilled its mission, bringing beauty and luck to all of us.

Having outdone even her triumphs of previous years, Spiridoula headed home. I stayed alone in Agia Paraskevi for a few minutes to admire our handiwork. Two old women, both under five feet tall, came in, dropped on all fours, and crawled under it slowly and deliberately, like inchworms. 'The Epitaphion looks beautiful,' one said, latching on to the bishop's throne to haul herself up to a standing position. 'But you forgot the *daphne*.'

'Is *daphne* supposed to be good for the Epitaphion?' I asked tentatively.

'*Daphne* has been considered "good" for over three thousand years,' she replied and hobbled out, shaking her kerchiefed head as if thinking, 'What a rookie!'

I knew that *daphne*, or laurel in English, was an important plant. I just didn't know what it looked like. The goddess Gaia turned a wood nymph being pursued by Apollo into *daphne* to protect her virtue, the Olympic victors were crowned with it, and the Pythia at the oracle of Delphi inhaled the smoke of the burning plant to induce visions. But I hadn't realized that Jesus wanted *daphne*, too. I was not about to make an executive decision to run out and collect what I thought was *daphne*, then add it to the Epitaphion without Spiridoula's approval. After my mishap with the *mai*, I suspected I was just as likely to pick poison ivy, so I decided not to mention our oversight to Spiridoula.

That evening, we all assembled in the *plateia* in front of Agia Paraskevi for the funeral procession of Christ. But although the church bells had rung, indicating that a service was starting, Father Prokopi was nowhere to be seen. We stood around, holding our lambades. Finally, a car stopped and a figure in a long black robe and stovepipe hat started running towards us, with a crowd of churchgoers cheering him on as though he was a marathon runner rounding the halfway mark.

Once we were all inside, I stood near the Epitaphion so that I could gloat over its beauty during the two-hour-long liturgy, which is a full funeral service ending with a procession through the village. Father Prokopi circled the Epitaphion three times, splashing it with myrrh. Towards the end of the service, my six-year-old friend Popi came and slipped her small hand into mine. We watched as four men acting as pall-bearers attempted to lift the Epitaphion to bring it outside. There was brief but heated controversy: should they use the long wooden sticks to carry the Epitaphion? It turned out to be impossible to manoeuvre through the church doors with the carrying sticks, so they grasped the funeral bier with their bare hands and heaved it off the table into the air, shaking under its weight. The whole congregation followed, holding their lighted candles, with Popi and me right behind the Epitaphion.

As we made our way down to the church of Agia Triada, the entire extended village fell in line behind us; I wondered if there were any Liotes left in Athens. At every crossroads the procession would stop for a short prayer, and at Agia Triada we turned to retrace our steps. Families whose homes we had passed on the way down had splintered off and were now standing in front of their doors, glowing in the candlelight, as the procession made its way back.

Once we reached the neighbourhood of Agia Paraskevi, Father Prokopi stopped in front of Marianthe's house, which had a large black bow tied around its gatepost to indicate a household in mourning. There we sang the mourning hymn, praying that her husband and son – who had been here last Easter, had died within two weeks of each other and were now lost to Lia – would live in everlasting memory. As I stood among the candle-bearing worshippers, I realized how deeply everyone felt their loss, how the absence of two vital neighbours had left Lia a little hollower this Easter. Then we continued the few steps to Agia Paraskevi. At the outer gate of the churchyard, the pall-bearers raised the Epitaphion on to their shoulders so that the rest of us could pass under it for luck before it was placed back inside the church.

I stayed in the courtyard, watching people's faces illuminated by their candles as they passed by, wishing each other «Και του χρόνου», 'And next year.' I had always assumed that this phrase, uttered on every special occasion, meant, 'May we be together again this time next year.' After singing the mourning hymn, I realized it also means 'May we be alive, safe and healthy to celebrate again next year.' It wasn't just being together that mattered. It was being able to come together, and lucky enough to find your loved ones waiting for you when you arrived.

Then I noticed that everyone was clutching flowers. The *filakta*! I ran into the church. The Epitaphion was transformed, almost back to its pre-Good Friday wooden shell. Still, I managed to retrieve a few wildflowers and one rose to place behind the icons in the house. Next year, I've got my eye on some *daphne*.

The rest of Greece went to church on Saturday morning for the First Resurrection. But there was no service in Lia — Father Prokopi needed to rest up for the evening. Most of us took this as a special dispensation to throw ourselves into pre-Easter preparations. Five separate women visited my house, bringing me Easter cookies, bread, and the local version of *mayeiritsa*, the soup used to break the Lenten fast after the Resurrection service. *Mayeiritsa* is a medley of greens, herbs and sweetbreads, which means that I've never indulged in more than a taste of the real thing; I draw the line at offal. Since you're supposed never to return someone's plate empty, I gave back the visitors' china filled with my decorated eggs, which were an especially big hit with people who were in mourning and therefore weren't supposed to dye their own.

By eleven p.m. on Holy Saturday, all of Lia except those who were in mourning had gathered in Agia Triada to wait for the climactic service of Holy Week. We were all dressed in our best, and carrying our Easter lambades (plain white for us grown-ups). Popi had new red shoes, and eleven-year-old Leonidas was devastated at having left his soccer-themed lambada in Athens.

Father Prokopi was there, having arrived out of breath, dashing over from Babouri, where he had completed an artificially early Resurrection service. We would have the real thing, climaxing at midnight. The interior of Agia Triada glowed, as light from the heavy gold chandelier reflected off the ornate wooden iconostasis shielding the altar and the new icons of saints on the wall, which replaced those that had been damaged during the war. Wherever you glanced, eyes stared back at you, whether from the ceiling fresco of Jesus looking down, saints peering from every angle, or villagers winking hello.

Tonight the church interior was even more impressive than usual – garlands of Greek flags hung from the church ceiling, criss-crossing each other, and the icons were ringed with flowers. Father Prokopi chanted and we stood, sat and stood again, praying and chanting in response, until he suddenly noticed that it was almost midnight and signalled to the cantors to jump ahead in their hymn books.

Just before twelve, the lights were turned off. As the midnight bell began to toll and we all stood in the darkness, Father Prokopi emerged from the altar, carrying a single candle. Several boys holding lambades rushed forward to be the first to receive the flame; soon it had been passed on throughout the church, and we were all illuminated by candlelight. We sang the Resurrection hymn, and outside people shot guns in celebration, causing all children under the age of three to burst into tears. Father Prokopi tried to continue the service, but everyone was too excited to stay. So the cantor flipped the switch that makes the bells ring their most jubilant chime, and we all streamed into the courtyard to shake hands, say 'Christ is risen,' and answer 'Truly He has risen.'

There was a sense of disbelief in the churchyard. It had actually happened – we had a priest, we were all healthy and together, and once again, at midnight, Christ had risen. All week, whenever something good had happened, like Father Prokopi recovering or me getting my ID number, I had joked, 'Look, it's an Easter miracle.' But Easter itself was the miracle.

I headed home just as my elderly next-door neighbours were making their tentative way on foot down the sloping road to our houses. The husband of the frail couple, Barba Prokopis, had been ill recently, so after exchanging 'Christ is risen' greetings I asked, 'How are you doing?'

'Fine,' he replied. 'It does my soul good to see the church full.'

'He had to go, even though he was sick,' his wife piped up.

'I would have gone even if I was dead!' he said. Which, considering that the souls of the dead had been among us since Thursday, was entirely possible.

By now it was almost two a.m. I was invited to break the fast at Dina and Andreas's house, where we cracked eggs together to see who had the lucky strongest one, ate *mayeiritsa*, drank wine and laughed. Andreas won the egg game, either because his egg was the strongest or because he was especially skilled at egg-cracking after decades of practice. But I was feeling lucky myself, because, despite everyone's urging, I had successfully managed to avoid eating intestines, which were being served in two ways: *kokoretsi* (lamb's entrails wrapped in its long intestine and roasted on a spit), and *gardoumbes* (said entrails wrapped in said long intestine, cut into bite-sized chunks and oven-roasted).

One of the pro-intestine guests at the table was

Andreas's sister-in-law, an elderly widow who had been friends with my grandmother when they were both young mothers, but had survived the war and moved to the city. 'The last time I spent Easter in that church was over sixty years ago, and I was holding my daughter who was a newborn,' she told me. 'She started crying and your grandmother came up to me and said, "Let me take the baby outside so you can stay."' The old woman sighed. 'Tonight, I saw you standing next to my daughter, who is a grandmother herself now, and I remembered that Easter. See where life brings us?'

The next morning, the follow-up Easter Sunday service was held in Babouri. As a Liote, and one who had stayed up late listening to reminiscences, I felt entitled to skip it. I woke late, then strolled to the *kafenion* to watch Stella roasting lambs for people who didn't have their own spits.

Back in Motsala, Dina and Andreas's spit was empty, because roasting on a spit is a sign of great celebration that is not appropriate for people in mourning. Instead, Dina roasted lamb in the oven, with spices and potatoes, which was just as delicious. I gorged myself on wine, lamb and mountain views.

In the evening, when I finally rose from the table, Dina warned me not to fold my napkin – it would mean that I wasn't coming back again. So I left my napkin in a heap on my chair, and headed home to nap. When I had recovered from my celebratory gluttony, Thomas, the contractor, came over. With the passing of time and the intervention of Foti, Thomas and I had reached a compromise and settled on a price for the house's construction. Now he was here to sign the agreements.

An engineer friend of my father's had drawn up a contract, filling it with clauses meant to satisfy the innate

Greek suspicion that everyone is out to cheat you. I wasn't really suspicious of Thomas, and I don't think he was wary of me, but there were other, less reliable parties involved. For example, when it came to the steel rods for the frame of the house, Thomas had to go to the steelyard to oversee delivery himself. Otherwise, they might try to pass off cheap Bulgarian steel as good Greek steel. The document was also very clear about dates, so that there would be as little delay as possible. The walls of the house should be done by the festival of the Prophet Elias, 20 July; the roof, by the end of August; and the interior by St Nicholas's Day, 6 December.

Once the contracts were signed, we celebrated by drinking *tsipouro*. I would like to be the kind of girl who downs a shot of moonshine without blinking, but I think it looks, smells and tastes like methylated spirits. So I dumped mine into the sink once Thomas had left. Then I picked up *Calendar Customs of Greece* to finish reading about Easter. I turned the page to the Festival of Saint George. 'St George's Day marks the beginning of the summer semester, and it is virtually the beginning of the year as far as working contracts are concerned,' the author writes. 'All agreements used to be signed on St George's Day.' Normally, it is celebrated on 23 April, but since festivals can't be celebrated during Lent, which extended past the twenty-third this year, St George's Day was to be observed the day after Easter. Tomorrow.

I had been worried about our delay in getting approval. First the Building Department rejected Zervas's plans because they were in pencil, not regulation blue pen. Then the engineer submitting our proposal was informed that it was missing some newly required documents. He had to drive from Igoumenitsa to Ioannina and back again to get them, only to be told, 'You should have known to submit them in the first place – you're a civil engineer, aren't you?' But by now he had given me both approval from the Forestry Service and a project number which proved we had submitted the proposal. I still needed the OK from the Archaeological Service, but we could keep working in the meantime. And thanks to St George, spiritually speaking, we were one day ahead of schedule.

I made some tea and brought the contract out to the verandah, to admire it while watching the sunset. I had vowed to my aunts that I would become a part of everyday life in Lia, but secretly I had worried that without a job, my family or people my own age around me, I would be bored and lonely. And in the beginning, I was. But during Easter, I had been so busy with matters both spiritual and mundane that I hadn't even had time to notice that I was neither of those things. Having participated in the ritual of Easter, I felt reborn as a member of the village, on my way to being a bona fide Liote. I had been thinking of my year in Lia as a worthy digression from my real life, but I was beginning to realize that 'real life' exists wherever you are. And I was here.

I had a house about to begin construction. I had made friends, albeit on the outer ranges of the age spectrum. And the Haidis house finally had a working computer and stove, a kitchen floor that no longer flooded, and a noticeable lack of squirrels and scorpions. I was starting to belong in Lia. Soon I might even learn to like spoon sweets.

4

PLAYING WITH FIRE

«Η φτώχια θέλει καλοπέραση.»
'Poverty needs a good time.'

18 May

*I am sitting on my terrace, drinking tea and watching the
veils of morning mist drift up from the valley below. The
mountain tops rising above the clouds look like a Japanese
painting. I didn't sleep much again last night, listening
to the squirrels roll walnuts around the ceiling and the
more troubling, unidentifiable thumps, creaks and sighs
the Haidis house makes. Now I am enjoying the peace
morning always brings, and a farm-fresh egg courtesy of
Foti's hens.*

'Eleni!' *A piercing voice calls. It's Dina, inviting me
over for breakfast.*

'Guess what I have for you today,' *Dina gloats once I
am installed at her kitchen table.* 'It's milk, fresh from

the goat!' She places a full eight-ounce glass of creamy liquid in front of me. 'I told Iphigenia, the shepherdess, that you've never had fresh goat's milk and she gave me this for you — it's so healthy!'

And so disgusting looking. The most milk I can handle is a little semi-skinned in a bowl of cereal. But this is a gift, two times over, both from her and from Iphigenia. Apparently, in Lia, goat's milk is a delicacy. I pick it up and drink. It's gamey, like liquid lamb. I force down half a glass.

'Thanks!' I say. 'I feel healthier already. I'll save the rest for later.'

That afternoon, when Dina and Andreas are taking their siesta, I pour the goat's milk on to a paper plate, where it pools like an oily blob of eggshell paint, and leave it for Scrappy, the stray dog who frequents my yard. His tail wags in rapture. In Lia, there is always enough of a good thing to share.

Epiros is the poorest region in the European Union, a fact I often heard cited by Epirotes bemoaning the indifference of their politicians. It's a dramatic statement and is meant to be startling. What shocked me most was that my neighbours didn't look poverty-stricken — not like the people I'd seen in New York, anyway, where a lady begs near Lincoln Center wearing only a bin bag. Instead, the region's poverty manifested itself in more subtle ways, such as the lack of jobs, that drove young people out of the area, emptying villages of all but pensioners and migrant workers like Vlad and Net. Lia was rural, but we had plumbing and electricity, which had arrived in the village in 1967. Everyone else had TV, and I had Internet access. What more could a community want?

I could tell the villagers weren't well-to-do, however, because on the first Friday of every month the *kafenion* filled with Liotes eager to meet the postman and pick up the Greek version of Social Security cheques (many Liotes, having worked in the US, happily collected those too). But my neighbours were so generous with their food, drink and company that I felt we were living large. Then I overheard the saying 'Poverty needs a good time,' and realized that, in Greece, sometimes you live large because you're poor. Which explains why, once the solemnity of Lent and Easter ended and summer began, Lia's social calendar kicked into high gear. Having seen how Easter brought the village together, I was determined not to miss any uniquely Epirote event, anything that my aunts and grandmother might have attended when they lived here. So with ninety-one major saints' days and eleven national holidays to celebrate, life became a non-stop party.

In Manhattan, a party meant brightly coloured 'signature' cocktails, faux comfort-food hors d'oeuvres, and 'goodie bags' filled with freebies that rich urbanites fought over when leaving. Here a good time consisted of homemade wine in recycled water bottles, hunks of roast lamb, and a band that really wails. And I do mean wails. I realized this the night of Easter Sunday at the first festival of the season, in the village of Glousta. Dancing was about to begin and the clarinettist struck up what I considered to be a rather mournful tune, the traditional Epirotic music that Patrick Leigh Fermor wrote in *Roumeli* was 'Exactly the kind of long-drawn-out and wailing song in a minor key, whose waverings . . . bewildered and irritated Byron's Western acquaintances.' I was neither bewildered nor irritated, but I wasn't exactly humming along. So I was shocked when I noticed the young woman sitting next to me gyrating in her chair, drumming her fingers in front of her mouth, playing 'air clarinet'. She leaned over to me, sighed and said, 'It just wouldn't be Easter without the clarinet.'

I found more to celebrate after Easter when my mother, Joanie, called from Worcester with a news bulletin. I had sent her an enlarged photo of the coin Net found on the cornerstone of the Gatzoyiannis house, and she had taken it on a fact-finding mission to Bahnan's Market, a Mediterranean grocery shop where my aunts stock up on filo pastry, olive oil and other imported products. A Lebanese sales assistant scrutinized the Arabic letters in the image, ignoring the queue of irate shoppers forming behind Joanie, before informing her that it read 'One arsa, Constantinople', and the date was 1277. Explaining that Muslims date the year from Mohammed's journey to Mecca, and that the current year was 1423, he worked out that the coin was minted in 1856. Some time after that, but before my grandfather's older brother was born in the 1870s, the Gatzoyiannis house had been built by one of my unknown, unrecorded ancestors, who had placed this coin on the cornerstone to give the house strength and wealth. And perhaps to leave something for me to find one day.

With the Worcester grocery research, the excavation of the foundations had become a bicontinental endeavour. And it was far more than just simply bi-cultural. The coin had been minted by Turks, used by Greeks, found by Albanians, and identified by a Lebanese man working from a blown-up photo clutched by an inquisitive Midwesterner, who had married a Greek and got sucked into the mysteries of reconstructing his ancestral home. All roads now seemed to lead to Lia.

*

During the Easter feasting at Dina and Andreas's their visiting relatives, the Mouzinas, had invited me to celebrate my forthcoming nameday at their home in the northeastern city of Thessaloniki. I accepted eagerly, because I knew this would give me a chance to witness a famous – and infamous – ritual that takes place each year near Thessaloniki, when a religious group known as the Anastenarides walks barefoot on burning coals, clutching icons of Saints Eleni and Constantine. Traditionally, in Greece, birthdays aren't celebrated; you receive gifts and good wishes on the festival of the saint you're named after, without anyone ever mentioning how good you look for your age. My saint, Eleni, was the mother of St Constantine, the emperor who put the 'Holy' in Holy Roman Empire, converting his subjects to Christianity in the fourth century AD. Both saints are celebrated on 21 May.

Eleni is one of the most popular Greek names for women, as Constantine is for men. When I arrived in Thessaloniki, half of Greece was paying nameday calls on the other half, the government was at a standstill because the president, prime minister and several ministers named Constantine had to take time off to be adored by friends and family, and the radio station was playing twenty-four hours of songs that had the names Eleni or Constantine in them. Living in America, I felt my nameday never got the attention it deserved. So here in Greece I was determined to observe the day in a blaze of glory. Literally. That's where the Anastenarides came in.

The Anastenarides say their bare feet never get burned while dancing on the coals on the big day because St Constantine protects them. They've been doing their dangerous dance for centuries, most likely to commemorate a miraculous event that occurred in the thirteenth century, when villagers entered a burning church to save the icons of Saints Constantine and Eleni – who were crying out for help – and walked out unscathed. The American folklorist Anne Gault Antoniades, who in 1953 described the firewalking ritual as 'a Christianized remnant of a pagan cult', argued that it dates back even further, to the ceremonial dances for the wine-god Dionysus that were held in ancient Thrace.

Officially, anyway, the Orthodox Church would say that 'pagan cult' is right on the money. In recent history, the Anastenarides met with opposition from both Orthodox clergy (who don't have much of a tradition of saints 'possessing' worshippers) and the local gentry (who thought firewalking was primitive, and, well, tacky). But after the Second World War, foreign scientists started studying the rite, and folklorists began arguing that it was a unique aspect of Greek culture worth preserving, or at least tolerating.

Even today, the Mouzinas were divided on the value of the ritual. At lunch, Mrs Mouzina told me that the Anastenarides had sacrificed a bull that morning, adding, 'That is pure idolatry!' I wasn't sure that a bull sacrifice was any more idolatrous than roasting a lamb at Easter, but I was glad I had skipped the bloodletting to sleep late, and peacefully, in a house full of people.

As for Mr Mouzina, he was pro-firewalking. Driving me to Langadas, one of several villages that are home to the Anastenarides, he thundered, 'The church calls the Anastenarides heathens. I say, let the bishop walk on hot coals if he's closer to God!'

Amen to that. In Langadas, we went straight to the *konaki*, the whitewashed hut where the miraculous icons are kept. When I arrived, a wide-eyed boy was drumming and a middle-aged man was playing the *gaida*, an inflated bladder with a reed sticking out of it, like a bagpipe. Spectators ringed the periphery of the room, and in the middle, the Anastenarides began dancing to the rhythmic music, holding the icons above their heads. I had imagined that the movement would resemble Greek line dancing, but instead, the Anastenarides hopped and shuffled back and forth, like Native Americans in those old cowboy-and-Indian movies, who jump up and down saying 'Hi-ya, hi-ya'. Instead of hi-ya-ing, the Anastenarides were sighing heavily. (*Anastenazo* means 'to sigh'; people say the name Anastenarides derives from the fact that they sigh while firewalking.)

The music intensified and I pressed myself against the wall. I felt as if I was watching an ancient mystery, and worried that if I looked too hard I would be turned into a pillar of salt – or that someone would challenge me to walk across the burning coals, and instead of striding nobly across, I would end up char-grilled. During Easter, at church in Lia, I had been just another worshipper caught up in the miracle. Now it felt odd to go back to being an outside observer. I wanted to participate, but I was afraid, both of the heat and of my lack of divine protection. So I wandered out of the *konaki* towards the pyre, a teepee-shaped pile of sticks in the middle of a square of earth enclosed by chicken wire, and searched for Mr Mouzina, who had been swallowed by the crowd. There were hundreds of people, but only Anastenarides, their families and a few TV cameramen were being allowed inside the chicken-wire enclosure, where the Anasterides would dance on coals. Four policemen were on crowd-control duty; I heard one say into his cell phone, 'Happy nameday! . . . I got the Anastenarides again. Firewalking should be over at midnight, so I'll meet you then.'

Suddenly, I felt Mr Mouzina's hand on my back. 'Let us through,' he yelled. 'This girl is a reporter from America – you have to let her in!'

I'd seen this kind of aggressive, do-you-know-who-I-am approach tried by velvet-rope crashers in New York, and it never worked. So I was shocked when the policeman with the late-night-party plans parted the chicken wire so I could pass.

Deciding I'd better act like an American journalist, I moved towards the person the cameramen were interviewing, a portly gent in a chair, who turned out to be the Archanastenaris, the 'chief sigher'. I stepped right up and bravely asked if he was the president of the Anastenarides. He chuckled and sat up a bit straighter.

'I guess you could say that,' he said, grinning.

'Um, so is the talent hereditary?' I asked.

'It is,' he said. 'But it can skip a generation.' He smiled, Buddha-like.

'Why?' I asked. 'How do families decide who firewalks and who doesn't?'

'They don't decide,' the chief laughed. 'As for why – a person dances because the saint calls him.' He made it sound so simple. But I wondered, if a saint were to call me, would I hear?

For two hours, kids ran around the glowing fire, until the pyre had burned down to coals, which were raked into a circle with a stick. Loud singing emanated from the *konaki*. The four-person band filed out and the Anastenarides began shuffling around the circle of coals, some holding icons, others swaying their arms and upper body as if in a trance. They all looked intensely focused, with knitted brows and wild, blank stares. There were nine men and three women, including a heavyset old lady with a bandage trailing from her ankle, who looked like everybody's yia-yia. She also looked to be about two hundred pounds, so I worried about her crossing the coals safely.

They danced around the circle as the music crescendoed. One of the middle-aged men strode across the coals. We held our breath collectively. He made it across and looked none the worse for the experience. In fact, he seemed much happier than before, smiling through his sweat. Another man followed. Soon all the Anastenarides were shuffling, hopping and whirling in ecstasy in the middle of the glowing circle of coals. I was shocked at their transformation – they suddenly looked radiant, not freakish.

Although I was listening hard, I didn't get a call from the saint. I half hoped I would, so I could share this transcendent experience and leave as a different, perhaps better, person. Who knew what spiritual and physical transformation fire could perform? Maybe the crucible would even purify me of my ovarian cysts. But you can't fake a saint's call, and if I had tried it and ended up with third-degree burns, Mr Mouzina's wife would never let him forget it.

In his book *Firewalking and Religious Healing*, anthropologist Loring Danforth quotes several articles that insist that anyone can walk on coals as hot as 1,200 degrees Fahrenheit, because coals conduct heat poorly. But he doesn't recommend that you try this at home. As for me, I wasn't sure whether physics or piety protected the Anastenarides. But I knew I admired their faith, their willingness to walk into the fire, certain they would be transformed, better off for having faced the flames. My year in Greece was a leap of faith, so I could think of no better way to celebrate my nameday than with people who were testing their faith on the most basic level and emerging unscathed.

Back in Lia, the landscape was totally transformed, as if it, too, had shuffled over hot coals. In April and early May the village had had a subtler beauty, with sage-green mountains, slate-blue skies and woodsmoke in the air. Now everything was sharp, spotlit by the sun, and the lizards running across the road had turned the bright green of a Maybelline mascara wand to blend into the mountain. Everything was vivid and pungent, with the air smelling like plants, manure, and an occasional strong hit of star jasmine. Spanish broom exploded from the side of the road in great yellow masses, and smoke-bushes, which resemble fragile old ladies with lavender-tinted hair, were starting to bloom in lacy bunches. The magenta flowers of the Judas trees had disappeared, and a white-blossomed tree called *fraxos* clamoured for attention in their place.

I had only been gone a few days, but I was astonished to notice how beautiful the village was, overflowing with plants and animals. It seemed we had now entered tortoise season: they crossed the road slowly and deliberately, occasionally turning their necks just a little to stare, annoyed, at my car. There were infant animals everywhere. When I stopped for a glass of wine at the Xenona at sundown, a fleet of baby bats learning to fly kept springing unsteadily from the cracks in the stone walls of the inn, unable to swoop artfully like their parents. At Spiridoula's house, Thomas had strung wire along the corners of the verandah in front of the swallows' nests, so that the youngsters had a swing on

which to practise their take-offs. And as I drove towards
the Haidis house, I realized it was the first night of fire-
fly season; floating bursts of light surrounded me.

I arrived in Motsala as darkness was beginning to fall.
This was my favourite part of the day in Lia – the long
hours of the afternoon and early evening, when the
workday was done and people woke up from their post-
lunch naps to do exactly what they wanted, whether that
meant strolling through town or sitting to drink moonshine. Vlad, Net and Xalime were chattering in
Albanian, old Barba Prokopis and his wife, my next-door
neighbours, were sitting on their verandah, and the
house at the top of our path was now inhabited by
Athina and Grigoris Ganas. Athina, stocky with short
brown hair and wide glasses magnifying big green eyes
that watched over everyone's business, was tending her
hydrangeas when I said hello. She told me they'd be
staying until September, but had to return to Athens
once a month for Grigoris's chemotherapy treatments.
He had lung cancer, but although he was bald and
swollen, his baseball cap and booming voice when he
strode into the yard to greet me made it seem as if there
was nothing wrong.

I sat on my verandah until it was too dark to see any
more, admiring the huge green squash leaves that were
now filling my garden, then went inside to make some
tea. As the hot water gushed out of the tap, something
skittered across the sink – another scorpion! I thought
about calling Net to kill it for me. But he'd think I was
ridiculous, not to mention helpless. Ever since Dina had
told me about the tomato-stake incident, Net's way of
smiling made me uncomfortable – I couldn't tell if it
meant, 'I'm a shy Greek-as-a-Second-Language fifteen-
year-old and you're a foxy American adult,' or 'How

come I have to work all day clearing the ruins of your house while a capitalist pig like you sits on her butt playing on a computer?' So I picked up my shoe, bashed the scalded scorpion and scooped it up with a paper plate.

Exhausted after the slaughter, I climbed into bed. That's when I heard it . . . a tap, tap, tap sound coming from nowhere in particular. I had been annoyed that my aunts kept calling to check if I was sure I still wasn't scared, alone at night in the house. Now I wished they were here. It was three in the morning here, but only eight p.m. in Boston, so I dialled my sister, Marina. She wasn't there, but her room-mate's visiting sister was.

'Would you mind just staying on the phone while I look outside to see who's tapping?' I said to the stranger on the line.

'No problem,' she replied. 'I made my mom stay on the phone last week when the cable guy came unexpectedly — how did I know he was really a cable guy?'

In New York, I, too, had worried about crafty thieves and rapists posing as cable guys. Now I was in a Greek village at three-fifteen a.m., begging a stranger to stay on the line as I checked for wolves, ghosts, or psycho-killers in the dark. I was clearly going crazy. When I stepped on to the terrace, the yard was peaceful, glowing under a bright moon. So I thanked the stranger in Boston, hung up, and managed to fall asleep by four.

At ten-thirty the next morning, I was blasted awake by a car honking on the road above the house. Then I heard a man shouting, 'Eleni . . . Elenaki . . .'

Some kind of emergency, I thought. Rabid wolves? War with Albania? I pulled a sweater on over my blue daisy-print pyjamas, ran up the path and saw the postman, smiling in his red hatchback. He had a letter for me and the guys at the *kafenion* had told him I was home, so he thought he'd bring it over. I took the envelope, which turned out to contain a comic strip from one of my former colleagues, and said, 'Thanks so much!' But what I really meant was, 'Great, now the entire neighbourhood thinks I lie around in my pyjamas all day while they cook, clean and build houses.' I made a mental note: Get a grip. Sleep more. Start waking up at eight.

While I was watching the Anastenarides in Thessaloniki, the Gatzoyiannis house had undergone its own trial by fire. The Albanian family had disassembled the ruins into individual rocks to use in the rebuilding, and had torn down the outer door to the courtyard, carefully saving the arched stones. Now the place looked less spooky, but more forlorn – an empty lot instead of a ruined home. There were new trenches for the foundations, following the footprint of the original building. Vlad and his family had cut back the bushes and vines that had consumed the ruins and I could see clearly the outlines of the original dark basement. When Thitsa Tina returned to Lia for the first time, thirteen years after her mother's death, she had discovered a last message from her mother tucked into one of the walls of the Good Room – a small paper icon of the Panagia on which my grandmother had written her name, a prayer to the Virgin and the words, 'Don't be upset, I am all right. Mana.'

The house had yielded that treasure to my aunt and the Ottoman coin to Vlad. I had told Net I'd give him five Euros for each item he found, and so far I'd paid for a broken coffee cup, a clay pipe and two horseshoes. Today I looked around to see if the house had a message for me hidden somewhere, but all I saw were piles of rocks and churned-up soil. The mulberry tree stood like a skeletal sentinel, watching over the workers digging up the yard. The setting depressed me. I wasn't sure it could ever be a place that made me happy instead of anxious, a home instead of a pile of memories. At night I often wondered whether rebuilding the house was just a waste of money and energy, or, worst of all, something that would alienate the villagers. I knew that my aunts cried every time I mentioned the house, and that in Lia no one except Vlad, Net, Xalime and Thomas ever offered advice on the rebuilding or even visited the site. So although the Liotes seemed to enjoy attending festivals or sharing meals with me, a rare young person, I couldn't tell if they supported my project or not.

A week later, I was in the *kafenion* trying to imagine what the house would look like finished, when impassioned shouting jolted me to attention. An argument had erupted over who makes the better sausages, Greeks or Germans. In one corner, representing Germany, was a Liotan lady who had married a German, settled in Munich, and was here on holiday. In the other corner was everyone else, loudly protesting on behalf of the Greeks and particularly the Ifantis sausage dynasty, whose patriarch had been born in Lia. I slipped out before the heated argument could intensify into overturned chairs and flying beer bottles. But I felt a little better. Maybe my house project was misguided, but at least I wasn't the most obnoxious foreigner in town.

That night, over dinner at Dina's, I told everyone about the Great Sausage Debate, the newcomers at the *kafenion*, and how inflamed they all were by culinary chauvinism.

'It's exciting to have lots of people around,' Vangeli

Panagiotou said. 'But the village is really best in spring and autumn, when it's just a few of us.'

'What are you talking about?' Dina retorted, setting baked feta on the table. 'You'll hang out with anyone who strolls into the *kafenion* and buys you a beer.'

'That's true,' Vangeli answered. 'But you know what they say: With the shepherd wanting it and the artist not wanting it, even Jesus wears mountain boots.'

Everyone laughed, dug into the cheese and began listing the merits of Ifantis sausages. I knew I had missed something. 'What was that about Jesus and the boots?'

Vangeli, never one to ignore an audience, started to explain. 'Well, there's this shepherd, see, but he's made some money, maybe he sells his goats' milk to the Dodonis factory to make feta or something.' I was with him so far.

'Anyway, he commissions this artist to make him an icon of Jesus, but he wants Jesus portrayed as a shepherd. The artist says that's fine, and then the shepherd answers, "And he has to be wearing mountain boots like mine." The artist says, "Hold on. In all the icons of Jesus I've seen, none show him wearing mountain boots." The shepherd says, "The one I'm paying for will!" So with the shepherd wanting it and the artist not, even Jesus wears mountain boots. You've gotta do what you've gotta do.'

I wished I had some guidance as to what it was I had to do – to continue rebuilding the house or to respect my aunts' reluctance ever to see it again. The ground was ready for the foundations of the Gatzoyiannis house to be laid once more, approximately 150 years after the Ottoman coin was placed on the first cornerstone. But I wasn't sure of the wisdom of my mission.

And then, I received a mini-miracle, or at least the

kind of divine protection afforded to the firewalkers. George Zervas appeared in Lia to supervise the pouring of the foundations. I had called him several times to let him know we were ready, all in vain because of his scorn for telecommunications. But one morning I hiked up to the Gatzoyiannis house and there he was, looking around in a daze. I realized that he was following the jagged path of a metallic-hued June bug buzzing drunkenly through the air.

'Look, *chrysomiges* [gold flies],' Zervas said. 'When I was a kid, we would catch one, tie a string around it and watch it fly, like a kite. If you get a few, you can have races.'

I considered the bronze bugs, which had always struck me as looking like repulsive mini-aliens. Somehow they now seemed beautiful as they darted around, sparkling, like flying sweets wrapped in shiny paper. But I had no time for childhood reminiscences, or even for seeing nature in a new light. Zervas was going to wax philosophical no matter what; I had to keep my eyes on the prize. There was business to take care of here; a gaping square trench waited in the ground for the foundations to be poured in. Neat piles of stones that would once again join together to form walls ringed the excavation. I was determined to get the foundations poured today, while Zervas was here – who knew when he would return? I needed to see the cement in place, a concrete result that would prove my stay here had a good purpose, and that I was making progress.

'We're all ready to go,' I told Zervas proudly.

'Great.' He snapped out of his bug-induced daydream. 'Where's the rooster?'

'What rooster?'

'The rooster for the foundations. You know, when

you build a house, traditionally, you kill a rooster over the cement, leave the head in the foundations, cook the body and have a feast for the workers.'

'But why?' I asked, wondering why my aunts, with all their voluminous advice, had never told me this apparently essential bit of information.

'Well, all traditions have a practical and a spiritual basis,' Zervas explained. 'Practically, in the old days, people didn't eat meat often, so a rooster feast was a good incentive for the workers. And spiritually, the sacrifice makes the house stronger.'

'I don't want a weak house!' I shrieked. I turned to Foti, who was helping me supervise. 'Foti, do you have a rooster?'

'Sure,' he said. 'But just one, and I don't want all my hens to be widows.'

'Don't worry,' Thomas said, not about to let a poultry shortage make him late for lunch. 'We'll kill a rooster when we lay the foundations for the second floor.'

Zervas nodded. 'Let's get started then. Where's the priest?'

Oh yeah. The priest. I called Father Prokopi from my cell phone to let him know we had a spiritual emergency. He was available. Within fifteen minutes, Thomas had incised a cross into a slab that would serve as the first stone, and Father Prokopi was standing at the edge of the trench in his long black robe, red and white ceremonial alb and stovepipe hat. He instructed me to write the names of all the people who would live in the house on a piece of paper, then he shook his censer, filling the air with sweet smoke, and began chanting blessings for the house and its inhabitants.

As I wrote the names of my family, and of my aunts

and their children – the descendants of the original Eleni Gatzoyiannis – I wondered if my grandmother was watching and if she approved. Was she glad that we were putting the tumbled rocks of her house back together, or was the house itself, the scene of so much of her suffering, a source of bad luck? Was I setting things right or somehow putting another cycle of violence in motion?

A drop of holy water hit me in the eye, knocking me out of my reverie. Dipping a bunch of herbs into a bowl of holy water, Father Prokopi splashed the four corners of the foundations, then said, 'May you all live happily in this blessed home.' Looking at Father Prokopi silhouetted against the green trees and the purple mountains in the distance, I prayed that the souls of all the people who had suffered and died there might finally be released from the grim confines of the ruins. Then Father Prokopi dipped a metal cross into the water for all of us to kiss. Thomas, Foti, George Zervas and I all took a turn, and so did Vlad, Net and Xalime, apparently untroubled by the fact that they're Muslims. I dropped the first stone into the wet cement and everyone clapped. There was no rooster, but it was still a beautiful ceremony.

In lieu of a rooster feast, I invited everyone to lunch at the Xenona inn, which Zervas had also designed in the traditional style, a large stone building with wooden balconies upstairs and a huge dining room and sitting area around an open fireplace downstairs. But it was now warm enough to sit outside, under the plane tree in the stone-paved *plateia* in front of the inn. Over lunch, Foti promised me he'd look for a rooster with a big coxcomb for the foundations of the second storey; when it comes to lucky roosters, the bigger their coxcombs the better. I hoped Father Prokopi wasn't listening; I suspected that rooster killing might be as idolatrous as the Anastenarides' bull sacrifice. But he was chatting away with Thomas. George Zervas, however, still had roosters on his mind.

'You know, I didn't give you a good answer when you asked about killing the bird,' he said thoughtfully. 'I should have told you it's an ancient Greek ritual that survived, a sacrifice to appease the gods so they'll allow you to raise the house.'

Having lived here for three months now, I had sort of figured that out.

'So many things in Epiros have survived from Ancient Greece, like the folk songs,' he continued. 'In *The Odyssey*, Odysseus returns to find his father an old man, ploughing. He says, "I'm your son," and his father wants proof. So Odysseus says, "I know these are our fields," and the father responds, "Anyone could have told you that." Odysseus says, "Here's the scar from when Penelope's father's dog bit me," and the father says, "We all have scars on our ankles from something." Finally Odysseus describes the day they planted the crops together, and his father embraces him.'

'We have a song about that?' I asked. This was news to me.

'Not about Odysseus, but about a woman whose husband returns after years of working abroad. She wants proof that he is her beloved. He says, "In our yard an apple tree grows." She says, "That's true of most yards." He says, "By our door a fig tree grows." She responds, "The neighbours could have told you that." So he says, "On your breast, an olive grows" – meaning a beauty mark – and she embraces him.'

'That's racy!' I said.

'That's Homer,' he answered. 'Some people say all of Homer is just a series of folk songs strung together. I've collected three hundred songs from my grandmother and I want to turn them into a poem. Of course, it depends on my abilities whether anything good will come out of it. But I think it's a possibility.'

Zervas's life seemed full of possibilities, even at seventy-seven. He was so full of optimism that I suddenly felt positive as well. My life here in this ancient place would be epic poetry in motion, the house would be rebuilt beautifully, my cysts would shrink to nothing, and when we found a rooster to sacrifice, it would have the largest coxcomb on record.

By late June, the village was full of visitors looking for a good time. School had ended and Liotes who had emigrated poured back into town to join in the summer fun. Suddenly, my social calendar was full. Andreas took me to pick oregano, teaching me to choose stems that had white buds on them, so they looked like lily of the valley and smelled like a well-grilled steak. Dina showed me how to 'open' handmade filo pastry using a broomstick-like rolling pin, a talent which is the apotheosis of every village wife's cooking career. (Even the thitsas in Worcester don't have the patience to make their own filo pastry.) And everywhere I went, I met people who knew me, although I didn't know them. After church one Sunday an old woman in a black kerchief came up and planted a moist kiss on my cheek, explaining, 'Your father is my cousin.' I smiled and nodded. 'I'm so glad you're rebuilding the Gatzoyiannis house,' she con-tinued. 'That was my neighbourhood too.' Tears spilled out of the crimped corners of her eyes. 'May the Virgin Mary assist you!'

I always felt uncomfortable when old women I didn't recognize saw me and started to cry. It had happened before, on a visit to Lia, when one of my grandmother's neighbours, now dead, burst into tears, saying I looked so much like my grandmother it was like having Eleni standing before her again. As the tearful old woman walked away, a middle-aged man in a well-tailored suit tugged at my arm to introduce himself. 'I was the boy whose umbilical cord your grandmother ate so she could have a son,' he explained. I nodded, pretending I knew what he meant. Apparently, my poker face needed practice. 'That's what they did in those days,' he explained. 'She had your aunt Tina afterwards, but then your father, so it worked eventually.'

He smiled; a literature professor, he knew that genetics did not support the theory that he played a role in the conception of my father. But he was explaining that we were related, however mystically and illogically. I was used to living in a city of strangers, where we only knew what we told each other about our personal histories. Now I felt naked, not because of my lack of kerchief or my strappy sundress, but laid bare emotionally, when strangers came up and told me things that my relatives did not even know about themselves. I missed my anonymity, but I knew that this is what I had come for; to have my family's past greet me at every turn, with no escape, and to let our past inform my future.

As for everyone else, they had come because it was *panegyri* season, a non-stop succession of festivals that would culminate in the Virgin Mary's holiday on 15 August. *Panegyria* happen all over Greece, although the songs played by the band and the food served from spits and communal pots differ from place to place. But everywhere, a *panegyri* is fun for the whole family: little kids run around, teenagers show off their dance moves and old people gossip about everyone else. My own, unsubstantiated theory is that the word *panegyri* comes from the word *gyro*, for circles, and the god Pan, because Pan liked to party hard and kick up his little goat heels in circles.

I was kicking up my own heels all over the mountain range. I threw my donation into the basket at the *panegyri* for Agios Prokopi in Lista. (It's pay by donation, Foti explained, because the Listans figured out they make more money that way than by charging for food — everyone wants to be seen tossing in an impressive amount.) In Agia Marina, I listened to old men harmonize as they squatted in a circle recalling words to a forgotten Epirotic tune. I even supervised ten-year-old boys running from the churchyard to the cemetery in Glousta during the festival of St John the Baptist.

But my favourite celebration occurred at the *panegyri* of Agia Triada, right in Lia, when I joined my fellow villagers in a parade to show off our icon of the Holy Trinity, which was framed by pink and fuchsia hydrangeas for the occasion. At the end of the evening service in the central Agia Triada church, Antonis Makos, the Church Council president, picked up the icon and took the lead, followed by Father Prokopi wielding his censer, Spiro and Sofia the cantors, and several boys who had come on holiday with their families and been given the important task of carrying the gold standards used in church parades. We proceeded towards the church of Agia Paraskevi, in front of the men drinking coffee at the *kafenion* who rose to cross themselves as we passed, singing hymns devoted to particular saints.

In the middle of one hymn, Costa, the eight-year-old

son of the *kafenion* owners, yelled, 'A car's coming!' We stayed put, singing, figuring that any car could wait for the Father, Son and Holy Ghost. That's the risk you take driving along the one road through the Mourgana mountains: sheep or saints could stop you at any turn. I was flushed with the thrill of power. Lia may be small, poor and remote, but when we got together to make a joyful noise unto the Agia Triada, we stopped traffic.

There were a few secular celebrations as well. Net turned sixteen, and we marked the occasion with souvlaki and fries around Andreas's homemade swimming pool. Net and his parents had been working on the Gatzoyiannis house's walls for over a month now, and they had a system all worked out: Net poured water into the concrete mixer, Xalime carried concrete and stones to the foundations in a wheelbarrow, and Vlad laid rocks and concrete on top of each other. I was surprised that Xalime did the heavy lifting, until I realized she was probably the strongest of the three. In any case, I wasn't about to volunteer to replace her, so I kept my mouth shut.

By the first week in July, the basement was finished and we were ready to pour foundations for the ground floor. I knew what this meant: it was time for a rooster to meet its maker. Part of me found the idea of a sacrifice disgusting and barbaric. But I knew you didn't raise a house in Lia without decapitating a rooster, and as a new villager I had to play by the rules. Besides, this was a free-range rooster, who had inseminated lots of hens and lived to a ripe old age, and I planned to put every part of him to good use, cooking his body to nourish citizens of three different nations (Greece, America and Albania), and immortalizing his head in a building. What more could a rooster ask?

For all my rhetoric, I still felt guilty when Foti pulled a struggling rooster out of his truck by its legs, which were tied together. An old black rooster with an impressive coxcomb, he was less than feisty. Maybe I was saving him from a long, slow death from disease, and giving him a glorious martyr's end. I had almost convinced myself that I was doing him a favour when Foti handed me an axe and said, 'Here you go.'

'No way!' I said, dropping the axe. 'I mean, I think the chief builder should do the honours – besides, I need to take pictures to document the ceremony.'

No one argued with me, so I stood in the semi-circle of spectators around Thomas and the rooster: Net, Xalime, Vlad and Foti. Even Grigoris Ganas had insisted on coming up to the house, although his wife had said he should rest, since he was weak from chemotherapy. But Grigoris had been in the construction business himself, and loved a good rooster ceremony, so he stood next to me as I gripped my camera.

Thomas put a board on the edge of the wet cement, laid the rooster's neck on top of it, raised the axe and let it fall. It took a few hacks to sever the head, and the rooster jerked a bit. But he didn't jump up and run around with blood spurting from his neck stump, which is what I'd expected. As I snapped photos of the severed head before Thomas covered it with more cement, Net walked over to Thomas and asked, 'Why did we kill a rooster? Isn't there enough blood in this house already?'

The villagers had told him that after the Civil War, they'd uncovered the bodies of thirty-seven people who had been killed by the Communist soldiers and buried in the yard of the house. It was a gruesome statistic, and Net was just a clever boy making an observation. But I still felt heat rise to the tips of my ears. Did he think

I was being ridiculous and callous rebuilding this house? Did all the villagers, who could be counted on not only to know my business, but also to have an opinion on it, agree?

If they did, what was it to me? I thought, striding angrily towards the car. I didn't need Net's approval, or my aunts'. All old houses have ghosts and tragedies. A home is a place where people's lives take place, and life includes pain and suffering. I wanted a rooster sacrificed because there was blood in this house, and I refused to let it languish as a former cemetery. I was going to turn it into a home again, and I needed all the help I could get. If three thousand years of Greek tradition told me that that meant killing a rooster, so be it. Anger pulsed throughout my body; I had whipped myself into sixty inches of indignation when Grigoris caught up with me, wheezing from the exertion. 'Wear the white dress you wore last night,' he said. I looked up, cross and confused. 'To the rooster dinner,' he continued. 'You look pretty in that.' He smiled and my anger dissipated. Grigoris and Foti had come to see my building site, after all, and we all had rooster blood on our hands (just figuratively speaking, thank God). At least now we were in this together.

Net wasn't complaining about the rooster when we gathered at Foti's house that night to eat it. Normally, the task of preparing the rooster fell to the *noikokyra*, the lady of the house. But I had never even imagined cooking one, so Spiridoula, as wife of the contractor and all-around expert, rose to the task, transforming a scrawny bird into a delicious wine-flavoured stew over spaghetti. Foti, having donated the rooster, allowed me to hold the event at his place, since I didn't have enough chairs. My contributions were an apple pie and a toast: 'To the rooster! May his memory be eternal!'

Lia was down one rooster. But she was gaining inhabitants daily, as people streamed in for the high point of the social calendar: the festival of Prophet Elias. Most Greek villages have a chapel to Prophet Elias on one of the highest peaks in the area, where the temple to Helios used to be in pagan times. Helios was the sun god and needed to be high up so he could ride his golden chariot to the sun. The Prophet Elias never actually died, he just rode up to heaven on his golden chariot, so he likes a sky-high chapel himself. (Father Prokopi once told me that before the end of the world, God is going to send Prophet Elias down to Jerusalem to be martyred, so he can leave his physical remains on earth like the rest of the saints. 'We won't know who he is,' Father Prokopi added thoughtfully, 'but maybe we'll see it happen on TV.')

In Lia, the saint's day of Prophet Elias is an even bigger to-do, because he is the patron saint of the village. Ever since his church has existed (and probably back when it was a temple to Helios), Liotes have climbed the mountain to pay their respects on the day of the festival, and celebrated on the nights before and after. It was during the festival in 1939 that my grandmother sent for the *mami*, the midwife, to come down from the dancing and help her give birth to the baby who would become my father. Since the Germans burned the village's records, the only way my father established his birth date – 23 July – was when, as an adult, he learned from an old woman in Lia that he was born on the third day of the festival.

So when my parents heard how many Liotes were returning for the *panegyri*, they decided to come and spend my father's birthday in Lia. I was excited to see them. With two other people in the house I would definitely sleep better, I could force Joanie to help battle the killer mould that had invaded my closets, and it might be fun to celebrate as a family. After all, how much trouble could a couple of parents cause?

We were in happy family-reunion mode on 19 July when we headed to church for the service and litany of the Prophet Elias. Only two of us actually made it to Agia Triada, however; my father felt the call of the *kafenion* as profoundly as Joanie and I felt the call of the saint, so he was drinking *tsipouro* with his cronies when we streamed out with the congregation, following Father Prokopi in the procession of the prophet's icon around the village.

Later that night we reunited in the churchyard, ready to party. A woodcarver from Metsovo was selling his wares, another pedlar hawked roasted corn, and Stella the *kafenion* owner sliced pieces off a lamb revolving on a spit. Local dignitaries arrived: members of parliament, a deputy mayor, and two mayoral candidates in forthcoming elections. Soon, four hundred people from nearby villages had poured in — a good showing, considering that many Liotes could not attend because they were in mourning.

The president of the Liote Brotherhood invited Father Prokopi to lead the first dance. At first, he demurred — he had a sore foot after the icon parade. But it is a tradition in Lia for the priest to kick off the *panegyri*, so he removed his hat and led four consecutive dances.

The first song was an Epirote tune about a handsome priest (a nod to Father P, whose cassock was flying out behind him as he kicked and twirled). I danced, my father danced, and, proving the adage that poverty needs a good time, Vlad and Net danced more vigorously than anyone else. As new immigrants, they were Lia's poorest residents, living rent-free in Dina and Andreas's one-room shack. But they stayed, because Vlad seemed to feel that the twenty-seven Euros each of them made per day rebuilding our house (along with the health insurance we paid for them each month in Filiates) offered them a better life than the one they had left behind in Albania. As the clarinet wailed, they leapt and stamped and flicked their wrists like aristocrats.

The following morning, we were up at six forty-five to participate in the centuries-old ritual of climbing to the mountain peak. My father drove me and Joanie to the old border-guard post, handed us two walking sticks and said, 'Have a good time.' He couldn't climb, he said, because of his heart condition. So my mother and I hiked up the dirt paths, passing friends on the way. Everyone was in high festival spirits, despite the early hour. Everyone except me. I've never been a morning person, so when we finally made it to the jam-packed chapel the size of the freight lift of my building in New York, I sat outside on the edge of the cliff, baking in the sun like a salamander.

Father Prokopi would occasionally step outside to waft the sweet smoke of incense over those of us who were worshipping al fresco. In between censes, I listened in on my fellow villagers. 'Kyrie Vassili, I haven't seen you here in years,' said one old man to another. 'It was the Occupation, 1944? I was nine years old.'

'That's the last time I made it up,' Kyrios Vassilis agreed. 'I wasn't sure I'd be able to again. But here I am.' He turned to admire the view, leaning on a stick.

Eventually, even we bystanders were swept up in the service as two efficient women carried a table out from the church, unwrapped several huge, round, frosted breads, and sliced them into hunks. They passed pieces around as Father Prokopi emerged smiling, carrying a metal cross for us to kiss, and waving a clump of basil to splash holy water on us. «Χρόνια Πολλά παιδιά,» he said. 'Many years, children.' «Και του χρόνου!» 'And next year!'

'Next year, God willing,' responded Kyrios Vassilis.

'Now if you'll hold on a bit, I'm going to do a brief memorial service for Elias,' Father Prokopi continued, referring to Marianthe's forty-year-old son, whose wife had taken the kids shopping one morning and returned to find him slumped in his chair, dead from a heart defect he hadn't known he had. Suddenly, in the middle of a blessing, Father Prokopi stopped chanting. His thin frame started shaking and he sobbed quietly for several minutes as the rest of Lia stared. Soon we were all crying, too, frustrated that for all his good intentions, none of Father Prokopi's chanting would bring back this lost member of the village, a man whose life we should have been celebrating today, on his nameday, instead of mourning his death.

Eventually, Father Prokopi composed himself and finished the service, and everyone kissed each other goodbye and started climbing down, some to pick oregano, others heading straight home, scattering across the mountainside like the holy water Father Prokopi had splashed over us. Joanie and I started down and bumped into Thomas driving his pick-up, the only four-wheel-drive vehicle that had made it up to the top, ferrying several loads of people too old or too citified to climb.

'Hop in,' said Spiridoula. 'There's room.' There were

nine of us squeezed into the back of the pick-up, eight women and one old man. Father Prokopi, striding by with a gym bag full of holy articles, declined a ride. He knew what he was doing, I realized, as we bumped down the mountain over rocks and clods of earth, with villagers waving at us and Thomas yelling, in his best gypsy-grocer voice, 'Nice fresh women. Take your pick.'

We got out at the Gatzoyiannis site, halfway down to the village square, where the growing grey walls were just beginning to take on the outline of a house. Vlad and his family had skipped the service and, with the basement done, were now starting to pile stones and mortar on top of each other to form the very beginnings of the second-storey walls. My father was also there, toying with an old hand grenade Net had found on the building site. People passing by on their way down from Prophet Elias glanced at the work in progress, but it was still just the suggestion of a house, not a finished home, and they had nameday calls to pay on all the local men named Elias, so they kept moving.

Back at the Haidis house, as Joanie and I lay down to rest from the morning's exertions, I said, 'It's only one o'clock, and it's already been a great day.'

At one-thirty, my father walked into the house, blocking the light coming through the bedroom door. 'Get up,' he said.

Joanie did. I didn't. I needed my rest.

'The bad news is I totalled the car,' he said. 'The good news is I'm alive.'

I sat up in bed, trying to understand this. He had taken the car to go and visit some friends, he explained.

'Right, you took my car, and then?' I asked.

Well, these friends had a long narrow driveway, and

instead of making them move their car so he could turn around, he thought he'd reverse out of it. Except that he'd reversed off the driveway; the car had rolled over once and landed on the road below.

I was in shock. So was he. I stood up. He went to lie down. 'Your pants are torn,' I said. I went into the living room to collect my thoughts, and Joanie came into the bedroom to investigate. My father had scraped his legs and butt, she reported.

I heard the gate slam. Foti rushed in, tears welling in his eyes. 'What happened?' he cried. 'I saw the wrecked car near the Xenona.'

'He drove off the road,' I answered. 'The car flipped over, but he's OK.'

'It was a miracle,' Foti said, sighing. 'The saint saved him.' He walked to the bed, kissed my father on the cheek, and made the sign of the cross. Looking at Foti, I knew he was right: my father was alive because Prophet Elias had given us a miracle.

'It was the evil eye that drove you off the cliff,' Foti continued, putting everything into perspective. 'Everyone passed by the house today, saw how quickly it was being built, and felt jealous. They praised it and they gave you the evil eye.'

Foti was losing me. I thought the careless brain was more at fault here than the evil eye; my father should have known better than to reverse off a cliff. Besides, I refused to believe that the house could be responsible for my father's accident, even indirectly. That would make this all my fault.

'He's bleeding,' Joanie said. 'Nick, take off your pants to show Foti.'

Everyone paused. Foti turned to me. 'Do you want me to take you to see the car?'

I did indeed. Looking at the mashed hunk of metal, I realized that when Prophet Elias performs a miracle, he does not mess around. Each window was broken and the windscreen had buckled. If Joanie or I had been in the passenger's seat instead of sleeping off our trek, we'd be dead. If the car hadn't hit the huge rock that had held it in place, it could have rolled right on down the mountainside. I was shaky with gratitude and disbelief.

By the time Foti drove us home, my father's calf had swollen to the size of a honeydew. Always eager to help, Foti offered to drive him to the hospital in Ioannina to get checked out, while I waited for a recovery vehicle to retrieve Asymina's crushed carcass. I thought back to the moment in Athens when the Avis clerk told me insurance cost an extra six Euros a day. 'That's 180 Euros a month!' I'd said, outraged. But I'd heard NickGage's voice saying, 'Get the insurance.' So I did. The Prophet Elias plans ahead.

That afternoon, a tow-truck driver in red overalls arrived, attached a huge cord to Asymina's earthly remains and pulled them on to his truck. Seeing that I had separation anxiety, he handed me a clipboard and said gently, 'Fill this out. I'll need twenty-four Euros for the ferry to Athens.'

Although I knew we were lucky that my father was alive, I was really annoyed at not having a car – and even angry that, while I had been a responsible driver for months, within one week of arriving in Greece my esteemed father had trashed my car joyriding around the village. But as Asymina receded into the distance on the back of the tow truck, I realized that steel can be fixed and humans can't. Prophet Elias had made the right choice.

Back at the house, I was just starting to calm down when the phone rang. 'Lenitsa!' a voice screeched so loudly that I had to hold the receiver a foot away from my ear to prevent hearing loss. 'What happened? I have to know the truth! If you lie to me I curse you, so you marry a man who lies, lies, lies all the time.'

'Hi, Thitsa Kanta,' I said, amazed at how quickly news had spread from Lia to Worcester. 'NickGage is fine. Foti took him to the hospital, just to be safe.'

'Oh, the shepherd's with him. Good.' She calmed down. 'Why didn't you go?'

'I had to stay because the tow truck was coming to pick up the car – it's totalled and smoke was coming from the engine,' I explained.

'Oh, *Panagia mou!*' Thitsa Kanta keened. 'You don't need to tell me that. You just like the doctors today, they tell you everything. I tell my doctor, if something wrong, I don't need to know, but someone got to make plans. If I'm gonna die, you call my son.'

'Well, no one's going to die today, Thitsa Kanta,' I assured her.

'You better be telling me the truth,' she repeated before hanging up. 'Otherwise someone else in the village will, and you know, my curses work. God loves your thitsa!'

In the end, I didn't need to worry about curses. We knew my father was fine when he returned from the hospital beaming and reported that even without insurance, the bill for all his tests and X-rays came to less than sixteen dollars.

We were all exhausted from the long, dramatic day. But the only way Thitsa Kanta and assorted Liotes of Lia and Worcester would believe that NickGage was all right was if they heard he had danced at the *panegyri* as he had the night before. That was what it meant to live in Lia: the entire village became your meddling extended family, relatives who love you too much to leave you in peace. As I watched my father dance opposite the clarinettist, I realized that I knew what the sceptics who had studied the Anastenarides hadn't been able to figure out. Life is risky, and people get burned. So you'd better pray that you have saints — or even civilians — looking out for you.

5

MOTHER TONGUES

«Πολλοί άνθρωποι, πολλές γνώσεις.»
'Many people, many opinions.'

29 July

*'Look what I found,' Net yells, striding towards me with
a heap of tangled metal.*

*'Thanks!' I grab the rusted, lyre-shaped object, which
has a hook hanging from it. 'So what is it?'*

*'You don't know?' Net asks. He turns it around, hold-
ing it by the hook so the lyre now hangs upside-down,
like the letter π, with two curved legs. I shrug.*

*'It's a tsellinge!' he bursts out. 'You put it on a rod
in the fire, for to hang the meat and roast.' Now Net is
laughing so hard that he snorts.*

*How could I have known that? I'm not exactly in the
habit of roasting meat on a hook above a roaring fire.
I give him his five-Euro finder's fee and thank him
again.*

'No say thank you,' Net protests. 'Not mine. Tsellinge *belong to your family.*'

He's right. I rub the rusted metal and think that the last person who touched it may have been my grandmother, who did roast meat above the fire on the rare occasions she could get some. The coin had been an interesting artifact, a clue to the history of the house. But these hooks are something more: direct contact with the grandmother I never met. As the house yields more clues, I am starting to consider my grandmother's life more than her death. Holding the tsellinge, I see her for a moment, bending over the fire in the space where the fireplace once was and soon will be again.

I turn to thank Net again. He and Xalime are mixing mortar for Vlad to spread between the stones of the slowly growing walls, chatting in Albanian.

If I came to Greece to 'find myself', when I got there, I found everyone else. And they each spoke their own language. I had travelled enough to know that 'Greek culture' is not one concrete, monolithic category: there's island life, mountain villages, hectic cities. Even the language has several different registers, levels of formality, and dialects. But I thought that by moving to the remote province my family came from, I was narrowing my options to one cohesive cultural milieu, characterized by an oatmeal-mouthed village accent. By midsummer, however, I realized there are almost as many obscure cultural groups in Epiros as in any liberal arts university that touts its 'diversity'.

Even in Lia, which in late July was nearing its full capacity of three hundred or so inhabitants, only about half were native Liotes. There were several Northern Epirotes – the Christian, ethnic Greeks from Albania –

including a family of three master stonemasons I had hired at great expense to do the really difficult stonework Vlad wasn't skilled enough to handle, and to speed up the building process. Then there were the mostly Muslim Albanians, like Vlad, Net and Xalime, who were still working for me, under the master stonemasons' supervision, starting to build the second-storey walls. And a number of widows and widowers, here for the summer, had acquired caretakers from the Ukraine to cook, clean and, in at least one case, boss them around like army generals. (A seventy-year-old, diaphanous-blouse-wearing Ukrainian vamp hired Vlad and Net to rid her employer's house of old junk by dumping it into the ravine, creating a grotesque landfill of beds, bureaux, olive-oil tins and bedspreads.)

I wasn't happy about the newly created rubbish dump, but on the whole I liked the formerly Communist Bloc new arrivals in Lia. All except the Yugoslavian-made Skoda we had been given by Avis to replace Asymina, the Hyundai my father had destroyed. A squat blue vehicle with upholstery that featured female robots in triangular miniskirts dancing a kick line, the Skoda's main drawback was that it had a gearstick, which I could not operate. Avis said an automatic car was impossible to find now that it was high tourist season and all the other isolationist honkies who were too lazy to learn to drive a manual car had already rented them. (They didn't say exactly that, but it was implied.) Since I was not the one who had committed vehicular homicide on Asymina, I reasoned, it was not my responsibility to find myself another automatic; it was my father's. But he didn't seem quite as troubled by my lack of wheels as I was; there was plenty of excitement right here in town, he said, now that

Lia was full of old friends to visit. Who needed a car?

My father was in denial about his accident; I had moved on to anger. But Thitsa Kanta was more interested in blame, calling from Worcester to lay it directly at my feet. 'You didn't believe the curse, and look what happened,' she boomed into the phone.

'The curse?' I asked.

'When my mother say goodbye to me and your father, she make us throw black stones behind us and promise not to come back to Greece to live or we would have her curse,' she explained. 'It's OK to come for vacation like I do, one–two months, but not to live like you. That's why NickGage had the accident; it was a warning he should go home, take care of his family, not worry about that cursed place.'

Just what I needed – another reason to feel guilty about my presence in Lia. Of course, I didn't really believe that my father's dead mother had crashed my rental car with him in it as a subtle warning. On the other hand, Thitsa Kanta knew more about curses than I did.

A few days after Asymina's untimely demise, we went to lunch at the home of a woman everyone called 'the Papadia' – the priest's wife – although her husband, the village's former priest, had been dead for several years. (Actually, *presvytera* is the correct term for a priest's wife; Papadia is a village nickname, as some Athenian girls I met once were kind enough to point out. They were the same girls who clued me in to the fact that fireflies should be referred to as *pygolambides*, 'bearers of light', instead of the village term my aunts had taught me: *kolofoties*, or 'ass-on-fires'. In Lia, the tiny, white-haired widow was delighted to be called the Papadia.) As we ate, she asked about my travels. I told her about visiting Metsovo at Easter, how surprised I had been to see women in native costume chattering away in Vlachiko.

'Did you see any Sarakatsanis in Metsovo?' the Papadia asked. 'There used to be a family with a summer place in the mountain there.'

'Like a vacation house?' I asked.

'No!' her nephew burst in, laughing. 'Sarakatsanis are nomadic shepherds, who graze their sheep in the mountains in summer and in the lowlands in winter. You used to see their straw huts in the countryside. There are probably only about five nomadic Sarakatsanis left now. The rest are doctors, lawyers, whatever. But they're proud of their history. They're organized into federations all over Greece. A friend who was president of the Epirote federation told me they gather every first weekend in August at a village of huts in the Zagorohoria.' He tore off a hunk of bread. 'I could put you in touch.'

I'd never expected to see straw huts or nomads, even reformed ones, in Greece. The first weekend in August was three days away. I told my father he had seventy-two hours to find an automatic car. By Saturday he'd located one at a small firm in Ioannina. Now I just had to get myself there. My parents needed the Skoda, so they could return it on Sunday as they left for the US. I was worried, but NickGage had all the answers.

'My friend Babis is driving to Athens this afternoon, so he can take you to Ioannina,' he told me on Saturday. 'I know you'll insist he leaves you at the rent-a-car place, but he offered to drive you all the way to the Sarakatsani meeting, which would be much safer.' (Since his accident, my father liked to pretend I was the bad driver. I believe mental-health professionals call this 'projection'.)

Babis looked like Billy Bob Thornton: bald, thin and with an insane gleam in his eye. He already had three passengers in his car, so I squeezed in between two strangers as rain started to fall. Pressed thigh to thigh, we were making uncomfortable small talk as Billy Babis sped along the curving road to Ioannina. On one hairpin turn, the car began to skid. The woman on my right screamed and Billy Babis swore as his car slammed into a copse of trees that blocked us from rolling down the cliff. No one spoke. Billy Babis got out, checked his BMW for damage, then got in, reversed out of the grove and sped on without a word. The woman on my left spent the rest of the ride hunched over, her head in her hands. I no longer had to make small talk, which was just as well because I didn't think I'd be able to; I was too painfully aware of the fact that now two members of my family had almost died driving off the mountain, nearly fulfilling a curse I claimed not to believe.

In Ioannina, I bid farewell to Billy Babis, wished his passengers good luck and signed a contract that brought me together with my new Hyundai, a twin of Asymina although she was gold instead of silver. I named her Chrysanthi, 'Golden Flower', and we sailed towards the Zagorohoria, a collection of forty-six grey, misty villages which cling to the edge of the mountains like barnacles on a ship, scattered around the periphery of the Vikos Gorge, the deepest gorge in the world. I motored through miles of unpopulated forest on to Giftokambo, a pine field that is home to the Sarakatsaniko Stani, a group of straw huts representing a seasonal Sarakatsani village. Leaving my new best friend in an open field-cum-parking lot, I walked towards the entrance past hundreds of tents full of Sarakatsani families; over five thousand guests come to the *Antamoma*, or 'meeting', each year.

At the arched wooden entrance to the park I found Christos Raptis, the former president of the Epirote Federation of Sarakatsanis, who had been told to watch for me. With red cheeks, blue eyes and a white moustache, Raptis was a walking embodiment of Sarakatsani goodwill; there was nothing he liked to do more than talk about Sarakatsanis, and the Stani in particular.

It was a collection of eight round thatched huts called *kalives*, and one rectangular one, a later innovation. This was a smallish village, he explained; anywhere between two and fifty huts was the norm. He pointed out the *kaliva* where the teacher lived and taught students sitting on tree stumps, and the mini-me hut that was the chicken's own poultry *kaliva*. Each human hut had a circle of stones that functioned as a fireplace in the middle of the dirt floor, an icon on the wall, and a cross and a thorn branch sticking out of the rounded roof, to keep evil spirits from coming inside. On the floor was a pile of blankets where the family slept: grandparents at one end, parents at the other and kids in the middle, so they couldn't wander out. 'Everything happened in this same space,' Christos said cheerfully. 'Sleeping, meals, sex.'

It all sounded so ... unsanitary. But somehow Christos made the situation seem cosy, waxing nostalgic about how men milked the sheep and women wove together. 'This was the first commune,' he said in a blissful tone.

'Does anybody actually remember this kind of rustic lifestyle?' I asked.

'Well, there's me – my family was nomadic until I was twelve,' he answered, striding towards the sheep pens. 'My wife's until she was eight.' He pointed to a brunette in a peach trousersuit who looked as though she didn't go anywhere without a travel iron. 'Most families stopped travelling in the sixties. Greece was modernizing, people wanted to educate their kids, give them opportunities. It's a hard life being a nomad.'

He led me to a picnic table at the edge of a stone dance floor with a huge bonfire in the middle, then plonked a feast of souvlaki and wine in front of me. A band started playing and scores of tall young men and girls in tight jeans ran up to form concentric circles of dancers.

'The aim of this gathering is for younger generations to get an idea of what nomadic life was like, to learn to value our traditions,' he explained, pointing out his two teenage daughters.

A secondary goal of the event, I gathered, was to party hard. The next day, when I found the Raptis family, the girls told me they had stopped dancing at seven-thirty that morning, when the band took a break so people could attend church. Now the Sarakatsani youths, having napped in their tents, were milling around the huts, dressed in traditional garb, ready to perform in the Sarakatsani dance exhibition. The girls wore black pleated skirts and blouses embroidered with geometric patterns, sometimes accessorized by chains of coins crisscrossed across their chests like bullet holsters. Some boys wore scratchy-looking white woollen trousers and others, even luckier, were in *fustanelles*, the traditional white pleated miniskirts, and black tops with wing-like panels hanging off the shoulders.

I sat on a tree stump as the Federation president rose

to speak. 'Sarakatsanis were the first Greeks, the first Europeans,' he intoned. 'We have never been conquered!'

This sounded a little like nomadic propaganda to me. But most anthropologists do think that since the Sarakatsanis were such an insular community, seldom intermarrying with outsiders, they are the closest 'race' to the Ancient Greeks. Then the dances started.

'Sarakatsani women were so modest they used to dance with their eyes cast downwards, because it would compromise them to look into a man's eyes,' Christos explained. His daughter, a civil-engineering student, winked at us as she danced past.

Having visited the Sarakatsanis in the 1950s, Patrick Leigh Fermor described them as 'true nomads . . . they hover on the outskirts of ordinary Greek life as fleetingly as a mirage'. But today, the politicians and housewives around me were nothing if not mainstream. Since they speak Greek, look Greek, and now live like other Greeks, the only way for Sarakatsanis to preserve their identity as a community is by celebrating together, dancing their dances and recalling the past. It's an elusive balance, but perhaps what we all want – the romance of the virgin forest and straw hut, and the hygiene of a bathroom and separate bedrooms. I was doing the same thing to a degree: living my family's past for a bit, trying to preserve what's important for our future.

As if to replace my parents, who had returned to the US, a new foreigner had arrived in Lia – Vlad's eighteen-year-old daughter Dorina, whose boarding school in Tirana had broken up for the summer. We met over dinner at Dina's; Dorina had adorable dimples and a compulsion to chat. She didn't speak Greek, but her school was run by Italian nuns, and I had studied Italian for a year in college, so we got by. As we dug into our lamb chops, she described her home (Albania is beautiful but poor), her fiancé (a twenty-two-year-old soldier who wants to move to America) and both her grandmothers (one was Catholic and the other Orthodox Christian, but both converted to Islam at some point, then gave up religion under Communism). She told me lots of other things, too, but I couldn't quite make them out. 'You speak Italian like a Spanish person,' she said, grinning.

I did understand when she said, wide-eyed, 'I can't believe we're all in one room. I told my father this is no way for a family to live! There's no room for any more people over here.' I looked around. Dina and Andreas's courtyard was cluttered with tubes and rocks: Andreas was building an artificial waterfall, fed with mountain water that rushed into his pool. Ever since his son died, he had dreamt up one home-improvement project after another to keep busy. He reminded me of sharks, who die if they don't keep moving.

'You can stay with me until my sister comes to visit,' I told Dorina. She smiled, then ran next door to get her toothbrush.

The next morning, I took her on a walk up to the Gatzoyiannis house to visit her family at work. Vlad, Net and Xalime thought it hilarious that we had walked up in the hot sun by choice. It didn't seem to make Dorina uncomfortable that her family was lifting stones and mixing cement while we strolled around, doing nothing useful, but I felt awkward, so I continued on to a house above. To the left of its new white aluminium front door was an old wooden one with broken hinges and coats of variegated blue paint that looked like the different depths of the ocean. It was an ancient lye-based paint, worn and faded by time.

'Hey, Net,' I called. 'Do you know what they're doing with this door?'

'Throwing it out.'

'Really?' I said. 'Can you bring it to me in the truck when you come home?'

Net stopped spreading mortar on a block of stone and looked up at me, shielding his eyes from the sun. 'What do you want that old door for?'

'I just like the colour,' I replied. He kept staring at me, expecting a more reasonable answer than that. 'Maybe I'll make it into a table,' I improvised.

He laughed and said something to Dorina in Albanian that made her dimple.

That afternoon, Dorina and I were eating at Dina's when her family came home from work.

'Dina, can we have some buckets of hot water, please?' Net called.

'I keep telling you, just use our shower,' Dina yelled back. But she took him his bucket anyway. 'Sometimes Vlad and Net use the shower, but Xalime never does,' she whispered to me. 'I think they're not used to showers, but because the girl lives at a school she is. That's why she's so glad to stay with you; you have one.'

I was happy to promote good hygiene. And Dorina only came over to shower and sleep. I didn't feel obliged to entertain her, so I would occasionally hop into Chrysanthi and drive off in search of adventure.

One night, at a dinner in the harbour city of Igoumenitsa, I met Georgia Vaya, a brunette in a smart navy suit who was married to the mayor of Arta.

'On Saturday I'm going to be the *koumbara* at a gypsy wedding in Arta,' I heard her say to the hostess. (The *koumbara* and *koumbaros* are the wedding equivalent of godparents.) 'I can invite anyone I want. Do you want to see the gypsy neighbourhood?'

'I do!' I jumped at the chance. Even when they lived in pick-up trucks and walked around barefoot, all the gypsies I'd seen had gold jewellery, working TVs and a unique fashion sense – they fascinated me. But most of my fellow Liotes were less entranced by the pedlars who drove through town daily hawking tables, sheets and live poultry. The Liotes warned me that gypsies would try to cheat me and were known to steal babies, so it was a good thing I didn't have any.

'How come the gypsies are still so poor and nomadic?' Nikki the innkeeper asked one night over dinner in the Xenona. 'Look at the Albanians – they came here and in ten years they've built homes, got jobs, lives. But the gypsies are cursed to roam. I'll tell you why. It's because a gypsy smith made the nails used to crucify Christ.'

'That's funny,' Antonis Makos replied. 'In the army, a gypsy soldier told me that the Romans were going to use many nails to crucify Christ, but a gypsy stole a few, sparing him some pain. So Christ blessed the gypsies with permission to steal for ever.'

Despite the warnings, I was determined to see the gypsies up close and personal. So three days later, I was in Arta, standing outside the Byzantine church of Agia Theodora with Georgia, her husband the mayor, a nervous nineteen-year-old groom in a grey suit, and several of his sisters who were ululating and gyrating their hips while holding large trays of *boubounierres* –

traditional Jordan-almond wedding favours – high above their heads.

The church, one of many important monuments from Arta's Byzantine past, was dedicated to Queen Theodora of Arta, whose husband killed her after he took up with a prostitute. Then he felt bad, and built several churches in her honour. This one, just across the road from the gypsy neighbourhood, was the gypsies' church of choice.

Georgia and her husband the mayor had baptized the bride, Efstathia, here eighteen years ago. Now nineteen, Efstathia was the eldest of six children of the Panagiotopoulos clan, a gypsy family that always votes for Mayor Vaya. The groom was one of eleven offspring of the Karafatalos family, a clan that votes for the opposition despite Georgia's best efforts. 'You would not believe the number of coffees I've made for old man Karafatalos!' she told me. Now Arta's two most power-ful gypsy clans were merging; a month ago, Mr Karafatalos had called Mr Panagiotopoulos to ask for his daughter's hand on behalf of his son.

While we awaited the bride, Georgia pointed out the major players to me and her other guest, a matron in a pearl-grey suit. 'See that girl, the groom's sister? She's twenty and has four kids! But two of his other sisters married Greek guys,' she said. 'In a few generations gypsies will be completely absorbed into Greek culture. Look how the younger girls have started to dress like us.' She indicated some gypsy lasses in flowing gowns with spaghetti straps.

'No, dear,' replied her friend, raising an eyebrow. 'We've started to dress like them.'

The grey lady was right – this was a particularly Stevie Nicks moment in Greek fashion, replete with lace, gauze and handkerchief hems. Disregarding the trend, the gypsy women over thirty favoured brightly patterned long skirts and voluminous tops that hid a pouch of valuables secured at their waists. All females older than five wore make-up and jewellery; even the toddlers had hennaed hair. Overall, the Karafatalos clan was very good-looking, including the groom, whose only flaw was a little teenage acne.

I was knocked out of my reverie by the sound of a tambourine, a clarinet, and rhythmic shouts of 'Heh, Heh, Heh, Heh!' The bride was arriving! A J.Lo look-alike in hennaed ringlets and a white, sequined, full-skirted confection, she was escorted by a retinue of dancing women, and one effeminate male relative with long hair and a hologram shirt that glinted in the sun-light. The gyrating crowd parted so the bride could do a little shimmy of her own, arms raised above her head, wrists twisting, gold bracelets gleaming. Then her father, debonair in a pinstripe suit and black moustache, led her to the church door where her groom awaited, holding a bouquet. He handed it to her as the onlookers shouted for a kiss. The couple shyly complied, then entered the church.

The ceremony was like other Orthodox weddings I've attended, but with even more throngs of children running around, some topless, others in Pokémon T-shirts. But once it was over, the drummer started drumming, the clarinet began wailing, and we danced out of the familiar, fragrant world of the Greek church, gyrating en masse across the street into the gypsy enclave of dirt roads and whitewashed cottages. I snapped photos on the way and was soon besieged by requests from the multitude of children. 'Miss, take my picture with the baby,' said a nine-year-old hoisting up a one-year-old sibling. 'Miss, you're pretty. Take me in front of our truck.' Flattery will get you everywhere, my young gypsy friend. 'Miss, I'm the brother of the bride — take me with this girl.' They may not have cameras, but one thing gypsies do not lack is self-esteem. I was the lone paparazzo in a neighbourhood full of superstars.

We swarmed over to the designated honeymoon suite, the house of one of the older Karafatalos brothers. Before crossing the threshold, the bride stepped on a plate to break any bad luck and drive away evil spirits. Then everyone sat on the porch drinking *tsipouro* while the newlyweds' siblings gyrated to a tape of what must be numbers one and two on the gypsies' Top 40: a Greek song that complains, 'You snuff me out like a cigarette, toss me away like ashes,' and the Australian pop tune 'Daddy Cool'. Although all their relatives from the age of five to seventy-five danced energetically, the newlyweds remained seated. The groom beamed in relief that the ceremony was over, but the bride was sombre.

Mrs Karafatalos, a grandchild on her hip, offered to give Georgia and me a house tour. The large living room was consumed by the bride's dowry and gifts (except the gold items she was currently wearing on her wrists, neck, fingers and thumbs). Columns of folded quilts and blankets rose from floor to ceiling, and streams of china and cutlery flowed along the tables. The next stop was the bedroom, dominated by a king-sized bed whose pink silk quilt was strewn with rose petals. Mrs Karafatalos waved her hand regally over the bed, then pointed to the bedside table. 'That basket is where we'll put the virginity,' she said.

My eyebrows shot up. Seeing my expression, Mrs

Karafatalos explained, speaking slowly as if to a small child. 'After the dancing, the couple comes here to make love, and the woman bleeds.' (Here she indicated her groin to make sure I understood.) 'We take the bloody sheet and put it in this basket to bring to the party. The relatives throw money on it – fifty Euros, a hundred, whatever. It's a gypsy tradition.'

No wonder the bride looked nervous. Georgia, ever the gracious guest, said, 'How lovely!' Looking closely at our hostess, she added, 'You're not a gypsy, are you?'

'No,' Mrs Karafatalos admitted. 'My mother, she threw me away when I was born.' Suddenly she grinned, exposing two missing teeth. 'But an old gypsy lady took me in, so I became a gypsy. I even learned the language.'

I felt much more comfortable discussing language groups than bloody sheets. 'What's the gypsy language called?' I asked.

'*Giftika*,' she said. 'Because we're from Egypt, I guess.'

In an anthropology class I had learned that the prevailing theory holds that gypsies originated in India and their language is called Rom. But I was not about to question Mrs Karafatalos's authority. After all, as a gypsy she was an over-achiever, what with eleven kids and twenty-eight grandchildren.

We followed her out to the porch to find the mayor, a stocky seventy-year-old, boogying to 'Daddy Cool' and sweating in the heat. The man would risk a heart attack to secure those Karafatalos votes.

Luckily, Mr Karafatalos arrived to put an end to Mayor Vaya's high-risk hoedown and led us to the reception in the main square of the neighbourhood.

There, on a flatbed truck with one open side, a gypsy band from Athens was blasting out the endlessly requested 'You snuff me out like a cigarette' song, as tables were set around three sides of the square and relatives of the newlyweds carried the laden dinner plates, using as trays the tops of the plastic tables gypsy merchants sell door to door. Gypsies from all over Epiros ate spit-roasted goat, drank wine, danced to the cigarette song and had an all-out fabulous time – even Efstathia was smiling as she and her new husband led several circle dances. But I couldn't stop worrying about the sheet. The anthropologist in me wanted to see the ritual, but the rest of me was nervous for the bride.

At two a.m. the bandleader tapped on the microphone. 'OK folks, that was the last dance, because we gypsies have our traditions to uphold,' he boomed. 'I need a child from the bride's family and one from the groom's to come up here and receive the couple's money. Let's see which one of them raises the most for their new life together!'

People streamed up with cash and envelopes. Money poured in and the couple sat there smiling; this seemed to be the stress-free part of the evening. I hadn't brought a gift, so I beckoned an eleven-year-old and handed her fifty Euros for the bride, '"From Eleni" – no last name, please.' She strolled up as the announcer bellowed, 'Yiorgos Karafatalos is busy with his watermelon business on Corfu, so he can't be here, but he gives eight hundred Euros to the groom and two hundred to the bride.' My fifty came next. Everyone clapped politely, but after the Watermelon King of Corfu, it was an anticlimax.

Then I felt it – a drop of rain. 'That's it, folks. Good

luck to the happy couple,' the announcer said, ducking under the truck/stage. The band put a tape in the sound system and started packing their instruments as rain fell more steadily.

Georgia stood up. 'Looks like the party's over,' she said. 'We'll take you to the hotel.'

'What about the sheet?' I asked.

'It got rained out.' She shrugged. 'Don't worry; I'll call if there's a scandal!'

Both relieved and disappointed, I said goodbye to the smiling bride and left as the groom's sister, the twenty-year-old mother of four, continued to dance, twirling in the rain.

Driving to Lia, I wondered what life would be like for the newlywed gypsies' children. Would they assimilate into the Greek mainstream, as Georgia predicted? Two of the groom's sisters had. One, a chef's assistant in Athens, told me, 'I could never come back to live here; I'm used to another way of life.' But that left nine siblings who were still entrenched in the community. When you have eleven kids, chances are that a few will follow in your footsteps. But Efstathia only planned on having three, she'd told Georgia, so that she could educate them all. The gypsies were masters at choosing their own identity: were they thieves or chosen people, kidnappers or rescuers of orphans, gypsies or Greeks, or both? I started to wonder about my own children. Would they learn Greek? Would they even be interested in visiting their grandparents' home, which I was now rebuilding?

By the time I entered Lia, I had stopped mulling over my potential progeny and started worrying about Dorina's immediate future. In a few days Marina, my sister, would arrive, and I needed the bed for her. I'd have to send Dorina back to the crowded room with no shower. As I passed the Xenona inn, I saw Vlad flagging me down.

'Eleni, I have something for you,' he said.

I pulled up to the side of the road.

'Come see new house,' he insisted. I had no idea what he was talking about, but I often had a hard time understanding Vlad's broken Greek, so I followed orders. He led me to a house belonging to a Liote family who lived in Athens. Xalime, who was working in the garden, rushed inside to get me some cherry juice, while Vlad indicated that I should sit on the couch. Dorina and Net appeared from back rooms. Vlad handed me a silver coin he had found in the ruins of the Gatzoyiannis house; it had a hole at the top, so it must have been worn as part of a woman's dowry. Later, after Internet research, I learned it was a six-kreuzer Austrian coin bearing the grotesque profile of 'Leopold the Hogmouth'. But at first, all I could make out was the date: 1685. I wondered how this foreign coin had reached my grand-mother's house – did it serve as jewellery on her wedding day? – only to be discovered by Vlad 317 years after it was minted.

'Thanks,' I said. 'This is great. But what are you all doing here?'

Net explained that the owners of the house had come for a visit and agreed to let Vlad and his family live in it, in exchange for taking care of the place. Dorina broke in, saying in Italian that the house had two bedrooms, a living room, kitchen, bathroom, garden and washing machine. I realized that I had just sunk to the lowest rung on Lia's socio-economic ladder; I was now the only Liote I knew without a TV or washing machine. But I was glad for the family; this was a step up from one room.

'Congratulations!' I said. 'That's wonderful.'

Vlad sat down across the table, dejected. 'Dina and Andreas very mad,' he said. 'She spoke to me angry, said not take anything she had given us, even TV, which I pay seventy-five Euro to fix in Igoumenitsa. They not good people I thought.'

I had forgotten; Dina and Andreas had let the Albanians live rent-free in their one-room shack so that Vlad and Xalime would watch their house when they went on dowry-selling trips. Mourning two dead sons, they had started to think of Net as family.

Back in Motsala, my neighbours were abuzz with the news of the Albanian defection. 'Vladimiros had to take this opportunity,' Athina reasoned. 'He told me he hadn't been able to go to his wife for four months because they were all sleeping in one room.' You could always count on Athina, who had squirrel's cheeks but hawk's eyes, to disseminate crucial information.

'You're right,' her husband Grigoris nodded his bald head. 'But he should have told Dina that they might leave as soon as he knew, instead of springing it on her just after Andreas's son's memorial service, on the day they moved. She feels abandoned.'

'Look, everyone got mad at the time,' Vangeli Panagiotou chimed in. 'But Vladimiros should apologize now, say he appreciates all they've done for them, feeding them, housing them, introducing them to you, Eleni, who gave them the jobs on the house and let the girl sleep in your own home. Albanians are ungrateful people.' He shook his head definitively. 'They're not like us.'

I wasn't taking a racial-profiling view of the situation;

it made sense for the family to move on up to a bigger place. But I felt bad for Dina and Andreas. They didn't discuss the incident with me, I suspected because I employed the family. But Dina complained that the neighbourhood was so quiet it depressed her. And Andreas started expanding the kitchen, the latest in his self-prescribed course of movement therapy.

We had all got along so well for so long, eaten so much pita together in the courtyard. It was sobering to see how easily our community could fall apart, how quickly prejudices arose. But as my neighbours bickered, I was about to inject more international flavour into our local mix of nationalities; my sister was on her way to visit me.

I drove to Ioannina to pick Marina up, leaving a day early to check on my own internal drama: it was time for the sonogram that I'd promised my doctors in America I'd have every few months in Greece. When I made the appointment, it had seemed routine. Now, having learned about my grandmother's curse, I was nervous. My appointment was a crushing reminder of my lack of control over my fate. I was able to decide where I would live, what language I would speak, even my citizenship. My identity was up to me, but I couldn't choose to be cyst-free.

At Ioannina's University Hospital Dr Tsamboulis, a soft-spoken man who had been recommended by a friend, led me into the ultrasound room, where a young female doctor stood wearing jeans and a crop top under a lab coat. Normally, I wouldn't want to be examined by anyone with an exposed midriff, but I was new here, so I didn't protest.

'My patient is in the bathroom right now, so wait a moment, we'll be right with you,' said Dr Britney, as I liked to think of her. An old man shuffled out of the bathroom, boxer shorts visible above his unbuttoned trousers, and lay on the examination table.

'Turn to the wall,' Dr Britney commanded. I did, understanding that the gentleman wanted his privacy. 'Not you!' The sexy doctor burst out laughing. 'Him.'

Grandpa rolled over so she could X-ray his back. He seemed untroubled by my presence; if he wasn't embarrassed, I wasn't going to be either. The examination ended, the old man left and Dr Tsamboulis locked the door; my sonogram would have no studio audience, thank God.

Fifteen minutes later, he handed me my X-rays and a letter in English to send to my oncologist in America. My cysts had shrunk slightly, he said. That was good news. The bad news was that they were still there; I would have to return for a follow-up sonogram in three months. I was just happy that nothing was horribly wrong with my reproductive health, and that my grandmother wasn't cursing me for breaking my family's vow. I could ignore the whole thing for a few more months and take my sister on holiday!

Marina's ten-day visit was perfect, except for the fact that, as a French professor who had spent the last two years living in Paris, she was frustrated to discover that now her Greek was nowhere near as good as her French. One night at the Xenona, Foti Tsandinis bought us drinks. We chatted, and soon he turned to Marina and said, 'Honey, how come you don't speak Greek as well as your sister?' She muttered, 'I concentrated on French, and haven't been here in a while. But I understand everything.' Everyone was satisfied until Vangeli Panagiotou joined us and asked Marina the same question. This time she just glared.

On the walk home, we developed a plan. Later, at dinner at Dina's, Marina hadn't taken her first bite of pita when Grigoris said to her, 'You don't speak Greek as well as Eleni, sweetheart.'

Marina swallowed. 'My Greek's not that great,' she said. 'But *vozono alafiatika*.' ('I speak tinker language.')

There was a moment of stunned silence. Then a roar of laughter rose up around the table. Marina was now the most popular girl in Lia. She might not know perfect Greek, but she was fluent in the mother tongue.

After her triumph, Marina and I walked home. Looking out at the lights of a village on the mountain top across the ravine, she whispered, 'It looks like a constellation!' I had been here for so long, I had stopped noticing how striking my surroundings were; Marina had to remind me not to take Lia for granted. We stared at the glittering night sky and chatted for hours, then finally went to bed.

At three-thirty I awoke to someone stroking my hair. Then I realized that the hand patting me was an awfully tiny one.

'Turn on the light!' I yelled. Marina did, and then screamed, 'There he is!'

And there he was – a squirrel scampered across my bed and up the chimney. He kept popping his little head out of the fireplace, waiting for us to leave his house alone. Finally, Marina chased him into the hall, then shut the bedroom door as I sat there cowering.

I tried to convince Marina to stay, to improve her Greek and protect me from amorous rodents. But she had a summer course waiting. 'Look on the bright side,' she consoled me. 'With the squirrel around, you never have to sleep alone.'

*

I didn't have a chance to get lonely, because soon after Marina left, my father called to say a friend of his was bringing a tour group for lunch in Lia on their way from Corfu to Ioannina. I decided to stop by the Xenona to ask the group, who were mostly New Yorkers, what was new back in the city. I found thirty people in jeans, shorts and bum bags streaming off a bus; twenty-five of them appeared to be over sixty-five.

'Where's the bathroom?' said one grey-permed lady by way of introduction.

'Right down there,' I chirped, pointing towards the inn's basement.

'You mean there's stairs? Good Lord!' she groaned, hobbling off.

'Miss, is there cheese in this pie?' A tall man in glasses beckoned me. 'I have to take pills if I eat cheese. I'm lactose.'

Lactose! It was five months since I'd heard the phrase 'lactose intolerant'. In Lia, old people climbed everywhere and ate everything – the memory of years of starvation had inspired many of them to cultivate Santa-like paunches and force food on me. I was ready for some frivolous, bum-bag-wearing picky eaters. My fellow Americans!

The leader of the group introduced himself. An athletic middle-aged man with a grey beard and the voice of a news reader, Isaac looked like the head of a progressive private school, the kind of guy who would lead the entire student body on a hike to the top of a mountain, where they would then sit in a circle and 'share'.

'So, tell me what you all have done already,' I said to him, as the innkeepers Fanis and Nikki served *tiropita* and moussaka. 'How was Corfu?'

'Corfu was a wonderful, emotional experience,' Isaac intoned. 'I took everyone on the route the Corfiot Jews walked when they were deported, and asked them to be silent so that we could hear our footsteps on the cobblestones the way our relatives did as they were led to the boats headed for Auschwitz.'

Suddenly the bum-bag-wearers seemed a lot less frivolous. My fellow Americans, it appeared, were also my fellow Greek-Americans. Except that they were descendants of the communities of Greek Jews that had thrived before the Second World War.

'Now we go to Ioannina, where our relatives came from,' Isaac continued.

'I've passed by the synagogue tons of times, but it's never open,' I told Isaac.

'Well, the community is so small and elderly now, they don't usually have a *minyan*, the ten men required to hold a service,' he responded. 'But we're holding one on Friday. You're welcome to come.'

Over lunch, I learned that the New Yorkers were members of a Jewish community I'd never heard of, the Romaniote Jews, who had settled in Greece by the first century AD and lived there ever since. Unlike the Ashkenazim, who spoke Yiddish, and the Sephardim, who spoke Ladino, the Romaniotes spoke Greek and conducted their services in Greek. When a large number of Ioanniote Romaniotes emigrated to New York at the turn of the twentieth century, they founded the Kehila Kedosha Janina Synagogue on the Lower East Side, 'the only Romaniote synagogue in the entire Western Hemisphere,' Isaac told me. Most of the people travelling with him worshipped there.

Over lunch, I got to know the group; three were born in Greece, the rest had parents or grandparents who were. David's mother was from Ioannina, but he was born in 1919 in Egypt, where he learned eight languages, including Greek, which his family spoke at home. Markella, whose father was from Ioannina, was born in Athens under a false name while her family lived across from the German commanders' post during the war. 'My father said that it was the safest place to be,' she recalled. 'No one would suspect a Jew of living under the Germans' noses.' Nina had been born in Ioannina, and Belle was here because Ioannina was her father's birthplace, although he moved when he was two. 'For the descendants of Romaniotes in New York, Ioannina is a very big thing,' she explained. 'Growing up, you heard "Ioannina" all the time. So I had to see it.'

By the end of the meal, I'd decided to join them in Ioannina. I went to pack, leaving just in time to hear a lady tell Fanis, 'But you're even better looking than Anthony Quinn!'

In Ioannina we pulled weeds, branches and dirt off the graves in the Jewish cemetery, where a new wall to deter vandals had been built with funds from the KKJ in New York. Ninety per cent of the graves were overgrown, and the dense brush made it impossible for most of the New Yorkers to find the tombs of their ancestors, but many were happy just to be on hallowed ground.

'I always promised my mother I'd come visit the grave of my grandfather,' said eighty-three-year-old David. 'Now I've done it.'

The next day, we met at the headquarters of Ioannina's Jewish community on Joseph Elia Street, where the second synagogue had been located before the war. The Germans used it as a stable, so when 163 Jews returned from the Holocaust — all that survived of

Ioannina's 1,950 Jews – they tore down the ruins to create apartments and offices. Inside, New Yorkers in shorts and Nikes hugged tiny Ioanniote men and women in suits. Then they pored over the archives for their relatives' names. Occasionally their murmured questions would be interrupted by a joyous outburst. 'I found him! I found my Uncle Mordecai!' yelled a woman in a tracksuit.

As I left, a forty-year-old man with the kind of bushy moustache that identified him as Greek stopped me, pushing a shy thirteen-year-old boy ahead of him. 'You speak Greek, don't you?' he said to me. 'Well this is my son, Zachariah, and we were in there just now watching old people greet other old people. No one even introduced him. Tell your friends the community needs to do more to encourage young people's involvement. Zachariah's mother is Christian but he chose to be Jewish.'

The next day, as we sat outside the synagogue waiting for the service to start, I told Marcia, the other tour leader and the head of the American Friends of Greek Jewry, about the agitated man. She frowned. 'That's a big question for the Central Board of Jewish Communities in Greece, which holds free summer camps in Thessaloniki for Jewish children,' she said. 'Do they accept kids of mixed marriages or not? Technically, a child with a Christian mother, like Zachariah, is not a Jew unless he converts. But because the communities are so small and assimilated, intermarriage and emigration are the norm.'

'And soon these old people will die and the community probably won't exist any more,' said Judy, one of the younger New Yorkers. 'In the end, Hitler won.'

Her statement shocked me. I thought the fact that we

were waiting to attend a service in this centuries-old synagogue meant that Hitler hadn't won. But the story of Ioannina's Jews is a tragic one. Rae Dalvin's book *The Jews of Ioannina* describes how, after 48,674 Jews from Thessaloniki were deported between March and August 1943, the Ioanniote Jews considered taking refuge with resistance groups in the mountains. But a prominent local businessman, Sabethai Cabilli, visited the occupying German commander, who assured him that his community would not be harmed. Cabilli urged total cooperation, only realizing his fatal error on 25 March 1944, when the Jews were rounded up on the lakefront for deportation. 'I have sinned!' he cried. The elderly Cabilli was among the first to be killed on arrival at Auschwitz.

Elsewhere in Greece, some Jews did escape the Holocaust. Archbishop Damaskinos and Evangelos Evert, the Chief of Police, issued false identity cards to Athenian Jews, saving two-thirds of the community, including Markella and her family. And the 275 Jews on Zakynthos were unharmed after the Germans requested a list of Jews and the mayor and bishop gave him only two names: their own.

Most Greek Jews were not so lucky: about 87 per cent died in the Holocaust. Before the war, there were 78,000 Jews in Greece. Today, Marcia said, there were about 5,000 — 3,000 living in Athens, 1,200 in Thessaloniki, and the rest in small communities elsewhere, like the 50 in Ioannina. Life wasn't easy for them once they returned. Markella's aunt Estir, who still lives in Ioannina, said that when her husband came to reclaim his property from squatters, as was his right according to Greek law, a woman living in his sister's home said she would not let a Jew in the house. 'So he sued, and got it back,' Estir said. 'But the lady in his parents' house said, "Mr Laganas, this is your home. Let me make you a cup of coffee." Because of that act of kindness, we let her live with us rent-free.'

As darkness fell, the owlish community leader, Moises Eliah, arrived to lead us in for the service. The restored synagogue was breathtaking, with high arched ceilings, a wide central area and an *ieron*, a cabinet that houses the *tikkim*, the ornate wood-and-iron cases in which Romaniotes keep the Torah scrolls. These *tikkim* were two hundred to four hundred years old, Marcia explained, and were saved from the Germans by Ioannina's mayor during the war. I sat next to Rose, the president of the Sisterhood of the KKJ in New York. Tears filled her eyes as Samuel, a white-haired Ioanniote, began the service. 'I can hear my grandfather chanting this,' she said. I asked if Samuel was a rabbi or a cantor.

'He's just an elder,' answered Rose. 'His daughter lives in Israel, and his wife wanted to move there. But he said if he does, who will lead the services in Ioannina?'

The service ended, and at the farewell dinner afterwards, people found relatives they didn't know they had, identified mystery family members in old photos, hugged, kissed, cried, and exchanged information. Then, as president of the Sisterhood, Rose stood up to present an award to the Ioanniote community, 'for keeping Judaism alive in Ioannina'. She wept once more as she said, 'We consider Ioannina our home. It means so much to all of us to spend time with you, our family.'

I tried to leave the family gathering unnoticed. But David stopped me on the way out. 'I have a nephew,' he began. 'A doctor. He's thirty-three and he lives in

Great Neck. When I get back to New York, you call me and I'll put you in touch. He wants a girl like you, an old-fashioned girl. You're like us.' I appreciated the thought. But I lived in Lia now and was not about to start looking for long-distance love. Instead, I was searching for the same thing these senior citizens sought: a link with my past.

A few days later, as I drove out of Ioannina along a cobbled back street, I realized everyone was staring at my car. A boy on a bike rode up and yelled, 'You have a flat tyre!'

I pulled over, got out, and looked at the boy, a pudgy ten-year-old in a T-shirt that bore a picture of a tiger and the phrase 'Wild Thing!'

'I'll change it,' he offered. 'My father owns a garage and I help out.'

'But I don't have a spare tyre,' I cried.

Wild Thing looked at me as though I was the one wearing a stupid T-shirt. Then he walked to the boot, opened it and lifted the false bottom to reveal a tyre. Several older boys offered to help, but Wild Thing brushed them all off. Then the sound of laughter and gum-snapping alerted me to the presence of four teenaged gypsy girls, giggling at us.

'Is that your kid?' the ringleader said to me.

'No!' I yelled. 'He's helping me!' Did I look as if I could have a ten-year-old? The girls doubled over in laughter. Wild Thing was not amused.

Seeing Chrysanthi cured, I was so thrilled that I slipped Wild Thing forty Euros in my farewell handshake. Actually, I tried to slip it, suavely, as if he were a maître d', but Wild Thing held the bills in front of his face. 'Thanks, lady,' he said.

It was worth it. Wild Thing had given me back my mobility, but he'd also revealed to me a part of my identity that I couldn't escape. I did have a place in the community in which I lived. I was here to amuse everyone: the gypsy girls; Net, by asking for the old door; and the computer guy, who, when I brought my expensive machine for repair, chuckled, 'Where you are, there's the worst electricity, worst phone lines, worst everything. What are you doing up there?' I was a regional punchline. That was good enough for me.

Back in Lia, I discovered that, while the Romaniotes were searching for their roots, Vlad and Net had been literally digging up mine. While clearing the courtyard around the house they had unearthed a massive, rusted lock for the front door; one cartridge (unexploded); one *chibouk* (ceramic pipe); one *lichnari* (metal lantern); one enamel dish with green-vine and red-berry design; assorted forks, spoons and broken *flitjania* (coffee cups); and a glass oil lamp. I never knew how to read Net's attitude towards me, but both he and Vlad were very industrious in bringing me these knick-knacks, and sensitive too – once Vlad found a pile of bones, which he hid discreetly under a stone slab, in case they were human, until local experts identified them as goat.

I displayed the non-skeletal findings on the verandah. My favourite was a plastic medallion showing the Mother and Child on the front, and on the back a crown above the letter Φ, ringed by the phrase, 'The Soldier's Undershirt'. It must have belonged to a Nationalist soldier stationed in the house after the Civil War. People would knit socks and undershirts for the army, so any donation was called 'The Soldier's Undershirt'. The crown and the **Φ** meant this was a gift from Frederika, Greece's queen during the Civil War and mother of the last king before the monarchy was abolished.

I don't care much about Queen Frederika, but I have a definite fondness for the Virgin Mary. Greeks are big on patron saints: islands, people, even boats have them, and I've considered the Panagia mine ever since I wrote my senior thesis on the festival of the Dormition of the Virgin Mary on Corfu, an experience that made me yearn to live in Greece some day. Judging by the note my grandmother left on the back of a paper icon of the Panagia before she was killed, the original Eleni Gatzoyiannis felt a special bond with the Virgin Mary as well. So when Vlad handed me the piece of plastic, I felt it was a message from my patron saint, or perhaps even my grandmother, indicating approval of what I was doing – or at least negating her curse.

If it was a sign from above, it was the only family encouragement I was going to get for rebuilding the house. Shortly after Vlad gave me the medallion, I picked up Thitsa Kanta and her husband, affable Thio Angelo, who had come to spend two months in Greece. Thio Angelo had his own family house in Lia, so we wouldn't be living together. This was for the best; there might not have been room at the Haidis house for the three of us. Thio Angelo is trim and mild-mannered, Thitsa Kanta, like me, is only five feet tall, and she's slim, with a blond bouffant and round glasses. But although she may be small physically, she has a huge personality.

Thitsa Kanta is the only person I know whose self-esteem rivals the gypsies'. The minute she boarded the plane to Greece, she told the man sitting next to her that she was 'arch-right-wing, pro-junta', identifying herself as a fan of the military dictatorship that ruled Greece in the late 1960s and early 70s – perhaps the colonels' only remaining fan. Then she admonished the customs agent in Athens for not doing a more thorough check of her bags, telling him, 'In America, a man hid a bomba in his sneaks!' Thio Angelo, standing by in his black-rimmed glasses and driving cap, tried futilely to mediate, but eventually Thitsa Kanta placated the agent by showing him the non-stick Teflon pan she had brought so she could cook without butter. It turns out he had high cholesterol, too. This was all a clever diversionary technique; if he had checked her gigantic bags he might have confiscated her two tins of Maxwell House coffee. 'I love American coffee!' said Thitsa Kanta. 'God Bless America!'

Marina and I always felt self-conscious about mistakes when speaking Greek, and my cousins from Corfu were shy about their imperfect English. But Thitsa Kanta happily spoke a hybrid mix of the two, confident that people would understand her Kanta-ese. In Ioannina, when a waitress refilled her water glass, she said, 'Ευχαριστώ, honey!' At first I thought this phrase encapsulated the lifelong dilemma of the immigrant, an outsider who belongs in neither culture; in America, Thitsa Kanta's accent gave her away as Greek, but in Greece she couldn't stop using American words like 'honey', 'sweetheart' and 'relax'. But I soon realized that Thitsa Kanta doesn't feel like an outsider; on the contrary, she belongs everywhere. Her unique syntax represents exactly what she is: a Greek who moved to America, made it there, and now, with her Easy Spirit pumps and Maxwell House coffee in tow, is welcome anywhere, as far as she is concerned. And so was her vociferous opinion.

Shortly after they arrived, I took Thitsa Kanta and Thio Angelo to see the Gatzoyiannis house in progress. 'I told NickGage, "Why waste your money? Give it to me instead!"' Thitsa Kanta joked as we drove up. 'No, I don't want the money. But I don't want the house either!'

I was hoping the sight of her resurrected childhood home might change her mind. But when we got there, she just wandered around, crying quietly, while Thio Angelo patted her. I realized that, to her, it must be a depressing sight; everything was now erected except for the roof, doors and windows. I hadn't known how much a house that is rising up would look like one that is falling down. 'All right,' Thitsa Kanta said, walking to the car. 'I saw it. I don't need to come back.'

Over the next week, as I chauffeured her from my house to hers, to visit this old crone or that one, to Filiates to get her hair done, and to church, church and more church, I kept hearing the same litany of complaints. 'When I saw the basement, where my mother was a prisoner for twenty-five days, I could hear her moaning,' she told people. 'It was like she was there in front of me.'

One night, over dinner at the Xenona, Thitsa Kanta told friends she had a pain in her arm; maybe she was having a heart attack brought on by all the emotion. The arm wasn't sore because she'd slept awkwardly on the plane, or was tired from her journey. No — she was dying because I'd shown her the house; I was responsible for yet another family member's near-death experience. I felt bad that my aunt was upset. But I was starting to get annoyed. I was devoting a year of my life to rebuilding the house, taking a sharp detour off my career path, relinquishing another of my reproductive years to live as the only young, single person in Lia, all to watch it rise. If Thitsa Kanta was right about the curse, I was even risking my life. It was something I'd chosen to do, but I still wished she could appreciate my efforts to reconstruct her childhood home, just a little.

Foti ambled in and treated us all to another round. 'Not for me, Foti,' Thitsa Kanta said. 'I don't feel too good; I'm sick from seeing the house. I told NickGage he shouldn't waste his money. I don't know why he's letting her do this.'

This was more than I could handle. 'Because, Thitsa Kanta, if the house stays a ruin, then the people who ruined it have the last word,' I burst out, my patience exhausted. 'They tried to destroy our family like they destroyed the house, but our family was not torn down, it's still strong.'

'I know,' she said. 'But I got bad memories.'

'You do,' I replied, a bit more quietly. 'But what about Sydney, your new granddaughter? If she wants to come here in thirty years to see where you were born, why should she see rubble? She should see a strong, surviving symbol of the family.'

Thitsa Kanta drank her orange soda thoughtfully. 'OK, for that, for other people, it's good,' she said. 'Just not for me.'

Thitsa Kanta never complained about the house again. Instead she stuck to her other favourite topics: how she would never change her religion or her political affiliation, even if you held a knife to her neck; how, ever since she stepped on to the 'Blessed Land', she has never known a moment of suffering, and she and her family have prospered; and how she loves American coffee, God Bless America. As she talked, I would sit back and relax, and Thio Angelo would nod, and some-times wink at me.

A week after Thitsa Kanta and Thio Angelo arrived, I got an email from one of the New York Romaniotes. 'I just picked up my film and was thinking about what a wonderful trip we had, and how much I admire what you are doing in your village to honour your own family,' she wrote. 'It reminds me of what Elie Wiesel said: "We must remember the past, but we must not be prisoners of it."'

As I tried to turn a prison back into a home, I had at least one supporter. I thought about my visit to Ioannina's *kastro*, how two mosques, one church and one synagogue co-existed in a small, ancient place. I had met so many different ethnic groups that were as native to Epiros as the Liotes around me. They weren't always humble, or cooperative, or even tolerant of each other. But they had all been here, together, for aeons. I shouldn't have been surprised that there were so many cultures in Epiros; look at the different opinions, lifestyles and even languages that existed within my own family: Greek, English, French, Kanta-ese and, of course, *alafiatika*. Thitsa Kanta had the right attitude: each of us is our own civilization, no matter where we happen to be at the time.

When I was young and used to watch the Saturday-morning cartoons, I was so proud during the *Schoolhouse Rock* segment about 'America's Melting Pot' when a cartoon of a Greek immigrant with a handlebar mous-tache walked across the screen holding a sign that said 'Yiasou!' Then Reagan abolished the law requiring a minute of educational programming for each minute of advertising on morning TV, I grew up, and the 'melting pot' theory fell out of favour. It became more politically correct to describe America as a casserole: a combination of slightly mushy, somewhat soggy separate entities that join together into one delicious taste treat which can be reheated again and again. Epiros was also a casserole, just with different ingredients and sprinkled with a layer of feta. Thitsa Kanta is older and wiser. While I had to believe she was wrong about the house, she was right about one thing: God Bless America. And God Bless Epiros.

6

HOME SWEET HOMELAND

«Παπούτσι από τον τόπο σου, ας είναι και
μπαλωμένο.»
'Wear a shoe from your hometown, even if it's patched.'

10 August

*I'm shading my eyes from the sun, to get a better look at
the yellow digger tearing up huge chunks of ground in
front of the Gatzoyiannis house. The masons from
Northern Epiros, working with Vlad, Net and Xalime,
have erected the stone walls of the house in just two
weeks. Yanni, the master builder, taught Vlad how to
chip at the old stones with a pick, turning them into
squares for the house's corners, and curves for the graceful
arches above the gaping holes that will be windows and
doors.*

*Vlad, Net and Xalime will now build a low wall
around the property to define the courtyard. But before
that happens, the digger has to remove all the gnarled*

tree stumps, overgrown bushes and massive boulders that have accumulated over the past fifty years. As the masons admire their work, Vlad examines the uphill side of the house, where he'll use his new skills to build a small stone room that will be one of two modern spaces in the home, a kitchenette with a stove and running water. Before the war, the same space was the plistario, the washroom.

'Eleni, come see,' Vlad calls.

I climb up. The spot he's looking at has yielded a number of treasures — my family's broken spoons, an inkwell and medicine bottles. It must have been used as a dump by the soldiers who took over the house during the Civil War. But once I hike up there, I realize Vlad hasn't found anything. He's just pointing at a large boulder.

'That's a big rock,' I say. 'It must have rolled down the hill.'

'No, this,' Vlad insists, pointing to an iron rod curving up from under the stone.

'What is it?' I ask.

'Who knows?' says Vlad. 'Must move rock for to build kitchen.'

I have a quick consultation with the man driving the digger. A few minutes later, Vlad, Xalime, Net and I watch as the swinging, grasping metal claw reaches for the rock, wedges under it, and lifts it in one swooping arc. While the rock is being dumped into the empty lot across the way, Net darts forward to pick up the curved metal. He holds it up — a tangle of intricate Art Nouveau curves, joined in places by rusted metal flowers. As my eyes adjust, I solve the puzzle.

He has unearthed the iron bed that my aunts used to jump on, a piece of furniture that helped condemn my grandmother. My grandfather Christos had ferried the iron bedstead up the mountain on a donkey during a visit *to Lia, because he'd learned in America that 'sophisticated' people slept in beds, not on pallets on the floor. Although my grandmother seldom slept in it except when her husband was at home, at her trial some of her neighbours, resentful of her iron bed, Singer sewing machine and other fancy American innovations like a wind-up gramophone, testified that the 'Amerikana' had buried her riches somewhere to hide them from the invading Communist army.*

Before the Civil War, the bedstead was a source of pride, a family showpiece. I look at its tangled remains and pick up the curving frame, ignoring Vlad's warning that I'll get dirty. I hand Vlad a twenty-Euro finder's fee, a bonus for such a valuable find, and for working so hard in the hot sun. In August 1948, Eleni Gatzoyiannis was a prisoner in her own cellar. It's August 2002 when we find her cherished iron bed.

August in Greece means one thing: the *panegyri* of the Virgin Mary, a festival focal point which falls smack in the middle of the month. On 15 August, Greeks celebrate the anniversary of the Virgin Mary's dormition, the day she 'slept' and her soul ascended to heaven. The event isn't just observed or commemorated; it is truly celebrated with feasting, music and dancing, because it is considered a happy occasion. After all, when various apostles crowded around her deathbed crying and keening, the Panagia, knowing she was about to be reunited with her son, commanded them, 'Don't turn the moment of my joy into a time of sorrow.'

Greeks have followed those instructions ever since, by partying heartily on 15 August at one of the hundreds of *panegyria* held throughout Greece to mark the occasion. And virtually everyone takes part in the other traditional

August ritual: taking a holiday, whether it's the two weeks leading up to the festival, the two weeks following it, or the whole damn month.

In August, even Lia becomes a tourist boomtown. 'Last night, I counted 220 people in town,' reported Foti, stopping by for coffee early in the month. Before the Civil War, Lia's population numbered more than a thousand, but these days, 220 meant packed to capacity; I worried we might be breaking some fire code.

All over the country, my Greek friends were getting awkward tan lines on sunny beaches and dancing at open-air clubs until early morning, then sleeping in until afternoon, when they'd get up to drink iced coffees that would give them enough energy to repeat this vicious cycle of diving, dancing and drinking. But in Lia, I went to bed at midnight, rose at eight and spent the day chauffeuring Thitsa Kanta and Theo Angelo around or cooking with my senior-citizen friends. Occasionally I'd check my emails and turn down invitations to various summer homes. Everyone else was on holiday, but here in Lia I was constantly on duty. I couldn't leave now — who would take Thitsa Kanta to Filiates to get her hair done every week? Even without my driving duties, I had to stay to make sure the masons resisted the many temptations that could draw them away from building walls in the hot sun.

My latest native guide was Andoni, the Papadia's son and self-appointed keeper of Lia's flame. When he was four years old, Andoni was one of the many Liote children taken by the retreating Communist forces at the end of the Civil War across the border to Albania and then to Hungary. The plan failed in his case: he was not re-educated to be a good Communist. But he was left with a yearning for his lost home in Lia that could not be sated, even when his family returned to the poverty-stricken village in 1954 and his parents had to put him and his sister in an orphanage until they could grow enough food to provide for them. Andoni, who is tall, gaunt and mustachioed, a millennial Don Quixote, has lived his whole adult life as a lawyer in Athens. But he has spent the last ten years writing a vast history of Lia. He considers himself the leading Lia expert. Which he probably is; he doesn't have much competition.

Andoni saw me as the latest-model Lia fan, a younger, female, less hirsute version of himself. Naturally, he was committed to passing his lifetime of knowledge on to me. Now in town for the festival, he was determined to show me Maleshovo, or what I liked to call The Lost Continent of Lia. In the 1750s, Maleshovo was abandoned by villagers who moved up the mountain to found Lia in its current position. No one's sure why; Andoni suspects that a plague hit, forcing the survivors to move onwards and upwards. His cousin, the shepherdess Iphigenia, sometimes grazed her sheep near the ruined village, and took him there fifteen years ago. Now suffering from foot trouble, she had sent her son, an orthodontist named Gregory, to guide us to the abandoned village in her place.

The three of us started down a sloping path, armed with walking sticks, water bottles and pita the Papadia had packed for the journey. The last time the men had seen Maleshovo, Andoni said, they had found two ruined churches, one dedicated to the Lifegiving Well and the other to Agios Giorgos. Gregory said you could still see painted wall icons inside the shells of the ruined churches; Andoni wanted me to photograph them for his book on Lia.

'It may be the last time someone photographs them

before they deteriorate completely,' he said, outlining the historical importance of our mission. It may be the *first* time anyone photographs them, too, I thought as we descended deeper into the brush. We passed an irrigation pipe and a number of large cowpats, then the area became increasingly thorny and isolated. Not even Gregory was sure we were going the right way. He offered to go on a fact-finding expedition to see what was ahead, using the carved-oak *bastouni* he'd borrowed from his mother to clear the brush in his path.

'We'd have to slide down on our butts,' he reported, climbing back towards us. 'We could get to the next valley, but I'm not sure how we'd get back up.' I could tell that Andoni wanted to keep going, but he looked tired already. He was sixty now, fifteen years older than the last time he'd made the trek. And Gregory didn't want to be responsible for one of us twisting an ankle. Defeated by the topography, we agreed to go back.

'Maleshovo is lost for ever,' Andoni sighed. 'Forget her.' He sounded so sad that I imagined our village disappearing into the grey mountain mists.

'Come on, Andoni,' Gregory responded. 'We lost the battle, not the war.'

We trudged back uphill to the road, as Andoni and Gregory remembered other landscapes of their childhood that had been abandoned by people and devoured by the wilderness.

'Everywhere else there is deforestation,' Gregory said. 'In Lia, we have the opposite problem.'

I wondered if our entire village might one day be a huge, vertical vacant lot, a lost continent of its own.

'I'm too old to get to Maleshovo,' Andoni sighed. 'But maybe you'll try again next year, Eleni.'

The continent might be lost, but Andoni wanted to resurrect the possibility of rediscovering it. And with the Gatzoyiannis house progressing rapidly, it was no secret in Lia that rediscovering the past was my business.

Andoni returned to Athens, leaving strict instructions with his sister and mother to invite me when they made *trahana*, a cream-of-wheat-type substance that kept the Liotes from starvation during the German occupation, the Second World War, the Civil War and all the lean years that followed. For many Liotes it represented a difficult but purer past, when men were men and women spent three days cooking homemade mush. A Proustian breakfast cereal, it is traditionally made in August when the weather is hot and dry. *Trahana* preparation is a three-step process. On Day One, the Papadia and Vasso, Andoni's sister, made the dough, taking large quantities of milk that had soured into a yoghurt-like substance, pouring it into a tub of flour, adding *progemisma* – dough saved from an earlier batch of *trahana* – and knead, knead, kneading. Then we left the dough to rise, covering each tub with a huge pita pan and each pan with four blankets. The tucked-in dough was set on top of the Papadia's wooden *casella*, a chest carved with a double-headed eagle, which had once held her dowry.

'Ah youth, that it would come twice and old age not even once,' sighed the Papadia, admiring her *casella*.

'We had to work so hard when we were young,' added a neighbour who had come to help. 'If I had my youth again, I'd have a wonderful time. But I wouldn't overdo things like they do today, going on TV in their underwear. You know what I mean?' She threw a glance at the straps of my tank top.

The next morning, I showed up more modestly

dressed to watch Step Two. Vasso separated the dough – now three times its original size – into round balls, which she placed next to each other in large pita pans and shoved into the huge wood-burning beehive oven. Once the loaves were baked and golden, we spread a clean sheet over a double bed to prepare for Step Three. Using a *koskini*, a reversible grater-sifter made expressly for *trahana* production, we grated the loaves into hailstone-sized crumbs. Then we flipped the *koskini* over, using the sieve side to sift the grated *trahana* on to the sheet. There it would dry in the sun for several days, until it could be packed up to be boiled on cold winter mornings and served with cinnamon and milk for a sweet dish, or chopped hot peppers for a spicier taste treat. Mushlicious.

When I told Thitsa Kanta about my *trahana* seminar, she said the Papadia was doing it wrong; it's cheating to bake the dough so it gets hard enough to grate. Her mother used to just leave it in the sun until it was ready. I wasn't surprised that the *trahana* didn't get her seal of approval. While I was throwing myself into village life, Thitsa Kanta was practising her own favourite pastime: remarking on how much worse everything is here than in America. Nowhere was sacred, not even church.

As we sat in front of the elaborately carved, worm-eaten iconostasis in Agios Demetrios, waiting for the nightly countdown to the 15 August service, Thitsa Kanta leaned over to a middle-aged blonde in a stonewashed denim dress, smiled, and informed her that, 'In America, the priest gives communion every Sunday.'

'Why would you take communion every Sunday?' demanded the petite blonde, wrinkling her brow. 'To make sure you get enough? You need to prepare for communion. These women who take it every Sunday, don't they have husbands?'

'Sure,' Thitsa Kanta said. 'I mean, some are widows, but most do.'

Father Prokopi began chanting, but was ignored. His flock was busy following this theological debate taking place in the back of the church.

'Well then,' said the blonde triumphantly, 'they must be having sex.'

'But with their husbands!' Thitsa Kanta was indignant. 'That's not a sin!'

'So?' The blonde paused for effect. 'You're supposed to abstain from sex before getting communion!'

I had not been taught this in Sunday school. Of course, Sunday school only lasted until eighth grade, so perhaps the administration felt that sexual prohibitions were not essential information. Now that the info was flowing freely, I was riveted. So were the other worshippers. I'd never seen it happen before, but I think Thitsa Kanta was blushing.

'Oh, look, church started,' Thitsa Kanta said, giving the blonde spitfire a friendly tap on the arm. 'And the men are listening to us!'

'Let them listen!' insisted Blondie, not even whispering. But both she and her worthy opponent finally quietened down and let Father Prokopi command centre stage. Agios Demetrios had performed another miracle – Thitsa Kanta had met her match.

In Lia we may not have communion every Sunday, industrial-sized washing machines, reliable electricity, or really good steak (which, I have to agree with Thitsa Kanta, I missed too). But we did have our share of high culture. The entire village had been eagerly awaiting a performance by polyphonic singing troupes who were touring the region. I wasn't sure what polyphonic singing was, but I didn't want to seem culturally illiterate, so I pretended to be excited, too. The Goura, the tree-lined square near the historic plane tree under which St Cosmas once slept, was transformed into a *Midsummer Night's Dream*-like grove for the occasion. A retired electrician siphoned electricity off the village electric pole to power a string of lights hanging in the trees, and plastic chairs were set on the flagstones under the trees' spreading branches. I secured seats for myself, Thio Angelo and Thitsa Kanta. By nine-thirty a crowd of over 250 Liotes and friends had assembled; there's nothing Epirotes love more than a good polyphonic tune.

These turned out to be Epirotic songs in a minor key, sung *a cappella*, in close harmony. But of the five groups, only two were from the region I thought of as Epiros proper; the remaining three consisted of a troupe of Northern Epirotes – ethnic Greeks from Albania who sang in Greek; Albanians who sang in Albanian; and a soulful-looking trio of Serbian women in traditional dress.

'Tonight our performance transcends borders,' said the bearded, ponytailed young leader, who looked like a graduate student in Ethnomusicology. 'We'll start the way we begin every festival in Epiros: with *moirologia*, mourning songs!'

The crowd applauded heartily. One of the Romaniote New Yorkers had emailed me this joke: 'Short summary of every Jewish holiday: They tried to kill us, they lost, let's eat.' I quickly realized that the short summary for every Epirote song could be: 'I'm miserable, I'm going to die in a foreign land, let's dance.'

After the first two and a half hours of nasal whining, I'd had just about enough polyphonic revelry, but the rest of Lia was one enthusiastic fan club. Towards the end of the performance, the leader stepped up and asked for audience participation. Despite her sore foot, Iphigenia the shepherdess leapt forward, as did several other Liotes. I was surprised to see Grigoris Ganas's round face smiling out from under his straw fedora as he sang along. That morning I had driven him home from the *kafenion* because his cancer medication had left him too winded to walk back. But tonight he smiled as he sang a love song that a local man had written for his wife. Sophocles said, 'None love life as much as those who are growing old.' Watching Grigoris, it seemed that none sing as loudly as those who suspect they might not be able to join in the song next year.

After almost four hours of polyphonic pleasure, the event ended and we walked towards the *kafenion* for a well-deserved drink. Thio Angelo called to a debonair gent in the Albanian troupe. '*Merminges*,' he said. The singer smiled and responded.

'What did you say?' I asked.

'"Hello,"' Thio Angelo answered. 'You didn't know your uncle speaks Albanian, did you?'

No, actually I didn't.

'Oh yeah, I live there for six years,' Thio Angelo continued. 'My father and uncles owned two tinker shops in Albania — in Leskoviki and Premeti. You ask the old-timers there, they still remember the Stratises.'

Thio Angelo was seventy-six, so just how old were these 'old-timers', I wondered. Instead I said, 'You've been back and asked around recently?'

'Oh no. We left in 1941, during World War Two, when the Italians invaded, and the government throws out all the Greek citizens. The Northern Epirotes, the Greeks who were Albanian citizens, they stuck there, but I walk over the mountains for five days to come back here. Fifteen years old. I saw lots of dead soldiers.' Thio Angelo paused to take a sip of *tsipouro*. 'Then after the war the Communism came, the border closed. The Northern Epirotes, they can't leave Albania, and the Greeks like me, they can't visit. I haven't been back for sixty-one years.'

Thio Angelo wasn't the talker in the family, but when he did say something, he often surprised me. Maybe it was the *tsipouro*, but he became a bit tearful, recalling his formative years in Albania. Shouting from the next table distracted me and I turned to see Thomas, the contractor, waving my architect's blueprint under the nose of Yanni, the head stonemason from Northern Epiros.

'Zervas wants this roof to last for ever,' yelled Thomas. 'That means you pour six inches of cement on to a wooden frame to create the pitched roof, then press the slate tiles into the wet cement.'

'Then you'd have to wait a month for the cement to dry, before you can take the wooden supports out from under and get inside to plaster the walls,' Yanni shouted back. 'I've never poured that much cement into a pitched roof; I'm not sure we can do it.'

I jumped up. I didn't want to delay construction for a month only to find that the pitched cement roof had been done all wrong and was going to collapse. Besides, we were already two weeks behind schedule because of the time it had taken to find and transport the old traditional grey slate roof tiles. All the new-fangled village houses had roofs of orange ceramic semi-circles placed in neat rows.

'So, Yanni, how would you build a slate roof?' I enquired.

'I'm glad you ask, because building a real roof is very different from creating a roof on paper,' Yanni said, shooting a look at Thomas. 'I would make a flat ceiling of cement to hold the walls together, then set the pitched beams for the frame of the roof. On top of that would be a layer of wood, then a layer of aluminium sheeting, corrugated tin, more wood planks, and then I would attach the slate tiles with mortar.' He sat back with a smug smile, resting his case.

'But the other way – with the pitched cement roof – will last for ever,' Thomas insisted. 'NickGage wants this house to be as secure as possible. He said even if someone rolled a boulder down on to the roof, it should remain standing.'

I laughed, imagining one of Lia's senior citizens heaving a boulder down the hill on to the Gatzoyiannis house. But my outburst was blocked by Thitsa Kanta's yelling.

'You listen to Thomas!' she screeched. 'Who knows what the Communists around here might do!'

I realized that my aunts' paranoia had infected my father as well. They all remembered too clearly the old hostilities and jealousies that had led Eleni Gatzoyiannis's neighbours to testify against her at her trial. But right now, I had no time to ponder my relatives' psychological scars. I had to make an executive decision to put a roof over our heads. I turned to Thomas.

'Do it the fast way,' I said. 'As long as it's safe and strong.' It was better to choose a technique the workers felt comfortable with, I figured. But more than that, I wanted the house to look finished before Thitsa Kanta left. Right now it was a grey stone box with gaping holes where the windows should have been; if it looked more like a home, maybe she wouldn't be so opposed to it. In the meantime, we'd revisit Thio Angelo's childhood. After all the turmoil over the roof, I too wanted to be on an August adventure. I needed a little getaway.

'Let's go to Albania,' I said.

'What, now?' Thio Angelo asked.

'Sure. We can drive through customs control in Kakavia.' After all, Southern Albania was Northern Epiros; it was part of my heritage too. Operation Homeland was just expanding in scope. Thitsa Kanta was on board, eager to see something new, or maybe just to get further from her unpleasant memories. And Thio Angelo was ecstatic. I could tell by the way his upper lip twitched when he said, 'Oh, yeah. Let's go.'

'But don't tell anyone where we're going,' Thitsa Kanta advised. 'Better they shouldn't know our business. And what if NickGage thinks it's too dangerous for you to go and gets mad at us?'

'If you believe in the curse, staying here is too dangerous,' I argued.

But I told my pals at the *kafenion* that I would be driving my aunt and uncle around Epiros for a few days – which wasn't really a lie. All summer I'd heard Liotes describe Albania as Anarchy Central: a place where, if you parked your car, you might come back to a metal frame stripped of wheels, engine, lights, even the little icon hanging from your rear-view mirror. To ensure our safety, NickGage, who often travelled to Albania to do human-rights work for the oppressed Greek minority, put me in touch with Kyria Deena, a Northern Epirote politician who would pick us up at the border, along with her security guard and bulletproof SUV. This was good news; having already totalled one rental car by proxy, I was reluctant to drive Chrysanthi into the heart of darkness.

*

Driving towards the border-control centre in Kakavia, I became increasingly nervous. I was about to see a place that other Epirotes seldom visit but think about all the time. For Epirotes, Albania is the wrong side of the tracks, the really poor neighbourhood next to the lower-middle-class neighbourhood where they grew up. It's a place that makes Epirotes feel better about their own lot. And Albania is also a constant reminder of how their own lives might have turned out, if not for the vagaries of fate and international politics. Which, for people living in Lia, really amount to the same thing.

Legend has it that when the Great Powers settled the borders between Albania and Greece at the Paris Peace Conference that ended the First World War, they sent a committee headed by a German official to explore Epiros and draw up the border. The Xenona didn't exist back in 1921 – no inns did – so he stayed in monasteries, including St George Kamitsani, which is fifteen minutes away from Lia on the road to Filiates. I had visited it myself, getting the key to the church from the caretaking couple across the way, and I was mesmerized by the childlike frescoes with bright-blue backgrounds, and wooden bishop's chair carved with the faces of angels. Back in 1921 it was even more impressive, and the German official, who had, it seems, an eye for design, admired one of three candlesticks that Father Demetrios had on the wall.

'Take it,' the monk offered. 'It's yours.'

The German must have missed the 'Ethics: Say No to Bribery' seminar at the Paris Peace Conference. He clutched the candlestick and said, 'It's lovely. But how can I repay you, Father Demetrios?'

Father Demetrios kept abreast of local politics. So he

whipped out a map and said, 'Actually, there is something you can do for me, Mein Herr. See these three villages?' (Here he pointed to Lia, Babouri and Tsamanta.)

The German saw them all right – after all, he had a candle handy. 'When you set the border,' the monk said, 'I'd appreciate it if they stay on the Greek side.'

The official agreed and was as good as his word, although his promise caused the border to bulge awkwardly in that spot, ruining the line's otherwise graceful curve in a way that must have upset his precise German sensibility. But Lia remained Greek and the story confirms two firmly held Greek beliefs: all is determined by fate, and it helps to have powerful people obliged to you, so a nice gift here and there never hurts.

When Greece and Albania were under Ottoman control, they had a common enemy – the Turks – and ethnic identity didn't matter as much. But once the newly independent countries' borders were defined by the Great Powers in 1923, things got trickier. For the next decade and a half, people trotted back and forth. But the Second World War changed everything. After the war, the Communist dictator Enver Hoxha snapped Albania's border shut. Defecting was dangerous; occasionally refugees would make it across, but just as many were shot to death by Albanian border guards.

Once Communism fell in 1991, many Northern Epirotes were allowed to stream into Greece. Ethnic Albanians looking for work followed, especially those who, like Vlad, had lost their humble life savings in pyramid schemes. Now I was driving in the opposite direction, along with one sixty-nine-year-old auntie with perfectly coiffed hair, and an emotional uncle.

'Angelo's heart is flying to see his old house,' Thitsa Kanta said.

At the border, long lines of Skodas waited to cross into Greece. I parked Chrysanthi under the watchful eye of a fruit pedlar and we walked to the immigration building, where Kyria Deena and her Albanian driver Benny met us and helped us breeze through, flashing our American passports like Mastercards: 'So worldly, so welcome!' (People with Greek passports have to get visas to enter Albania, and vice versa.)

Driving into the country, I peered out of the bullet-proof windows of Kyria Deena's SUV. Two things overwhelmed me: Albania's beauty and its poverty. Southern Albania looked like Northern Greece except much, much dirtier. The scenery was gorgeous: mountains, rivers and grey-stone villages nestled into hillsides. But there was rubbish everywhere. There's already too much litter along the highway in Greece for my taste. But the roads in Albania were like paved dumps.

The scenery improved once we arrived at the imposingly beautiful fortress of Argyrokastro, which means 'Silver castle' in Greek. The castle had been used as a prison and torture chamber throughout the 1980s. But now it was just a tourist site with panoramic views. Gazing down from its grounds was like looking at the decline of civilization. Below the jewel-like castle lay winding cobbled streets of Turkish mansions, built around inner courtyards where life was meant to be enjoyed. Beyond were prefab Communist-Bloc apartment buildings, whose purpose was to compress as many people as possible into a small space where all would be equally miserable.

In his white, Velcro-fastened trainers, Thio Angelo climbed up and down the walls videotaping the history lesson below, with Benny close behind. By the time Thio Angelo and Benny returned, they were new best friends. Benny called Thio Angelo *piako*, which means 'old man' in Albanian. Oddly enough, Thio Angelo loved the geriatric nickname, maybe because the last time he was in Albania, *he* was calling people *piako*. We let him sit up front next to Benny as we drove to visit Kyria Deena's parents, who live in the village of Frastani, one of many Greek villages surrounding Argyrokastro.

With grandchildren climbing on their armchairs and an impressive garden out back, Kyria Deena's parents could have been any Yia-yia and Pappou. But as they chatted with Thio Angelo and Thitsa Kanta, her father revealed that he was one of the Omonia 5, leaders of the Democratic Union of the Greek National Minority in Albania, which formed after the fall of Communism to protest about the abuses against Albania's Greek-speaking minority. The party's leaders were charged with treason by the post-Communist government in 1994, and imprisoned for ten months until human-rights groups made it too uncomfortable for the government to keep them locked up.

'They held my friend in a closet-sized room,' he told us. 'And they would beat one of us in front of the others to demoralize us.'

'Oh, we've all suffered,' Thitsa Kanta responded, patting his hand. 'The poor little world! But good for you, you showed them. You're my kind of person!'

He described how ethnic Greeks were mistreated both under Communism and after. In 1987, five young Greeks from the village of Aliko tried to escape the Communist regime but were caught and disembowelled, their eyes poked out. The people of Aliko retrieved the bodies and carried them to the Ministry of Justice in

Agia Saranda. They were turned away, he said, but the gruesome spectacle raised awareness.

Now, under the new government, such excessive oppression is rare, but the assault on the minority took a more insidious form. Although international human-rights law states that a person's national identity is self-determined, the Albanian government has created 'minority zones', so Greek schools and churches exist only in the zones that are designated Greek. The illegal 'minority zones' are manipulated to the government's advantage, Kyria Deena's father explained. For example, although most of the six thousand citizens of the seaside town of Cheimara say they are Greek, the city is not a 'minority zone', and therefore cannot have a Greek school.

But the unjust policies did not concern Kyria Deena's father as much as the actions of the Northern Epirotes themselves. 'The government tried to stamp out Greek culture in Albania, where it has existed since antiquity,' he said wearily. 'Now that the borders are open, ethnic Greeks are leaving on their own and the result could be the same. The government tried to eliminate us, but we're doing it ourselves.'

I saw his point. But as we bumped along the road to Kyria Deena's house in Saranda, I understood why people were moving away. In Greece we had the same striking scenery plus paved roads, fair-to-middling litter removal, and all the churches you could possibly want! But next to me sat Thio Angelo, who enjoyed paved roads in both Greece and America, and was still desperate to see the place where he grew up. I once saw a nature programme that said mothers of all species are biologically programmed to love their children. Perhaps children are programmed to long for – if not love – their motherland.

*

The next morning, leaving Kyria Deena to meet other politicians, Thitsa Kanta, Thio Angelo, Benny the driver and I set off on the Return to Leskoviki. Thio Angelo kept talking about how beautiful Leskoviki used to be; 'a second Paris'. The first thing he was going to do, he vowed, was drink from the spring where he had collected water every day.

As we drove into town, past concrete bunkers and high-rise council flats that loomed awkwardly amid the mountain scenery, it became clear that today, Leskoviki isn't even comparable to Paris, Texas. Thio Angelo looked bewildered. Suddenly, he pointed to a ruin. 'Look, that was City Hall!' he said. 'The Italians almost kill me and my father there – some locals shoot at a soldier, so they round up Greeks and Albanians to kill. But one Albanian guy speaks Italian, he convince them to let us go.'

All the times I'd seen Thio Angelo – in a suit at church, or wearing his jaunty paper hat at his pizza place – I'd never realized I was looking at a man who had cheated death by the age of sixteen. Now he wanted to find his old house, but with all the new streets, he didn't know where to start searching. So we headed up to the edge of town, looking for the spring he remembered, the fountain of his youth. As we approached, I noticed a shrivelled old woman in a housecoat and headscarf resting on her haunches in front of a broken-down Fiat. She looked like an old-timer to me; she had to be close to a hundred.

'Thio Angelo, let's ask that lady if she knew your father,' I suggested.

We pulled over, and Thio Angelo, too nervous to talk himself, instructed Benny to ask if she remembered

Nikolas the Tinker. Benny did, gesturing at Thio Angelo. The woman gave him a wide, toothless smile, pointing us in the right direction. Thio Angelo handed her five Euros, and she kissed him on both cheeks. The kisses must have emboldened him, because he said something to her in Albanian, and she chattered away, raising two fingers. Then he asked about the fountain, and she led us to the spring. Thio Angelo and Thitsa Kanta drank lustily as I snapped photos of them at this important site. After hugs, kisses and more Euros were exchanged, we drove on towards Thio Angelo's old street.

'What did the lady say?' I asked Thio Angelo.

'When I heard her name, I realize who she is,' he said. 'Her father worked for King Zog, and when the Italians come, Zog left Albania, but he don't take her dad with him. I remember she and her sister have a horse, but she say no, two horses.' I would have never guessed that the shrivelled old woman was practically royalty, but Thio Angelo was still caught up in her lost glamour. 'When she rode into the market on that horse, she look so beautiful,' he mused. 'I remember her much taller.'

Then he spotted his house, and just as he could visualize the toothless old lady as the stunning daughter of the richest man in town, I could imagine him as a twelve-year-old tinker's son home from the spring, not an elderly American with a camcorder. The good thing about having a poverty-stricken hometown, I guess, is that it's less likely that your childhood bedroom will be torn down to make room for the new multiplex.

Two young men were retiling the roof of the house, so Benny went up and asked if we could come inside to take some videos, explaining that the *piako* used to live here. Suddenly the home-improvement specialists ran down their ladders, bolted inside and slammed the door, yelling something in Albanian.

'They think you're here for the house,' Benny explained. 'According to Albanian law, if you have three witnesses who say it was yours before Communism, you can take them to court to get it back.'

A woman in the high-rise council block across the way stopped hanging her laundry on the line to scream at Benny.

'She says, "Where are they supposed to live now?"' he told us, shrugging.

'Benny, tell her we don't want the house!' Thitsa Kanta laughed. 'They can keep it! What we gonna do with a house here? We got one in America, one in Lia, and Eleni's building another one we don't want – that's already too many!'

Perhaps to steer us away from any impending property disputes, Benny drove us out of town to a nearby hillside so we could look over into Greece.

'That's Bourazani,' Thio Angelo said. 'I used to go back and forth there.'

I couldn't believe Bourazani was so close. A month before, I had visited the area with my cousin Areti, who took me to see the old villages, called the Mastorochoria because the men from the towns were *mastores*, builders who travelled around Eastern Europe and Asia Minor building stone houses. In Bourazani we had stayed at a hotel with its own wildlife park, then, just as I was now standing in Albania looking into Greece, we had walked to the guard post to peer down into Albania, at the border where three rivers meet. It was the same border crossing Thio Angelo had passed through often, and it was to reopen this winter after sixty-one years.

Before and After

TOP: The thitsas, NickGage and me enjoying the holidays in Worcester, Massachusetts. *Left to right:* Thitsa Olga, Thitsa Kanta, NickGage, Eleni and Thitsa Lilia.

BOTTOM: Leaving the thitsas (and the USA) behind for the mountains of Northern Greece, I soon found myself following this shepherd and his flock on the road to Lia.

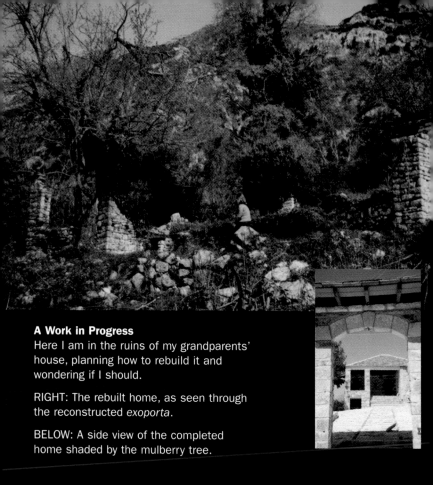

A Work in Progress
Here I am in the ruins of my grandparents' house, planning how to rebuild it and wondering if I should.

RIGHT: The rebuilt home, as seen through the reconstructed *exoporta*.

BELOW: A side view of the completed home shaded by the mulberry tree.

ABOVE: Foti delivers the unlucky rooster for ritual sacrifice over the foundations of the first floor.

LEFT: Father Prokopi blesses the trenches that were dug for the foundations of the basement.

Clearing the Air
Two different rituals to drive unsettled spirits away from the site, invite good luck and promote the building of a strong, happy home.

Making a Joyful Noise
Religious celebrations in Lia, *clockwise from right:* Admiring an icon of the Panagia in anticipation of the festival of the Dormition on 15 August. Candles lit in front of an icon of the Prophet Elias on his saint's day. Visiting Liotan boys lead the procession of the litany of the Agia Triada. Spiridoula directs me in decorating the crowning piece of the Epitaphion to prepare it for the Good Friday procession through the village.

A Moveable Feast

Celebrations all over Epiros, *clockwise from below:* Georgia Vaya, the mayor's wife, joins relatives of the happy couple in leading the gypsy bride and groom to their reception. The gypsy wedding ceremony. A Sarakatsanissa poses in traditional dress at the nomadic shepherd convention. The Anastenarides dance on hot coals. Sarakatsani youths perform one of their dances. The sister of the groom (and mother of four) in front of the gypsy bride's dowry.

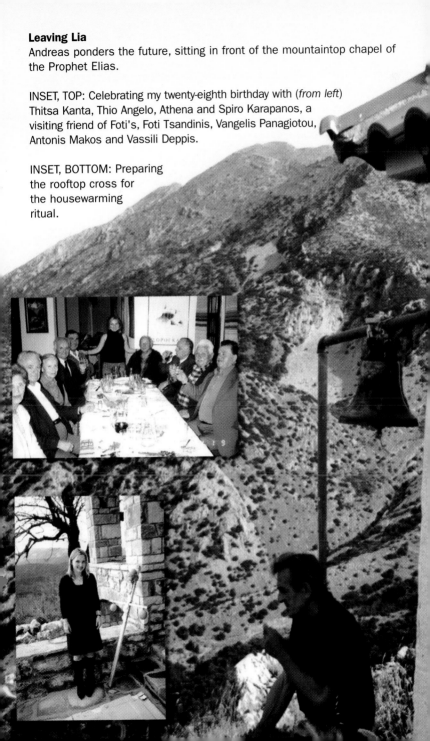

Leaving Lia
Andreas ponders the future, sitting in front of the mountaintop chapel of the Prophet Elias.

INSET, TOP: Celebrating my twenty-eighth birthday with (*from left*) Thitsa Kanta, Thio Angelo, Athena and Spiro Karapanos, a visiting friend of Foti's, Foti Tsandinis, Vangelis Panagiotou, Antonis Makos and Vassili Deppis.

INSET, BOTTOM: Preparing the rooftop cross for the housewarming ritual.

'It will be the largest crossing in all of Greece,' the lonely Greek soldier posted there had told me and my cousin. 'See the lights along the highway on our side? We put them there so that people will know they just entered Europe.'

I told Thio Angelo and Thitsa Kanta about the plans for the lights, and said that maybe the border crossing would revitalize Leskoviki. After all, these were historic mountains. The Italians had invaded Greece by coming over them from Albania at the start of the Second World War, and the outnumbered Greek forces had beaten them back, a victory for the underdog Greek Army that had riveted the attention of the world. Areti had pointed out a mountain near Kalpaki, where the word «OXI», 'No!' is written in stones. According to popular folklore, that is what Metaxas, the Greek prime minister, said when the Italian ambassador asked him not to resist the occupation. (What Metaxas really said was, *Alors c'est la guerre*,' but that would look awfully sissy carved into a mountain top.)

'Well, all I can say, Ange, it's a good thing the Italians come to kick the Greek citizens out of Albania,' said Thitsa Kanta, turning away from the historic view to walk to the bulletproof SUV. 'Otherwise, you'd still live here.'

Aristophanes said, 'Our country is the country in which we prosper most.' Thitsa Kanta would definitely agree. Today, having seen Leskoviki, she was feeling particularly red, white and blue. But Thio Angelo had six years of Greek-Albania in him, and on the way back to Saranda he wanted to stop in Premeti, where his family had owned a shop for two years before moving to Leskoviki.

Premeti was built along a river, and with the council

flats, mosque and river view, it looked just like the East 90s in Manhattan. I felt right at home, but Thio Angelo's past had not survived here as it had in Leskoviki. A modern town with wide streets, Premeti now had a large main square with a new church and school, right where the old church and Thio Angelo's house once stood.

We wandered into the old part of town, visiting the city's two other churches just to make sure that he hadn't remembered the wrong neighbourhood for his childhood home. In Agios Nikolaos a wizened old man entered the church and lit a candle, asking Benny who we were. His name was Vangelis too, like Thio Angelo, but he didn't know any Greek beyond a few pleasantries. Benny asked if he remembered Nikolas the Tinker who had lived here in the twenties, but Vangelis said no, he couldn't have known him, he was born in 1941. This *piako* was the same age as my mother, who was no doubt attending a power yoga class in Worcester at this moment. Stooped and grey, he looked about twenty years older.

We shook hands goodbye, and he told us his last name, Athanassios, which means 'immortal' in Greek. That seemed appropriate; he was still here, after all. He didn't speak Greek, but he was lighting a candle, as his ancestors must have done for centuries. The old man made me hopeful that Kyria Deena's father might be wrong, that there would always be a Greek presence in Albania, however stooped, grey and unfamiliar with power yoga.

As we drove back to Kyria Deena's house in Saranta, Thio Angelo napped. I wondered if he was dreaming of the now-disappeared streets of Premeti.

*

The next morning we were awoken in Saranda by ringing church bells; it was 15 August, the Panagia's holiday, and because Saranda is partly populated by ethnic Greeks, it was being celebrated here, too. We went to Saranda's shiny new church and attended the service, surrounded by Orthodox Christians who hadn't been allowed to practise their religion until Communism fell in 1991. There were no old ladies dropping to the floor with the assurance that comes from a lifetime of frequent genuflection, like the experts in Lia, but it was still a nice ceremony, with all the requisite incense, chanting and lighting of candles.

After church, as we made our way towards Greece, Benny suggested we stop in Klissoura, an ethnic Greek village just on the Albanian side of the border, which was hosting a huge *panegyri*. It was only a few miles out of our way, but they turned out to be unpaved, so we bumped along for an hour and a half until we arrived in a once-grand village of grey-stone houses studding the mountain. Dozens of the villagers' relatives from Greece had come for the occasion. The square was hung with a banner that read, in Greek, 'We thank you for making the effort to come to our remote village to celebrate with us today and beautify the solitude with your presence.'

The president of the village treated us to coffee in the *kafenion*. Today only sixty-five people live in Klissoura, he said, but before the war there were three thousand inhabitants, including traders who travelled all over Epiros. He pulled out a pre-war photo of children in front of the school, and Thio Angelo identified a friend he knew from church in Worcester. 'I gotta take some movie,' Thio Angelo said, whipping out his camcorder. 'Jimmy Bazooka gonna see where he grew up.'

Once Thio Angelo had finished adding to his oeuvre,

we set out for Greece; we had to get to Lia before evening, because there were *panegyria* in the neighbouring villages of Babouri and Tsamanta, and we wanted to beautify them with our presence as well. We kissed Benny and Kyria Deena goodbye at the border and drove towards home.

Paved roads! Clean villages! I think even Thitsa Kanta was happy to be back. When we returned to Lia, Vangeli Panagiotou asked where we had gone. 'To Albania,' I said. 'To see Leskoviki.'

'That's right, Angelo lived there as a child, so it pains him,' he responded. 'The way Cheimara, where I grew up, pains me.'

A place that pains you, in Greek vernacular, is somewhere you love. To love a place is to feel for it, to let it wound you so it leaves a scar, a permanent keepsake. When I had picked up Areti to start our field trip to the Mastorochoria, we had driven through Lia. 'These mountains make me think of the war,' she'd said as we neared the village. 'Probably because of the stories my mother told us about that time.'

Her mother's mother had been executed alongside my grandmother. In a way, Lia was her mother's Leskoviki, a place where she came to remember the past and realize how lucky she was that fate had carved out a different path for her, but a place that, even if it disappeared, would live on in her mind and pain her when she remembered.

That night, Thio Angelo, Thitsa Kanta and I went to Babouri, the village next to Lia. As we danced with dozens of Epirotes in Babouri and, later that night, hundreds in Tsamanta, I knew that all over the world, from Australia to Alexandria, Greeks were celebrating.

The next day, I didn't see Thitsa Kanta or Thio

Angelo anywhere in town. So I drove to their house, where I found them turning various shades of green, running back and forth to the bathroom.

'We shouldn't have drunk from the fountain in the damn Albania,' Thitsa Kanta whispered, clutching her stomach.

It was Leskoviki's revenge. A second Paris is not to be spoken ill of lightly.

A few weeks later, Thitsa Kanta had recovered enough to go into Ioannina and stock up on the candied chestnuts, feta and Turkish delight she was hoarding in anticipation of her eventual return to the US. After clearing out the Arvanitis Supermarket we were ready to return to Lia, and were cruising along when the car in front of me screeched to a halt. A matron in a jade-green suit got out to stand in a parking spot, while a woman with platinum hair and black roots leaned out of the driver's seat. 'Go backwards so I can park!' she screamed. 'Can't you see my hazard lights are on?'

Her snarl propelled me across a psychic border of my own, from my polite American persona to an in-your-face Greek driver. I rolled down my window. 'Oh, this is my fault?' I boomed. 'No, this is your fault! If you want me to do you a favour, you'd better ask nicely. I'm not going anywhere!'

I turned off the motor of the car, pulled the key out of the ignition and raised it into the air like the fist in a Black Panther salute. The blonde retreated into her powder-blue hatchback Fiat as the matron in the green suit pleaded with me. 'Please, Christian woman, just back up a little!' she entreated. 'There's lots of traffic!'

'There's traffic, but there's also the matter of civilized behaviour!' I huffed. But they seemed appropriately cowed, so I slowly backed up just enough to let them park.

Thitsa Kanta stared at me as we waited for the Fiat to wedge itself into its new-found home. 'Lenitsa, I'm shocked,' she said. 'I always thought you were a lamb, but you can be a goat, too. Good for you.'

I normally shun confrontation; in New York, I made my room-mate Katherine handle all potential confront- ations with real-estate brokers, plumbers and the like, ever since the Time Warner Cable operator reduced me to tears. After spending an hour on the phone trying to convince the operator to give me information about my own cable bill, I started sobbing audibly. 'Anything else?' she grunted into the phone. 'Yes!' I gasped. 'You should know (sob) that you are NOT (sob) a nice person.'

In Ioannina, Thitsa Kanta was amazed at my new alter ego, which was like the three Fates rolled into one sixty- inch natural blonde: fair, swift and so justifiably bitchy. We were in good spirits until, just as we hit the high- way, torrents of rain started lashing the windscreen. I pulled over to wait out the storm, but it was getting late and showed no signs of letting up.

'Lenitsa, maybe we call Kaity and George to stay with them,' Thitsa Kanta quavered.

It was a sensible request. But although the storm scared me, I was filled with a yearning to be home, and for me, now, that meant Lia. Plus, this was my chance to prove to Thitsa Kanta that there was nothing to be afraid of in Lia – no wolves, no ghosts and no curse. So I drove off towards the mountain. I knew I was being pushy, and my behaviour shocked me almost as much as it did Thitsa Kanta. I couldn't explain it. But maybe, while living in the village with generations of survivors,

I had grown stronger as the rebuilt house grew taller.

As we drove on, I thought the weather was improving. But then it started pouring again, lightning flashed, driving rain alternated with the rattle of hailstones and I clutched the steering wheel, terrified that I was leading my aunt to her death. I drove so slowly that a number of eighteen-wheelers passed me on the right-hand side. Thitsa Kanta was silent, but I noticed her crossing herself every time we turned a sharp corner.

Then, as driving rain gave way to blinding fog, she said, 'My mother was right. We're going to die in this village.'

Thunder crashed and I started shaking; it was the kind of storm that Greeks always refer to as δεύτερα παρουσία, the Apocalypse. Thitsa Kanta was here because of me. I hadn't forced her into the car physically, but I knew I would be to blame if we crashed and died. Still, I tried to convince myself, I had driven through worse. And I was almost home.

Suddenly, we were there. I pulled into Thitsa Kanta's driveway just as the rain stopped. 'We made it,' she chirped, gathering her packages. 'Good job, Lenitsa.' Now that we had arrived safely, it was as if she hadn't noticed the rain at all; the curse was forgotten. Despite my new-found assertiveness, I was too polite to gloat. Besides, I understood why Thitsa Kanta believed in her mother's curse, which would punish any of us who returned to the village. Lia's scenery and history are so dramatic, and my aunt's memories so tragic, it was natural that everything here seemed like a risk. In the village, life seems tenuous and death always close at hand. It's nerve-racking, but exhilarating as well.

By mid September, the late-summer rains had produced a new crop of wildflowers: yellow autumn crocuses and purple wild cyclamens, loud bursts of colour that glowed in the bright sunlight. The days were clear and the nights cool enough to build a fire, in which Thitsa Kanta and I would roast chestnuts.

'Lenitsa, want me to tell you why I woke up at four this morning?' she asked me one evening. She was still getting over her bout of stomach trouble, so I wasn't quite sure I did want to know. But my curiosity won out.

'I had a dream,' she rushed on. 'I was here in Lia, filling a barrel from the Motsala, like in the old days, when I hear my mother calling, "Oooh, Kanta." She slipped into the shrill tone village ladies use to yell to each other across the ravines. 'Suddenly, I was standing next to my mother above the Haidis house.' Thitsa Kanta swirled her hand in the air. 'She looked just like she did before the war, with two long braids. She held a loaf of bread – that's good; bread is a sign of strength.'

'So, what did she want?' I prodded.

'She says, "Kanta, I'm so glad you're here,"' Thitsa Kanta reported. '"I'm exhausted, I've been busy for so many months. Now that you're here I can go rest."'

'Go where to rest?' I asked.

'I don't know – I'm just telling you what she said,' Thitsa Kanta continued. 'I ask, "Why are you so tired?" and she says, "I've been watching the *kopela*" – that's you – "and the *paidi*" – that's your father.'

Kopela means young lady, which is about right, but at sixty-three, my father hardly counts as a *paidi*, a child, in my opinion. Still, I wasn't about to quibble with the dead. But Thitsa Kanta had no qualms about doing so.

'I ask, "Mana, what about NickGage's accident?"' Kanta continued. '"Were you watching then? He almost died!" My mother says, "I wasn't there right away, but

Nitsa stopped the car with her back so it wouldn't roll down the mountain. Then I broke the windscreen to get him out; see, I have a scar on my hand." My Aunt Nitsa had no kids, she always like NickGage best,' Thitsa Kanta mused. 'Maybe that's why she get there first.'

'Wasn't Yia-yia Nitsa buried at the Panagia church?' I asked. In Lia, because of the shortage of flat, consecrated land for burials, the dead are traditionally disinterred after five years, and their bones are stored in a box decorated with their name and sometimes a photo; I had just seen my great-aunt's bonebox in the ossuary next to Panagia. 'That's right below where my father drove off the cliff.'

'Of course!' Thitsa Kanta cried. 'Nitsa had her back to the accident, so she stopped the car!' She smiled.

'So what happened next, you know, in the dream?' I prompted.

'Oh, nothing really,' Thitsa Kanta replied. 'I said I'd stay and my mother disappeared. But when she was gone, I could still hear her saying, "Watch out for the kopela, the kopela." So I know, even with the stomach trouble, I can't go home early. I have to stay until October 10th, the date my ticket says, to look out for you.'

'You think your mother knows the date of your ticket?' I was sceptical.

'I don't know what she knows,' Thitsa Kanta said. 'She probably meant that she'll come back because she wants to see her house finished; she's glad.'

It's a good thing I was drinking iced coffee instead of hot, because I spilled it all over my hand. Two months ago, Thitsa Kanta had implied that her mother caused my father's accident because he'd broken his vow not to come back here. Now she thought my yia-yia was disrupting her eternal rest because she was so eager to watch the reconstruction of her house? I was shocked, but I was not about to point out the sea change in Thitsa Kanta's thinking. It all made perfect sense. Thio Angelo's visit to Albania and my own desire to live in Lia had taught me how strong the pull of home is on a living soul; why wouldn't that yearning continue after death?

Besides, I was thrilled by Thitsa Kanta's new attitude; she now had the otherworldly approval she needed to support me — and the house. And it seemed I had something even more valuable than my aunt's encouragement: divine protection. Perhaps the near-fatal driving disasters my family and I had suffered in Lia weren't caused by my grandmother in her anger at my breaking our family's vow; perhaps they were mitigated by her, so that my father and I were saved.

7

DOORWAYS TO THE DEAD

«Ο θάνατος είναι ο μόνος θεός που δεν
ικανοποιείται με δώρα.»
'Death is the only god whom gifts cannot appease.'

24 August

Rounding the turn just below the Gatzoyiannis house, I
hear shouting.

'If that's how you feel, take your cash and go!'
Zervas's normally melodious voice bellows. I hike up to
see two musclemen with crewcuts sputtering, 'But . . .'

'No! I will not work with extortionists!' Zervas throws
down some Euros and turns his back to the men, who are
twice his size. The cash lands on the low stone wall that
Vlad is completing while keeping one eye on the battle.

One of the Crewcuts bends down, scoops up the cash,
spits on the ground and storms towards a pick-up parked
nearby. The other follows him, then dashes back to
retrieve a red bundle that looks like a sweatshirt — only

it seems to be moving. He jumps into the truck and the men zoom off. I wave, as I do at every car that passes by here in Lia. Crewcut Number Two responds by shoving his hand, palm forward, out of the window. The ultimate hand-gesture insult! My mouth drops open — I've never had anyone *mountsos* me when I wasn't behind the wheel of a car. Zervas is pacing back and forth at the front of the site, where the outer door to the courtyard will stand someday. But apparently not any time soon.

'Who were those guys?' I ask him.

'Workers,' he shouts, raising both hands towards the sky. 'I brought them to make the frame for the outer door to the courtyard — the entrance gate is a house's most noticeable adornment, and the stonework has to be perfect.'

'Why isn't Yanni doing it?' I ask.

'Yanni!' Zervas spits. 'He's another one! Once he finished the roof, he demanded an extra five hundred Euros for the chimneys. I said I wouldn't even mention that to you — we had agreed on one price for the roof, and that means chimneys and all!'

I look at the slate roof and the adorable stone chimneys with their own sloping slate mini-roofs and latticed stone vents. They look like something out of a fairy tale. But not a fairy tale worth five hundred Euros.

Zervas is still fuming. 'So I call this pair who are from Albania, just over the border from my village,' he continues. 'We drive here, singing Epirotic songs, I buy us lunch at the Xenona, and bring them to work. Then this one gets involved.' Zervas shakes a bony finger at Vlad.

Vlad looks up brightly. Zervas glares at him. 'They laid the cement, then sat for a break, and this one starts talking in Albanian,' he said. 'Then the guys come up to me and say, 'Fifty Euros each a day is not enough. We need a hundred each to finish this project.' So I told them to take their money for today and go. Now this one's all happy, because there's more work for him. But he doesn't have the skills to make an exoporta. It has to be a showpiece!'

'Vlad already has too much to do!' I protest. 'The interior walls, the courtyard — months of work. But who's going to build the outer door?' I stare at Zervas, this tiny man who had managed to antagonize not one, but two teams of muscle-bound builders so they couldn't cheat me. Now I have my dignity, but no exoporta. When I first saw the ruined house, the outer door was the only part still standing. I thought of the stone arch each time I visualized my grandmother's home. It was the entrance to her world.

'I have to go back to Athens and find some other masons,' Zervas says, pulling on his natty sports jacket even though it's ninety degrees out. 'I'll be back next week.'

I groan, knowing he will be days, even weeks, late. Then I remember something. 'Kyrie Zervas!' I shout. 'What was the worker hiding in his jacket? It moved.'

'Ach!' He whirls around. 'They found a hedgehog and planned to kill it and make stew, but it skittered away. They must have trapped it again!'

I shudder. Hedgehogs are adorable — that's like eating a kitten! Zervas looks at the sky in despair and repeats the expression that Greeks always turn to in times of misery: 'Mother, why did you give birth to me?'

I wasn't surprised to hear a seventy-something man complaining to his dead mother. People in Lia communicate with the dead on a daily basis, lighting oil lamps at the roadside memorial shrines, adding fresh flowers to the plastic garlands that decorate the gravestones in the churchyard, and asking advice, out loud, of parents who have been dead for decades. Lia's geographical and political borders have a long history of controversy, but one border has always been fluid – the fine, shifting line between the world of the living and the world of the dead. Everyone talks to dead loved ones, and sometimes they get an answer back. Eternity is one long conversation; just because someone dies is no reason to stop talking to him. Like any relationship, the bond between the living and the dead is one of give and take. The living are obliged to light candles to the dead and hold memorial services in their honour, so the deceased know they're not forgotten. In return, the dear departed keep an eye on the world below, often popping in with a message or word of warning, just as my grandmother visited Thitsa Kanta in a dream, asking her to protect me.

I was an absolute beginner at communicating with the dead. But living in Lia, I realized that seeking their advice is a practice as old as Epiros itself. So when my sister Marina visited in July, I'd taken her to Hell and back, on a visit to the Underworld where ancient Epirotes chatted with their deceased loved ones. As we boarded one of many tour boats in Parga's harbour, we noticed plenty of Germans and Brits on the 'Party Boat' next to ours. But looking around our boat, I saw that only old people and Greeks were eager to go on an Epirote death trip up the Acheron, the River of Woe, to the Necromanteion, the Oracle of the Dead, in the ancient kingdom of Hades.

While Marina and I simply purchased ten-Euro tickets to Hades, the ancient Greeks used to place a coin under the tongue of a corpse, so that he would be able to pay Charon, the greedy ferryman who rowed the dead to the Underworld. (An updated version of this custom is still practised in Lia, where coins are placed on the eyes of the corpse. Famous for his unique sense of style, my grandfather asked that an American dollar bill be discreetly slipped into his coat pocket when his time came.)

Our Captain Charon started the boat's engine and we sailed across the cobalt sea for half an hour before reaching the mouth of the Acheron – the ancient river to Hell. The boat manoeuvred into a narrow stream of Gatorade-coloured water flanked by banks of reeds. Flipping through Robert Graves's *The Greek Myths*, I read to Marina about the many levels of Hades, such as the Asphodel Fields, where 'the souls of heroes stay without purpose among the throngs of less distinguished dead that twitter like bats'.

We saw no bats or heroes' souls, but there were throngs of distinguished dragonflies in deep, rich blues, purples and greens, turtles sitting on mangled stumps, and the grasping branches of overhanging willows. I tried to photograph the dragonflies, but, like souls, they proved to be too ephemeral. The surroundings seemed like death itself – both frightening and beautiful. 'This is like the Jungle Cruise at Disneyworld,' Marina said. 'You know, only real and with ghosts.'

Our enthusiasm faltered when the captain pulled up to the bank of a field (corn, not asphodel), and announced that he would lead us on a two-kilometre walk to the Necromanteion. It seems that the River Styx – a small tributary between the Acheron and Hades – had dried up. But there had been no mention of a hike; I'd assumed the ruins would rise majestically from the banks of the river, so I could photograph them from the comfort of the boat. Sort of like the Jungle Cruise.

As we trudged on, I told Marina that this was nothing compared to the rigours faced by ancient mortals, who had visited the Necromanteion to seek advice from their dearly departed. Pilgrims to the Oracle of the Dead had to spend a month in dark, dorm-like structures, eating only *nekrodeipna* – 'food of the dead' – that the priests conveniently provided. The taste treats included 'carbonized fruits', broad beans, lupin seeds and other foods that evoke visions, or, as the Necromanteion guidebook – the Underworld Zagat's – says, 'cause wind, indigestion, and a relaxation of the sense to the point of giddiness and hallucinations and allergic syndromes'. The priests would lead guests through labyrinths to a cleverly lit underground cavern where they would see visions, and then swear them to secrecy to avoid the wrath of Hades, king of the Underworld.

'So it was a scam, taking advantage of people who are desperate to talk to loved ones they've lost,' Marina said. 'Sort of like the Psychic Friends Network.'

We had only bottled water and a slight case of sunstroke as mood-altering aids. But we found the Necromanteion appropriately creepy. Surrounded by green fields, the Necromanteion looked dead itself, a grey, post-apocalyptic collection of dusty, sun-baked boulders and scattered cracked urns, and a small stone chapel rising from the rubble. A French tour guide was leading a group through the chapel, exclaiming on the 'humanity' of Greek churches, and pointing out the gashes in the wall icons where invading Turks had gouged out the saints' eyes. The Turks weren't the first invaders who tried to subdue the historic religious nature of the place. It had functioned as an Oracle until 167 BC, when Aemilius Paulus went on his anti-Epiros rampage. Then, in the eighteenth century, Christian leaders exhibited their knack for capitalizing on ancient holy places by building a church to St John the Baptist above the ruins. Today, below the chapel, flimsy metal steps wind down a hole in the ground. People circled it fearfully, no doubt wishing we had Teiresias, the blind seer and ancient tour guide to Hades, in the crowd.

'Hey, Mare,' I said, 'you go first.' In her twenty-five years as my little sister, Marina had learned her role well. She climbed down, a canary into a coal mine. I followed nobly, like Eleanor Roosevelt saluting the miners. Odysseus had visited the Oracle of the Dead on his journey back to Ithaka and communed with his fallen comrades from Troy; I had to consult the Necromanteion on my odyssey. So I descended into the scene that Circe describes to Homer's hero, 'the Great Hall of Hades and Persephone'. Built in the fourth century BC, this was where the hungry, drugged pilgrims were led: a barrel-vaulted chamber with slick stone floors, slimy walls and a powerful echo. The floor was slippery, gouged out in places to disorient drugged pilgrims even further. Some crevices in the stone were filled with pools of water, perhaps from the dried-up River Styx. The arched underground hall was infinitely scary and majestic, even to modern visitors who aren't half starved and on hallucinogens. 'It smells of corpses!' gasped an overexcitable Greek lady, shimmying down the stairs in her capri pants.

Later, as we sailed out of the swampy confines of the Acheron River into the kaleidoscopic waters of the sea, a yacht's tender passed us. At the front, like a carved mermaid on a ship's prow, sat a topless blonde in black bikini bottoms. I was sweaty, tired and disappointed, because I'd sat in the slimy cavern for twenty minutes and never heard a word from Persephone, Odysseus, or anyone else in the Great Beyond. But the speedboat mermaid looked cool and confident, and I envied the rich-girl moxie that let her ride bare-breasted into the mouth of Hell.

On our way back to Lia, Marina and I visited the monument to the fifty-six women of Zaloggo, who, with their babies in their arms, danced off a cliff in 1803, choosing death over the dishonour of being captured by Ali Pasha's Turkish army. We climbed 410 steps straight up to stand at the base of the towering stylized stone figures commemorating their dance of death. Below, a marble arch is carved with the song they sang as they leapt off the cliff: 'Farewell, poor world; farewell, sweet life.'

When we finally reached the statues at the edge of the cliff, I looked for a place where a dissenting Souliotissa might have been able to hide if she chickened out at the last minute. Of course, she wouldn't have, but I suspected that hiding is what I might have done, as I stared at the craggy cliffside and the fields below. A year earlier, if I had heard the story, I might have imagined myself gracefully leaping to my doom, a heroine. After living in Lia, where the dead and the idea of death were ever-present, I realized how attached I was to my own imperfect life. Now I found the story frightening, another cautionary tale about people trapped by fate and their homeland, doomed to tragedy.

My morbid mood didn't last long, because after descending the 410 steps, we drove on to the town of Glyki, where the narrows of the Acheron River begin. If the reedy, insect-infested length of the Acheron we'd sailed is the creepy part of the Underworld, the narrows of the Acheron must be its Elysian Fields. Marina and I hiked along the banks of the clear river, then, when the banks disappeared between rock cliffs, jumped in and waded through the narrows – a gorge which has 100-metre-high cliffs on either side and is two metres wide at its narrowest point. Mountain-fed streams bubble right out of the rocks, and although the river was teeth-clenchingly cold, we felt revitalized by its coolness in contrast to the oppressive heat of the day. The views were astounding – like being at the bottom of the Grand Canyon looking up. Marina waded ahead as the river got deeper. Unfortunately, I'm three inches shorter than my younger sister. I lagged behind, hoisting my camera above my head as the water level reached my nose. Suddenly a heavyset Greek man was at my side. He swept me up in his arms and carried me over to the shallow side.

'If that guy was Charon, you'd have to tip him,' Marina said as I reached her. But he was mortal, and on our hike back we didn't see any dead men wading. Our search for a calling plan to reach the spirit world had been invigorating, but overall, it was a bust. The dead seemed to be telling me, 'Call someone who cares.'

Once Marina left, I gave up on communicating with the dead. With early-autumn tomatoes turning red in my garden, and the heady scent of ripe grapes filling my terrace, I concentrated on tending my 'crops' and resurrecting the Gatzoyiannis house. But even though I stopped looking for death, to paraphrase Emily Dickinson, he kindly kept stopping for me. While I was in Arta to shop at the autumn bazaar, I visited the city's famous bridge, three asymmetrical stone arches sloping across the rushing Aracthros River. In the small folklore museum, a docent led me into a stone-paved, crypt-like room with seaweed on the walls. Pressing a button, she announced, 'Now you will hear the legend of the Bridge of Arta.' A familiar folk song started playing. 'Forty-five bridgebuilders and sixty apprentices,' a voice intoned, citing the men who in 1612 worked every day to build the bridge, and watched in despair as it fell down every night. In the song, a bird flies overhead, hears the men weeping, and informs them that for the bridge to stand, they must wall up the master-builder's young wife in one of its columns.

The next day she arrives with her beloved husband's lunch and notices him watching her. 'Why are you so sad?' she asks. A wily apprentice answers, 'His wedding ring fell down that pillar, and no one will go and get it.' Of course, she volunteers. As they start to brick the pillar up above her, she realizes what is happening and cries out:

> 'May this bridge shake like a poppy-head
> So may it shake and tremble
> And as the leaves fall from the tree
> So may the travellers tumble.'

But her ambitious husband, who sees the bridge as his key to immortality, reminds her that she has only one brother, and he is likely to cross the bridge. So she retracts her curse, and dies, allowing the bridge to stand.

When half of Arta was liberated from the Ottoman Empire in 1913, the border between the Greek side and the Turkish half was set at the highest arch of the bridge. But despite its important political past, it's the story of the master-builder's wife that elevates the bridge to legendary status. Even today, people cross it in silence, because the sound of whistling or music is said to make her wish she were alive, and the entire bridge tremble with her rage.

I crossed the bridge quietly, remembering a Romanian version of the same legend – only it was a church that the builder couldn't get to stand. The cross-cultural message is clear: it's hubris to try to subvert nature by building a bridge's arch over a river or a spire into thin air, and the gods require a sacrifice to appease their anger. Most often, history teaches us, that sacrifice is going to be a woman. After Arta, I felt much less guilty about the rooster head buried in my foundations.

In all my wanderings, I realized that, in Greece, death was regarded as rather like the postman: a frequent visitor who has a job to do. And the afterlife is a nearby, familiar place. Once, in Ioannina, I asked where a bakery I remembered had gone. 'The baker moved to Οδος Αναπαύσεως,' the new shopkeeper told me. It was only after he laughingly described the street as being located 'north of the city – very far north' that I realized the street name translated as 'Avenue of Eternal Rest'.

In America, death is a spectre that lurks in books and movies. When death isn't entertainment, people seldom think about it. But Liotes hold rituals to honour death with nonchalant regularity. The villagers are so used to people leaving, to go and work in a city or foreign country, and coming back, that the one thing they know to be eternal is a Liote's fierce homing instinct. It was only natural that people would hover around the village after they passed on to their reward.

One Sunday, when Father Prokopi was performing the liturgy in Babouri, I arrived at church late, just in time to see him outside in the cemetery swinging the censer over a grave, sending swirls of sweet smoke into the air. The service had ended and he was saying a *trisagion* in memory of an old woman who had died a year ago. Relatives of the deceased handed me a plastic bowl of *kollyva*: boiled wheat sweetened with raisins, nuts and icing sugar. The wheat symbolizes the Resurrection, as it is written in John 12:24: 'Except a corn of wheat fall into the ground and die, it abideth alone, but if it die, it bringeth forth much fruit.' Eating the *kollyva* indicates you've forgiven the soul of the deceased, a lady explained, handing me a packet with a plastic spoon, paper napkin, and a strip of paper printed with: 'We thank you for sharing in our sorrow – The Family.'

She also gave me a sweet bun wrapped in wax paper embossed with a gold cross and the word *mnemosyne*: 'remembrance'. The ancient goddess of memory was named Mnemosyne; she and Zeus conceived the Nine Muses who governed the arts, perhaps because all creative expression stems from the vivid power of memory.

After the ceremony in the graveyard, we sat in Babouri's *kafenion*, toasting the deceased with coffee and cognac. It was a sunny morning, but as people departed, many were in a reflective mood. One man opined to his elderly mother, 'Life is like a watch. Time runs out and eventually it stops.' She wailed, 'But you can take your watch to Filiates to get it fixed. You can't do that with a person!'

The old lady was right. Here I was sitting in the sun, happily chewing what I thought of as a 'death muffin'; but for an elderly woman in Babouri, this was the first anniversary of the day she'd lost her own sister and was left with the insufficient consolation of memory.

Although Liotes still talk to their relatives after they die, it doesn't fill the black hole left by their absence.

When Dina made *kollyva* for Andreas's son's memorial, she explained to me that it should contain pomegranate seeds, which are desirable for more than just their tart taste and pink colour. They are associated with Persephone, the goddess who became Queen of the Dead. She was picking flowers with her mother, Demeter, Goddess of Agriculture, when Hades thundered up in his horse-drawn chariot, kidnapped her and dragged her back to his Underworld kingdom, where he installed her as his queen. Devastated by Persephone's disappearance (and no doubt feeling guilty for not having kept a closer watch on her blossom of a daughter, instead of gloating over the beauty of the flowers she'd created), Demeter set the whole world on an involuntary hunger strike. She froze the crops and spread famine, creating the first winter. The other gods implored Demeter to relent, but she insisted that as long as Persephone languished in the Underworld, the earth would suffer as well. Meanwhile Persephone played the martyr, refusing to eat or drink anything, to accept Hades' hospitality and become a part of his world. Eventually Hades felt so awful that, according to Robert Graves's *Greek Myths*, he was 'obliged to cloak his vexation, telling her mildly, "My child, you seem to be unhappy here, and your mother weeps for you. I have therefore decided to send you home." '

At that point, Hades' faithful gardener reported that he saw Queen Persephone eat seven seeds of a juicy red pomegranate, therefore tasting the food of the dead – the one thing Zeus had told Demeter that Persephone must not do if she wanted to return to the world of the living. Technically, the pomegranate-tasting could have condemned Persephone to the Underworld for ever, leaving Demeter to mourn and the earth to starve. But Zeus negotiated a compromise: Persephone would spend nine months with her doting mother, and the rest of the year with Hades as queen of the Underworld. During those three months, Demeter was free to neglect her Agricultural Goddess duties, to let the crops die and winter cover the earth.

Because Persephone always returns to the world of the living, the pomegranate seeds in the *kollyva* represent resurrection, and because she ate them in the Underworld, they signify life after death. Today, even though pomegranate seeds are rich in significance, they're still subject to the whims of Demeter. When Dina made *kollyva* for Andreas's son in July, she sighed, 'Who can get pomegranates at this time of year?'

A few days after the Babouriote memorial service, I drove Thitsa Kanta to Filiates to get her hair done, and decided to stop by the *pantopoleion*, the Everything Store. Ever since the Everything Man had advised me to find someone to share my bread with, when I'd bought kitchen gadgets from him during Holy Week, I'd had a soft spot for the man, even though it took him fifteen minutes to find anything, because the store was such a jumble of irons, china, hunting gear and barbecues. But once he had done so, he'd insisted on carrying my purchases to the car, despite the fact that he was old and gaunt. So when I walked in and saw his son at the counter, I was disappointed. I took one look at his glazed eyes and knew I wasn't going to get any romantic advice here.

'Where's the old guy?' I asked.

He blinked and stared at the gas grill in the window.

'We lost him a month ago,' he said. 'Cancer of the liver.'

I said how sorry I was, and that he had made everyone who came into the store smile. But his son said nothing as I wandered back out into the harsh sunlight. The woman in the bridge of Arta and the dancers at Zaloggo had seemed romantic, mythical. Now I realized that they had once been individuals who had given advice and done people favours, and that after they'd gone they had been missed. Perhaps they had welcomed death in the end, knowing how scary it is to be left behind to seek messages from oracles, or to look for the fingerprint of a familiar hand on the shiny surface of a gas grill.

'What's wrong, honey?' Thitsa Kanta asked as we drove back. 'You quiet.'

'Nothing really,' I said. 'A man died. I didn't expect him to, but he was sick.'

'That's the worst,' Thitsa Kanta said. 'To suffer before you die, like being sick, or like my mother. I'm old, I want my children to be healthy, my grandchildren, to see my niece get married. I don't care if I die. But I don't want to suffer.'

'You'll live a long time,' I told her. 'So I have plenty of time to get married.'

But she didn't answer, and I knew she was thinking about her mother. It was late August, and in a few days we would hold a memorial service to mark my grandmother's execution fifty-four years ago on 28 August 1948. Also coming for the service were the daughters of my grandmother's sister-in-law Alexandra, who was executed alongside her. And, since nothing changes the fact that August is prime time to visit Greece, I had two friends from New York who would be passing through.

On the 27th I drove to Igoumenitsa to pick up Elsa from the ferry. By the time we pulled up at the Haidis house, the village was already buzzing with the news that young foreigners were in town. Anna, a Greek-American friend, had arrived the night before and had spent the morning charming all my retired male pals, who were now chauffeuring her around. They pulled over, and Anna, Foti and Vangeli stepped out of a borrowed van one by one to hug me and Elsa.

'They're taking me to see the execution site where your grandmother was murdered,' Anna said. 'I've wanted to go ever since I read your dad's book, and you can only get there in a car with four-wheel drive. You guys should come.'

'I'll get my camcorder,' said Elsa, rifling through her bag.

I was glad I didn't have time to think about this before I squashed myself into the van with the others. I had been here for five months and had yet to see the site; in twenty-five years of visiting Lia I had never gone there. When I'd picked oregano with Dina and Andreas I'd known we were nearby, but everyone was too tact-ful to mention it. I did want to go, to pay my respects, but I'd never asked anyone to take me, although I knew they would have rustled up a truck from somewhere if I had done. As we bumped along to the execution site, I was embarrassed by my reluctance, considering how important a place it is in my family's history and how close I had been all this time.

My failure is not exactly surprising; it took me years to summon up the courage to read the story of my grandmother's execution by firing squad, let alone make my way to the isolated ravine where it happened, where she and the others were given a final shot to the head and then tossed into a mass grave, and their bodies covered with rocks. We invent rites of passage in an attempt to have control over a transition period, because changes, even happy ones like weddings or births, are always stressful. Rituals are the sanitized celebrations of the really big, messy moments that happen off camera; there's a reason for having baptisms instead of parties in a delivery room. Visiting your grandmother's grave is respectful. But I didn't know the protocol for going to the place where she was executed. And although I no longer feared her curse, I was a little wary of standing on the same spot where the original Eleni Gatzoyiannis was killed, on almost the anniversary of her death.

When the van could go no closer to the execution site, we walked until Foti and Vangeli pointed out the area. The landscape of my nightmares turned out to be a lush green plateau surrounded by mountains and covered in wildflowers – wild roses, tiny blue flowers that bunched together in parasol-like shapes, and morning glory like ground cover. There is no marker; if someone wanted to put up a plaque, they wouldn't know where to do so. Even the people who recovered the bodies of the prisoners wouldn't be able to differentiate this exact patch of scrub from that one. Only God knows now. The vast, craggy field wasn't telling us anything.

As Elsa videotaped Foti and Vangeli describing the area in a language she couldn't understand, I had to smile. These were the perfect men to show me this site: Vangeli with his dramatic delivery and righteous indignation over wartime atrocities, and Foti trying to direct us to the nearby chapel of Agios Nikolaos, to gloss over the execution itself, just as he had tried to spare me from seeing the dead mouse that had chewed through the cable of the stove the night I first moved in to the Haidis house.

Following his lead, we tramped on along overgrown footpaths towards the tiny church of Agios Nikolaos, a comforting presence. From the outside it's just another nondescript white chapel on a mountain somewhere in Greece. But inside it's covered with faded, cracked but exquisite murals.

'This is the oldest church in Lia – they think it's from the thirteenth century,' said Foti. 'The outside was covered with frescoes, too, but the guerrillas used them for target practice during the Civil War.'

I imagined those two-dimensional folk paintings of saints with gold haloes and blue robes dancing with the Bamiyan Buddhas in a heaven for desecrated religious artworks. Something that expressive and powerful doesn't just disappear.

Foti led us inside; two candles glowed in the candle-stand. I wondered who had been here before us. A shepherd on his way up the mountain? Or someone like us, for whom this part of nowhere was their destination? Foti stepped through an arch to the altar, and I looked towards the spot where his candle illuminated a painting of the Dormition, with the Panagia supine and swaddled against a cobalt background, the eternal Mother, nurturing even in death.

On the way out, we stopped to add our own candles to the glowing sentinels by the door. Normally, when I light a candle I make a wish, a request to the saint, usually for the health and happiness of myself, my family, a friend, or for help with a particular project. But today there was no question as to the message my candle's flame should carry up to heaven: I lit it in memory of my grandmother, in gratitude for the sacrifice she made so that I could live free from the suffering that she had endured. And I was also grateful for her protection; after hearing about Thitsa Kanta's dream, I knew she had helped me avoid wolves and survive scorpions, floods and car crashes so that I could live in our village.

The next day, Elsa, Anna and I ran around ferrying people and things up to the mountainside church of Agios Demetrios for the memorial service. It wasn't really a memorial service, Thitsa Kanta kept reminding us – that would be a big deal, we'd have to invite lots of guests and serve them food. This was just a *trisagion*: a prayer in memory of my grandmother and the four other Liotes killed along with her fifty-four years ago today.

When we arrived at St Demetrios, the church my grandmother visited almost every day of her life until the guerrillas turned it into a stable, the daughters of her sister-in-law Alexandra were there. One was already crying; the mother of my cousin Areti, she had been eleven when she'd visited her mother in prison and had herself been beaten by the guerrillas. People kept shaking her hand, saying, 'It's a difficult day.'

Dina, who knew how these things went, having survived memorial services for two of her children, told Thitsa Kanta and me to sit in the middle of the church, behind a table that had the memorial bread and the *kollyva* on it. Father Prokopi chanted the *trisagion*, mentioning all five Liotes killed over half a century ago today on another hot August morning. Everyone held candles in memory of the dead. Afterwards, we stepped out into the blinding sunshine to distribute the bread and *kollyva*. People shook hands with me, saying, 'May you live to remember your grandmother.' I found these ritualized expressions of condolence to be a beautiful product of Greek culture, resolving the dilemma of what to say at a time like this. In Lia, everyone knew what to say: 'Long life to you,' 'May her memory be eternal,' and 'May you live many years to remember her.'

The survivors of the murdered women lined up for a photograph: me, Thitsa Kanta and Thio Angelo, and three daughters of Alexandra, who was executed with my grandmother. Their bones had been stored together in the ossuary at Agios Demetrios, until my grandmother's were moved to Worcester to be buried next to my grandfather after his death in 1983. In the photo we all look alike: heart-shaped faces with varying degrees of wrinkles, squinting in the sun, living to remember.

We were not the only ones keeping the dead alive in the memory. At the Xenona after the service, as we treated everyone to coffee and brandy, I overheard people mourning more recently deceased loved ones. Dina complained that the truck driver who killed Andreas's son had killed four other people at the same time, and still hadn't gone to trial. 'Our lawyer says he'll probably just get fined. He wasn't drunk, just a bad driver.' She sighed. 'It doesn't matter; nothing will bring them back.'

'Nothing will; nothing,' agreed the daughter of Marianthe, who lost both her husband and her son within fifteen days this past winter. 'My mother just can't cope. I tell her not to think about such things, but you think about it all the time.'

According to a popular Greek expression, 'There are twelve Apostles, and each cries for his own pain.' Like most folk sayings, it is undeniably true. But as I listened to my neighbours mourning their losses, I realized that they didn't cry just to soften the edges of their pain, but to sharpen the details of their memory. I had travelled to ancient oracles and visited lost civilizations to learn the secret of communicating with the dead, but in Lia I realized that the translator I'd needed all along was Mnemosyne. Through memory, the dead continue to live and the living to draw strength from them.

Once the blinding August sun mellowed into the golden light of September, and my visiting friends had left, I focused on the rebuilding of the Gatzoyiannis house, to honour the memory of a grandmother I'd never met. The candles I'd lit asking Agios Demetrios for help must have been well received; one afternoon, Yanni, the mason, called me to say he'd heard we were looking for someone else to build the outer door.

'Weren't you happy with my work?' he asked plaintively.

'Your work is great; your attitude is the problem,' I said. 'Zervas told me you asked for more money for the chimneys, which were included in the original deal.'

'They weren't included,' he objected, but softly. 'I never include the chimneys in the price of the roof. It was all a misunderstanding!'

He sighed. I sighed back. Finally, Yanni broke the heavy silence. 'What if I come to do the outer door at my old rate?' he suggested. 'Then, if you like it, you pay me half of what I asked for the chimneys – 250 Euros.'

He might have been taking me for a ride. But at least it was a ride in the right direction, towards completion of the house. And Vlad liked working with him, so I knew he wouldn't try to drive him away. I agreed to his terms.

Now, days later, I was at the house checking on his work, which I had to admit was impressive. Grey slate tiles covered the house's sloping roof, and the two expensive chimneys rose like ostrich necks. Except for the courtyard and the stones covering the cement pillars of the verandah, the outer shell was done. It finally resembled a house more than a demolition site.

Yanni was building the two stone columns of the courtyard's *exoporta*, which would be joined by the same arched stones that had curved above the original door my grandfather built when he remodelled the house in 1936. On top of that would be a small slate roof, just for the entrance, making the gate look a bit like a pagoda.

'The house looks great, doesn't it, Yanni?' I said, trying to be friendly. 'There's not much left to do now.'

'Well, there's the interior walls, then the plumber has to come, the electrician, and the carpenter for the windows, doors, floors and ceilings.' Yanni paused for breath. 'And of course you have to dig a septic tank, build the courtyard . . .'

I sighed, deflated. The house was now a beautiful shell, but I worried that that was all it would ever be. Vlad was building steps leading to the back door and Thomas, the contractor, was sitting in the sun doing nothing. I walked over to him.

'Thomas, what's next on the agenda?' I asked, smiling in encouragement.

'Nothing,' he said. 'Not until I get money to pay the workers. I want twenty-thousand Euros — half the remaining cost of the house.'

A sit-down strike! Solving the dispute with Yanni had been a stroke of luck, but I didn't really know anything about labour negotiations. I did, however, know that the hunting season was about to start, that Thomas was an avid hunter, and that if he got the rest of his money up front, he might not return to the house until the season was over in January. People always say honesty is the best policy, so I thought I'd give it a shot.

'Well, I'm a little worried about the house getting finished, Thomas,' I said. 'See, I know you like to hunt, and I'm not sure you'll have enough time to do both.'

Thomas stood, drawing himself up to his full five feet five inches. 'Hunting is my passion!' he shouted. 'Not even Spiridoula, the wife I have fed and clothed for twelve years, can keep me from hunting, and neither can you!'

I had no answer to that. He smiled at my dumbfounded expression. 'Of course, hunting is only allowed on Wednesdays, Saturdays and Sundays. I won't go every day. I'll still work on this job,' he promised. 'If I get my money.'

'I need more cash transferred to my account here, but there's a law in America that you can only wire five thousand dollars a month,' I answered, figuring that dishonesty is the second-best policy. 'If I give you five thousand, can you do the inside walls and courtyard?'

'I can start,' he said, leaning back against the wall. Labour riots had been avoided. I started to walk away.

'Hey Eleni,' Thomas called. 'Do you know how to cook wild boar?'

I paused, as if this were a question I was used to answering. 'Not really.'

'I'll get some for you and Spiridoula can show you how,' he said. 'The hunting season starts tomorrow, you know.'

I knew. The streets were full of trucks laden with camouflage-clad men toting guns, and barking dogs in cages in the back. That night at the Xenona, a table of hunters was laying into an early dinner. 'The hunting season lasts until January 1st,' one told me. 'A lot of people go for wild boar, but they're so ugly. I shoot grouse. Have you ever seen a grouse? Beautiful bird.' Once the men had retired, requesting a five a.m. wake-up call, Fanis turned away from the full moon to look at me. 'Poor little birdies,' he said mournfully.

I was a little mournful myself. Summer was over, the house construction seemed to be stagnating, and the air was sharp with the smell of woodsmoke again. Autumn is the most beautiful season in Lia, with pinkish-purple wild cyclamens sprouting everywhere, and trees turning rust and gold. But it is also the most poignant, as many villagers leave Lia to return to big cities. Autumn fills Lia with the allure but also the sorrow of maturity, the awareness that time is passing and winter approaching, bringing loss and endings.

One day, as I gathered tomatoes from my garden, my neighbour Athina Ganas called out to me. 'We're having an *efkelio* at four,' she said. 'Please come!'

'Of course I will!' I said. Then I called Thitsa Kanta. 'What's an *efkelio*?'

'It's part of the service that happens on Holy Thursday, when the priest reads seven of the Twelve Gospels and blesses everyone with holy oil,' she said. 'But you can have one at your house if you need blessing, and Athina is holding one for Grigoris's health. They leave tomorrow. With the lung cancer, who knows if they'll be back next year?'

By four we were assembled in Athina's dining room, surrounding a table set with a censer, some cotton swabs and a bowl of salt with seven candles lying next to it. Father Prokopi read the Gospels as we crossed ourselves.

At the end of each reading he prayed for us all by name, and Athina lit a candle and placed it upright in the bowl of salt. Once seven candles were burning, Father Prokopi dipped a cotton swab in the holy oil and made the sign of the cross on our foreheads, cheeks, throats and hands. I prayed for Grigoris, who seemed nervous throughout the ceremony, dashing out to get more salt. When it was over he was calmer, and we all sat down to some sweet squash pita.

Father Prokopi handed me a poem he had written while working at the monastery of Agios Athanassios, which dates from 1600 and which he was trying to restore:

> Before you speak, listen;
> Before you pray, forgive;
> Before you quit, try;
> And before you die, prepare.

'I've never written poetry before, but the words just came to me,' he said.

'It was the Spirit filling you – divine inspiration,' insisted Sofia, the cantor who had participated in the ceremony. 'It's rare, but it happens if you believe.'

By the time we left, the sky was illuminated with a pomegranate-coloured sunset much deeper than the flimsy pink ones of summer. Three-year-old Irini, my neighbour Spiro's granddaughter, ran up to hug me and I realized how much I would miss her screeching, once her grandparents sent her back to her parents in Athens next week. The next morning, as I watched Grigoris and Athina's car pull out, a drop of rain fell on me. Summer was officially over. It rained all day, and poured the next. By day three of the non-stop storm, the Motsala spring, which had dried up in August, was gushing like the Hoover Dam. That afternoon, Foti called with late-breaking news.

'There are waterfalls in Babouri,' he said.

'Where?' I asked. 'I've never seen them.'

'No, they just started,' he explained. 'This always happens when the rains start, but it's usually not until late December. You're lucky.'

I drove to the bend in the road on the border between Lia and Babouri, where the tiny white chapel of St Charalambos the Miracle-Worker stands. The saint must have been working overtime; the haze on the road parted to reveal two separate torrents of water, gushing out of the side of the rocky mountain high above and falling hundreds of yards. Rain was steadily hitting my pleather raincoat, but I didn't care. The waterfalls erupting from the cliff were here for a limited time only, a miraculous – if fleeting – gift from above.

The rain continued for two more days, and every house in the village except mine and the one below me lost its electricity. Dina kept popping over to use my hairdryer and to marvel, 'In the thirteen years since Andreas brought me to Lia, I've never seen weather like this!' The grapes were all ruined, so no one would be able to make wine. The tomatoes turned white and shrivelled. Everyone was upset about the lost crops and the unusually stormy autumn. But although the weather was dismal, I was no longer depressed. Watching the waterfall, a sense of well-being had surged over me. My gloom at the prospect of my summer in Lia coming to an end broke, and although I knew that I would miss my neighbours who were getting ready to leave, I was prepared to enjoy the autumn – no matter how dramatic its weather.

*

By the time everyone's electricity was restored, the outer doorframe of the Gatzoyiannis house was finished and Yanni was gone. In the arch he had placed the keystone that my grandfather had installed, carved with the date 1936, when he added on to the house. But on a stone on the side of the *exoporta* Yanni had carved '2002', the year I'd returned to rebuild the fallen home. I was now officially part of the physical history of the house, chipped into its entranceway for posterity.

I stood there beaming with pride that the project had come this far, then jumped when I heard a noise from within the house. It was Wednesday, and although Thomas was hunting, Vlad and Xalime turned out to be inside, building the interior walls which would separate the house into three main rooms divided by a hallway, just as it had been in the past.

'Can I add some bricks?' I asked Vlad. I wanted to contribute to the construction of the house, to try to earn the immortality conferred upon me by the carved '2002' stone.

'Sure,' Vlad said. 'I take your picture.'

I handed him my camera, then inexpertly added a few bricks as Xalime laughed at me and at our role reversal – me building and them photographing my progress.

'How's Net?' I asked. He'd started high school in Filiates, they told me, and boarded during the week, coming back at weekends to work. 'Many kids live together,' Vlad said. 'They have time for to work, to eat, for games. But language is hard.'

I made a mental note to buy Net a Greek–Albanian dictionary next time I drove to Ioannina, then left to meet Foti, Thitsa Kanta and Thio Angelo for dinner. Foti showed up in his camouflage ensemble – he'd come straight from butchering a wild boar caught after he and his cronies had driven out at five a.m. to beat the other packs of hunters to the best spots.

'I want to come on a hunt,' I told Foti. Autumn in Lia is all about the hunt, and I wanted to be a part of it, at least as a spectator. He opened his mouth to answer, but Thitsa Kanta interrupted, waving her hands for attention to indicate that we should wait for her to stop chewing. Then she turned to me.

'You cuckoo?' she screeched in English. 'Those men, they go crazy in the mountains. They gonna rape you and then come back to the village and talk about it!'

I looked at Foti, who had spent years running a pizza place in Massachusetts. He studied his salad, doing a pretty good imitation of not understanding English.

'What would be worse?' I asked. 'Them raping me or them talking about it?'

'Both are not good,' Thitsa Kanta insisted. 'You're not going.'

We chewed our tomato and cucumber in silence for a few minutes. Then Foti turned to me. 'Give me your cell-phone number, and I'll call you tomorrow if we catch anything good,' he promised. 'You can take pictures.'

The next day, at one thirty p.m., the phone rang. 'Wait for me at my house,' Foti's voice commanded.

I was sitting in front of his gate when five trucks thundered down the road. Seven camouflage-clad men, one camouflage-clad eleven-year-old and five dogs swarmed out of the car and around their prey.

'Bring them out so the girl can photograph them!' Foti commanded.

'Right away, Grandpa!' One of the men saluted. It took three hunters to drag the first spiky-haired boar on to the ground, a trickle of blood trailing behind her. She must have weighed 180 pounds. Then they dragged out the second – this one was only about 75 pounds. I had been hoping one would be a male, with tusk-like curved teeth. Most of the hunters' trucks had a pair of teeth suspended from the rear-view mirror to invite good luck and advertise the hunter's skill. Thomas told me that when he was little and his teeth fell out, he used to throw them backwards over his shoulder on to the roof of his house, saying, 'Old bone, give me teeth as strong as a wild boar's!' I masked my disappointment at the lack of tusks, because I knew Foti had had the hunters drag the pigs here just for me. Everyone lined up and I took a commemorative group photo that I knew would be copied, laminated and passed around for years.

We all piled into our respective vehicles and drove on to Louie's Grill, where two experts hung the boars upside-down from a tree on hooks, sliced them down the middle, removed gobs of intestines, made incisions at the hooves and started peeling the skin down. I had to photograph the process – I'll probably never see another boar being skinned. But I couldn't stay close without gagging because of the stench.

'Do all animals smell that bad when they're skinned?' I asked Foti. I was starting to consider vegetarianism as a viable lifestyle.

'All animals smell,' Foti answered. 'But only pig entrails smell that bad.'

I tried to adopt the hunters' nonchalant attitude. But when they started hacking the heads off the boars, I knew I wasn't man enough for this crowd. It was time for me to go.

Back in Lia, I saw Thitsa Kanta on the road outside my house.

'Where you been?' she asked.

'With Foti, skinning some pigs,' I said. 'I left the guys in Agioi Pantoi, waiting for the liver to be grilled so they can eat it. Where've you been?'

'I start walking here to find you, and I see some Germans looking at the sign that says "Eleni Gatzoyiannis Road". They speak a little English, so I say, "What you looking for?" and the lady answer, "Eleni's house." So I take them up to see it.'

'You did?' I asked. 'Did you cry?'

'Me?' Thitsa Kanta was shocked. 'No! But the German lady did. I put them in the basement and I show them how the soldiers used to come and stand in the door and scare the prisoners. I tell them there was fifty people in there, and she start crying.'

There were actually thirty-one prisoners in the basement, which was so crowded that they had to sleep sitting up. But I didn't correct Thitsa Kanta. She'd gone from fleeing the house in tears to leading guided tours to it; if a few details got mixed up along the way, I didn't care.

On the last Sunday of September, all tour-guiding and most hunting was suspended for the day. We had not one but two memorial services to attend. Sunday morning found all of Lia in church, chanting to the memory of Angeliki Bartzokis. She had died in the hospital in Filiates forty days earlier, and had, according to Orthodox belief, spent the forty days after death wandering the earth, saying goodbye. Angeliki had been one of the few women left in Lia who was approximately the age of my grandmother. While most villagers recalled Eleni Gatzoyiannis from a child's point of view, Angeliki had remembered her as a friend she'd lost long ago. On the festival of the Prophet Elias, a few weeks before Angeliki had had the stroke which killed her, we'd stopped by her house on our way down from the chapel. Angeliki had been slim in a black housedress, but had seemed in perfect health. I'd kissed her hello and she'd touched my face as tears filled her eyes.

'Eleni in name and in person,' she'd said, noting my resemblance to my grandmother. 'The same smile, same eyes.' She'd turned towards the tray she had set out on the verandah in anticipation of guests, muttering, 'Eleni *mou*, where are you now?'

Now Angeliki was about to find out, I thought, as I blew out her memorial candle at the end of the service.

Angeliki's family invited everyone for lunch at the Xenona, but since it was only ten-thirty and lunch wouldn't start before one, most villagers joined me, Thitsa Kanta and Thio Angelo at the next memorial service, seven kilometres away in Tsamanta. A flyer on the door of the *kafenion* advertised this annual ceremony, held on the last Sunday of September, honouring ALL those who had been killed during the Civil War fought in the Mourgana mountain range from 1946 to 1949. ALL was capitalized to indicate that the memorial, organized by the veterans of Filiates, would honour those who had died fighting, whether for the Nationalist or for the Communist side, as well as nonpartisan bystanders like my grandmother who had simply got caught in the middle, and had died because of it.

The service was held on a mountain top where a white marble obelisk rises from a series of marble slabs. Originally, the slabs bore the names of most of a battalion of 160 Nationalist soldiers who were captured by the Communists. After being told that they had the choice to join the guerrillas or return to their homes,

120 of them opted to leave. The guerrillas explained that they would lead them towards the next village at night, to prevent them being spotted and shot at by the Nationalist forces stationed on the Great Ridge above. But when darkness came, they tied the prisoners together with wire and shot them. Because the men had removed their uniforms – the guerrillas said they wouldn't need them as they were returning home – their mothers were unable to identify their bodies when the bones were found in lime pits below the spot where the monument now stands. So they left their sons' bones buried there, tangled together. The author Sotiris Dimitriou wrote, 'Today, during the festival of the Dormition of the Virgin Mary in Tsamanta you can hear their cries. It seems they're awakened by our songs, as if they're calling to their unlucky mothers to come find their bones and bring them home.' Recently, plaques with the names of the women and children who were also murdered, including Eleni Gatzoyiannis, were added to the monument.

Descendants and friends of the deceased had gathered for the service, which was presided over by a white-bearded Archimandrite – swathed in black robes and gold jewellery – and five priests, including Father Prokopi. After the priests led us in chanting 'Everlasting be their memory,' the head of the War Veterans of Filiates introduced various veterans, who lined up to lay wreaths at the base of the monument, each saying a silent prayer. Then a fellow Liote stepped up. Vassili Deppis had lived in Germany for years, and now spent most of his retirement in Lia. He had an admirable paunch, hair that managed to remain jet black despite his age, and the booming voice of a man who doesn't hear very well.

'Brothers,' he began, looking up at the monument, 'we fought for freedom together, and you fell and died for freedom. The cursed ones who slaughtered you also murdered women and children. They weren't worthy of killing men!'

Everyone around me applauded except the master of ceremonies, who reminded Vassili that this was a memorial for ALL the war dead.

It felt strange to hear a political statement at a ceremony that, for me, marked a personal tragedy. Yet I knew that my grandmother's death was politically motivated. After *Eleni* was published, the Greek Communist Party sent a reporter to the Mourgana mountains to research the story of her execution and expose any inaccuracies. Instead, he learned that her murder was one of a cluster of killings in villages across the mountain range that were organized to terrorize the local population. A leak had been discovered within the Party, and officials realized that locals must have assisted in spreading covert information to their enemies. Show trials and killings were ordered throughout the region to frighten the locals into silence and submission.

The reporter told my father this, but I didn't learn about it until he told me, this year, as we drove past the memorial on his visit. But it was still difficult for me to see my grandmother's death as a political act, when it had had such deeply personal repercussions for my family. I appreciated that her name was on this monument. But my grandmother wasn't a soldier; she was a mother. I believed that the Gatzoyiannis house, where she'd raised her children and which was growing to look more like a home every day, was the real monument to her, the place where I could talk to her and feel she was most likely to hear me.

The last wreath-bearer stepped forward, snapping my thoughts from the house in Perivoli back to the monument in Tsamanta. A slim, bald man with a white rose in his lapel and a black mourning band on his arm, he saluted the monument, placed his wreath against it and stepped back next to Thitsa Kanta, who was crying almost as much as he was. After a moment of silence, the master of ceremonies led us in the national anthem. By the time we reached the end, I was as tearful as the old man. I pulled out a tissue as Thitsa Kanta tugged on my arm. 'Lenitsa,' she said, 'we got to get to Angeliki's lunch.'

All of Lia was in the Xenona, feasting on lamb and pasta in Angeliki's memory. There was another Eleni Gatzoyiannis there, my great-uncle Foti's third wife, whom he'd married after his second wife, Alexandra, was executed alongside my grandmother. I kissed the other Eleni's crêpey cheek, thinking there were three Eleni Gatzoyiannises in the village: me, this reclusive old woman, and the spirit of my grandmother. A few days ago, I'd bumped into a villager who'd said, 'Some foreigners are looking for you – they were in Perivoli asking for Eleni's house.' I'd smiled at the misunderstanding; the visitors weren't looking for me, but for my grandmother's home. Soon she would have one again.

I wasn't the only one at the memorial service with the house on my mind. An energetic little man next to Thitsa Kanta called to me over the table, 'Hey Eleni, your aunt and I were neighbours before the war. Did you know that? I went past the house you're building and burst into tears; I was born in the house right below it!'

'It's a beautiful house,' Thitsa Kanta agreed. 'Just like the old days.'

Apparently, once the house has made you cry it grows on you.

We'd almost finished eating when Father Prokopi came up. 'Before you leave for America, could you videotape the inside of Panagia church in Babouri, so the Babouriotes in Worcester can see it?' he asked Thio Angelo.

At the church of the Panagia, Father Prokopi showed us a carved metal box that held some of Agios Athanassios' bones. Thitsa Kanta recognized the metal reliquary as one the villagers used to bring to sick children to kiss. 'They brought it for your father once,' she told me. 'It always works, but it only cures kids, not grown-ups.'

The sight that fascinated me most was an icon of a winged soldier. Dressed in armour against a sky-blue background, he stood on the shrouded body of an old man, pulling a tiny, gold, nude young man out of the corpse's mouth. 'These are from 1819,' Father Prokopi said. 'That's Archangel Michael; he collects the souls of the dead.' Apparently our souls are small, gold, naked and portable, like an Oscar statuette.

I drove back to the Haidis house so I could record my latest discovery in my journal and Thitsa Kanta could call her sisters to tell them all about Vassili Deppis's speech, which had thrilled her as much as learning what a soul looks like had excited me.

'You should have heard him, he really told it like it is,' Thitsa Kanta laughed into the phone. '"The cursed ones!" Isn't that what he said, Lenitsa?'

I confirmed that it was, and told her to say hello to Thitsa Olga from me.

'She says hi too, honey; she misses you. Next year we all got to come together, for the inauguration of the house,' she said. There was a pause and then Thitsa Kanta snorted into the phone. 'Of course I'd stay there! I saw the house, had my fright and got over it. I've been there dozens of times now.'

'Tell her she has to come,' I yelled to Thitsa Kanta. I knew that, as the oldest, Thitsa Olga would find it painful to see the re-creation of the house she had grown up in, where she had loved a family that was divided too soon. Thitsa Kanta had shown me just how hard it was to relive the sorrow. But I liked to think I had helped her overcome her pain in order to reclaim a little bit of the joy she had felt in that house. And we had both learned a lot recently, from people we had lost who sent messages we had to be perceptive enough to hear: my grandmother, as she appeared to Thitsa Kanta in her dream; and Angeliki, as she sprang to my mind at her memorial service.

I don't know exactly what happened to Angeliki, or the women at Zaloggo, or the Everything Man, once they died. But I suspect that when the Archangel Michael steps on our corpses, the golden part of each of us that he preserves is the love we have for each other. As Father Prokopi read from St Paul's letter to the Corinthians during Grigoris's *efkelio*, 'Love never ends.' And people who love you never stop talking to you. You just have to know how to listen.

8

POWER POLITICS

«Ας με λένε δημαρχήνα και ας ψοφάω
από την πείνα.»
'If they call me the mayor's wife, I don't care if I
die of starvation.'

1 October

*I'm sitting in an empty window hole on the main floor
of the Gatzoyiannis house, staring at the grey, speckled
interior walls, which look much the same as they did last
week and the week before. The weather outside is just as
grey and unsatisfying: a heavy mist surrounds me for the
third day in a row. Vlad and Xalime have stopped stuccoing
the walls; before they can be whitewashed, the plaster needs
to dry. But in this weather, will that ever happen? A stray
dog that makes it his business to guard the site barks; someone's rounding the bend, walking towards me. The hem of
a long black dress kicks into view through the mist. It's
Father Prokopi trudging up, gasping for breath.*

'Eleni!' he calls when he notices me. 'I was at Agios Demetrios, saying a trisagion over a few graves, and I thought I'd come and see the house.' He stops below my window, hands on hips, looking up. 'It's really moving along!'

I'm glad somebody thinks so. 'We've still got a way to go,' I say.

'Well, I wish the renovations at Agios Athanassios were moving as quickly,' he sighs. 'Yesterday I got into a fight with the prefect in Igoumenitsa about it.'

The prefect had managed to rouse gentle Father Prokopi to anger? Somebody in Igoumenitsa is going straight to hell!

'I asked him to donate public funds to restore the monastery, since it has historic significance,' Father P. continues. 'He yelled, "Get out of my office, zourlopapas [crazy priest]! If you wanted help, your wife wouldn't be running on the New Democracy ticket in Babouri!"'

I gasp like an actress in a Greek soap opera. I know the prefect is a member of PASOK, the ruling Socialist Party. It seems that Father Prokopi's wife is on the centrist New Democracy slate in Babouri, and the prefect is holding it against him.

'I said, "Is that my fault? Women do whatever they want these days!"' Father Prokopi sputters. 'But he kicked me out of his office anyway, as if I were a criminal.' Father P. shakes his head, his obsession with restoring the monastery stymied by the prefect's political chauvinism. My contractor hunts all day, my architect won't answer the phone, and even the weather seems to be conspiring against me. But at least I don't need to depend on the kindness of strangers to fund the rebuilding of our house — or the kindness of politicians, which may be an oxymoron.

*

It didn't surprise me that the priest's wife was running for office. One thing I'd learned in Lia is that everyone in Greece is involved in politics — or, at the very least, everyone considers himself an important political commentator. In New York, I read the newspaper out of a sense of obligation, to 'keep up'. Here, people glued themselves obsessively to nightly news broadcasts, which were often as bloody and sensationalized as an American cable TV series. Aristotle urged his fellow Greeks to be 'political animals', interested in the workings of society. The Greeks I met were more like political zookeepers, carefully observing the workings of society, always ready with advice.

By mid autumn I was as much of a political voyeur as my fellow Liotes. It was time for local elections, and even Lia was suddenly full of political animals who were ready to roar. On 13 October, all of Greece would be voting for mayors and prefects. I didn't think that anyone would take the election in Lia, with its hundred-odd voters, too seriously. We'd had the same president for the past eight years, Nikolas Skevis, a cherub-faced grandfather with a halo of curly white hair. I hadn't seen any of my elderly friends marching around with picket signs, demanding a change in power. All in all, it seemed as if this would be a calm election, as low-key as it gets.

Then, one night in late September, my cell phone rang. 'Lenitsa, I'm at Foti's,' Thitsa Kanta stage-whispered. 'We can't make it to dinner. You better come here.'

When I arrived, Foti was pacing up and down and Thitsa Kanta was watching him, wide-eyed and white-faced. I knew there was an emergency — I just couldn't tell what it was. I turned to Thio Angelo, who looked relatively calm. 'How are you?' I asked.

'Lousy,' he said.

'He got constipation, but he took two Correctal, so he should be fine,' Thitsa Kanta informed me. That was unfortunate, but not unusual. Why was everyone so highly strung? The door opened and in strode Spiro Karapanos, the church cantor. 'She'll do it!' he announced, smiling.

'Thank God!' Foti gasped, collapsing into a chair.

'Bravo, Spiro,' Thitsa Kanta added. 'I'll make some coffee.'

The last thing these people needed was caffeine. 'What's going on?' I shouted.

'Oh, don't worry, honey,' Foti said. 'There was a problem, but it's OK now. Athena Karapanou is going to run on our ballot. We needed a woman, and now we have one – and that turncoat is out on his ass!'

Apparently, Nikolas Skevis was not the teddy bear of a village president I thought I knew. Over the past eight years, Foti claimed, the only improvements he had made in Lia were in his own neighbourhood. 'The road by us, where your father had his accident, is terrible, full of potholes!' Foti yelled, banging his fist on the table. 'But Nikolas got the prefecture to pave the paths to his chicken coops!'

It seemed that because of his low approval rating in Lia, Nikolas had been told he wasn't welcome back on the Socialist PASOK Party ballot. The three-person consortium would consist of Cosmas Bokas, a former pizza-place owner from Massachusetts with curly black hair and big dreams; Vassili Deppis, the rotund, vociferous man with an ever-present stick who had spoken at the memorial service; and Spiridoula, the token woman and the wife of our contractor Thomas. Spiridoula had cooked our sacrificial rooster and led me in decorating the Epitaphion, and I would have liked to vote for her. But all my other pals were on the centrist New Democracy ticket: Foti, the denim-clad retiree and my self-appointed protector; Vangeli, the dashing raconteur who recalled my father's baptism; and Antonis Makos, who lived near the Gatzoyiannis house and was the church council president – and did a fine job at that.

I knew where my loyalties lay, but I was confused about the electoral procedure. 'Why are there teams?' I asked. 'Doesn't just one person get to be president?' Spiro, Foti and Thitsa Kanta were muttering amongst themselves. So, as he waited for his Correctal to kick in, Thio Angelo stepped forward. 'All this election stuff is done in groups,' he explained. 'Each side, PASOK and New Democracy, has to have a team of three or four candidates for village president. This local team is on the Party's ballot, and you vote for a village president, a mayor for the municipality of Filiates, which includes Lia, and two city council members, on the same ballot.'

I sort of understood – you had to vote along Party lines (no Socialist village president and Centrist mayor), or cast a blank ballot. I wasn't used to running for office being a group effort, but life in Greece seemed to be more about the community than the individual anyway. Still, I was a little confused. 'Isn't Vassili Deppis always saying he's New Democracy?' I asked.

'That's right,' Spiro broke in. 'He only agreed to join the PASOK ballot to keep Nikolas Skevis from running again. And you have to have a minimum of three people on the ballot, so without Vassili, Nikolas could sign on to PASOK whether Cosmas wanted him as a running mate or not.'

My eyes widened. Machiavellian machinations right here in Lia! 'So what's Nikolas going to do now that there's no room for him on the PASOK ballot?' I asked.

'What's Nikolas going to do? I'll tell you what Nikolas already did!' Foti yelled. 'Without asking us he drove down to Filiates and signed himself up as the fourth person on our New Democracy ballot! He changed parties like changing underwear, pardon the expression.' Foti's face was as red as a genetically engineered tomato. I worried that this added stress might give him a heart attack, given that he looks pregnant, has high cholesterol and eats nothing but fried cheese and lamb chops.

'But there's nothing to shout about, Foti,' Spiro interjected. 'My Athena agreed to run, and each ballot is supposed to have at least one woman. Just call the New Democracy office in Filiates and tell the city councillor that Nikolas can't be on the ballot because we got a woman; she just hasn't had time to come and sign up yet.'

'And I'll say that if Nikolas Skevis stays on the ticket, the rest of us are going to quit and there will be no New Democracy slate left,' Foti shouted. He stood up, knocking over his chair as he made his way to the phone. It was a good solution, I thought to myself. Athena was a popular local matron, known mainly for her piety, boiled squash blossoms and good skin. ND's female candidate was just as strong as PASOK's.

Foti ambled back to the table, his face slowly resuming its natural colour. 'It's done,' he announced. 'The ND chief in Filiates is going to call Nikolas and tell him we need to drop him to take Athena.' He sat down and smiled. We took this as our cue that it was safe to leave him alone.

On our way out, Thitsa Kanta whispered to me, 'The

last time I seen Foti so upset was when a hawk kill two of his chickens!'

Foti may have calmed down, but by early October, everyone else in Lia was overexcited. Since there were no public debates or speeches, campaigning consisted of candidates going from door to door, drinking Greek coffee and asking the residents who they planned to vote for, then reconvening to whip out a list of registered voters and handicap the election like a horse race. I got to listen in on a few whispered caucuses, because in early October I acquired two room-mates: Thitsa Kanta and Thio Angelo. Dina and Andreas had gone on a dowry-selling trip, and since the two other houses in downtown Motsala were now empty, Thitsa Kanta insisted that I couldn't stay home alone.

'I promised my mother I'd watch out for you!' she protested, when I said I wasn't scared of being by myself. 'I know you need your privacy, but Ange and I will leave during the day, and at night we'll sleep on the couches in the living room.'

'You can sleep in the other bed in the bedroom,' I suggested.

'Lenitsa, we old people,' she protested. 'Old people snore and fart and get up at night! Better we stay in the living room.'

When she put it that way, I wasn't about to argue. And amazingly, having senior-citizen room-mates was fun. Every night Thio Angelo would build a fire, and we would sit around it discussing the events of the day, which meant, of course, the election.

'Everyone I talk to say they going to vote for Antonis Makos,' Thitsa Kanta said, throwing a tissue into the flames one night. 'He's the only one going out there, talking to people. Foti and Vangeli doing nothing, they too lazy and shy to go to someone's house and ask for a vote. I bet they each get just one vote – their own.'

Lia's election was shaping up to resemble a sixth-grade student-council race. Because only 130 people were registered to vote, it was easy to analyse their loyalties and figure out who was the most popular candidate. So I decided I would vote the same way I had done in sixth grade: for the person I thought no one else would vote for, so their feelings wouldn't get hurt. And feelings were running high – having been frozen out of his old party, PASOK, the current president Nikolas Skevis channelled all his icy bitterness into campaigning for the opposition, New Democracy, specifically for Antonis Makos, the one candidate who hadn't been involved in boxing him out of a spot on the ND ballot. Arguments broke out daily in the *kafenion*, and opposing candidates scrupulously avoided each other. Sometimes I could hardly handle all the tension.

So I was more than happy to take my weekly breaks from Lia to drive Thitsa Kanta down to Filiates to get her bouffant lifted. As we sat in the salon, she befriended the other ladies having their bouffants inflated. 'Alexandra Stratis from Lia, but I live in Worcester, America,' she would say, extending her hand. 'Where are your people from?'

One day a matron said, 'You're from America? My father-in-law lived there.'

'In Worcester?' Thitsa Kanta asked eagerly.

'I don't know where,' the lady responded. 'He and my husband weren't close. But I do remember the day he returned after thirty years, with a suitcase full of American dresses for my mother-in-law, who was an old villager, dressed in black.'

'Did he manage to get her size right after thirty years?' I asked.

'I don't know.' The woman smiled. 'My mother-in-law opened the suitcase, then took the American dresses and threw them into the fireplace one by one. My father-in-law yelled, "What are you doing?" And she said, "Just like my youth went up in flames while I waited for you, so will these."'

In America, women had burned bras. Here they burned poly-cotton floral housedresses. This was just the kind of juicy break from political talk I needed. But it couldn't last; while Thitsa Kanta's curls set, I had to head over to the police station to secure a national ID card so I could vote in the election a week later.

On the ride back, Thitsa Kanta studied the temporary ID, with my photo, name and birthdate.

'Lenitsa!' Thitsa Kanta gasped. 'That's right – today's your birthday! We gotta have a party. You tell me who you want there, and I'll arrange it.'

'OK,' I smiled. 'Thanks, Thitsa Kanta.'

'What thanks?' she huffed. 'Of course I throw a party. I love you too much!' She looked over at me. 'But don't tell people you twenty-eight. You look twenty! Say you twenty.'

I told Thitsa Kanta I was fine telling people I was twenty-eight. And I almost meant it. I'd never felt younger than I did in Lia, where the median age of the people I ate dinner with was probably seventy. But at the same time, much as I was enjoying my extended childhood here, I knew that my American friends were continuing to mature. And here I was with no job, no romantic prospects, and no idea of how my life would be different when the house was finished (if it ever was finished) and I returned to New York. If I thought too much about the forthcoming year of my life, it made me nervous; I wondered if I would still fit into my old life when I returned. Luckily, I had plenty of distractions.

When Thitsa Kanta and I returned home, we found Antonis Makos and Thio Angelo sitting around the coffee table with voter-registration lists. 'If you could stay to vote, we'd definitely win!' Antonis told Thio Angelo.

'No, we gotta leave on the tenth — the flights are full,' he answered.

'I would never stay for the election!' Thitsa Kanta yelped. 'The village is gonna be crazy!' She still saw Lia as a political tinderbox about to erupt into violence. But I wasn't worried — seventysomethings have usually worked through their aggression.

'Oh, Lenitsa,' Thio Angelo added, looking up at me. 'The electrician and plumber came. They up at the Gatzoyiannis house. The electrician ask for instructions. I say, you know what to do.'

I left my elders to their political strategizing and drove up to the house. The jarring blast of an electric drill indicated that the plumber was still inside, hacking up the cement floors to lay pipes. The electrician was already packing up his van. For weeks nothing had happened on the house and now, in one day, the plumbing and electricity were well underway. It was a cosmic birthday present.

'That was fast!' I said to the electrician.

'I'm not finished yet, but I've done enough for today,' he replied. 'The electrical box is up. The meter reader should have no problem reading that.' He pointed to the front of the house. There it was, a big metal box sitting like a pimple on the face of an otherwise historically accurate re-creation of my grandmother's house.

'No!' I wailed.

'Are you all right?' the electrician asked.

'The box can't go there! Why didn't you put it under the verandah or round the back?'

'I'd have to break a hole through the verandah to bring the cable down,' he huffed. 'And it can't go on the back – the meter reader has to be able to see it.'

'But I put so much effort, and time, and money into making this house look like it did when my grandparents lived here,' I told him. 'Please, can't you at least move it to the side of the house?' He looked sceptical, but walked up to examine the box. It was time to bring out the big guns. 'It's my birthday today, and I can't take such a huge disappointment on my birthday,' I pleaded. 'It would be bad luck.'

'All right.' He strode down the verandah steps towards me. 'I'll move it next week, as a birthday present to you.'

'Thank you so much!' I gushed.

'But I'll lose a day of work elsewhere, so I'll have to charge you two hundred Euros.'

'That's fine.' I extended my hand. It had taken so long for Thomas to get an electrician to come up here, I was lucky this man was willing to return at all. There was nothing else I could do if I wanted the house to be right. I'd have to consider the two hundred Euros a present to myself.

That night at the Xenona, my twenty-eighth birthday dinner was attended by me and nine people over the age of sixty, making the average partygoer's age fifty-seven. Thitsa Kanta and Thio Angelo were there, of course, and so were five of Lia's seven presidential candidates: Foti, Vangeli, Antonis, Vassili and Athena, all trying to be civil to each other for my sake. There was election talk, but people kept raising their glasses, wishing that I might live a hundred years, be as strong as the tall mountains, and return next year as a bride, so that everyone could rejoice for me. Nikki and Fanis served a chocolate cake with 'Many Years, Eleni' on it and sparklers spitting out starbursts of light. I appreciated the sparklers, the cake, all the good wishes. But most of all I enjoyed seeing everyone else having so much fun. Forget turning twenty-eight – I had a lifetime of political intrigue and partying ahead of me!

The next week brought another celebratory dinner: Thitsa Kanta and Thio Angelo's farewell meal at a taverna in Keramnitsa, a village down the mountain from Lia. Nestled closer to the main cities in the province of Thesprotia, Keramnitsa was not abandoned by young people in the way that many villages higher up the Mourgana mountains were, and it still had a winter population of about two hundred. With just four days until the election, candidates for city council kept streaming through this hot spot, handing out flyers and kissing people hello. Thitsa Kanta, who loved the excitement, accepted handouts from everyone, telling each female candidate, 'You look beautiful in this photo, honey!'

I was just relieved not to be among the campaigners; in August a young New Democracy politician had come to Lia to ask me to run as a city council candidate. 'People would recognize your name, because of your grandmother's story,' he said. 'And it would be great to have a Harvard graduate on the ballot.'

'But I wasn't a government major,' I protested. 'I don't have any experience.'

'That's OK,' he insisted, staring at me with his earnest brown eyes. 'You just have to have ideas, to want to help the region.'

I did want to help, but I planned to return to the US eventually, so I didn't think it would be right to run. Now I realized that no one had ever expected me to serve on the city council, just to draw votes to the ballot, and therefore to New Democracy.

Aside from being a campaign hub, Keramnitsa was also home to the man everyone said was the best carpenter in the Mourgana. I had asked him to meet us, hoping to convince him to join my building team, but when a gent in a checked blazer and a salt-and-pepper pompadour strolled in, I assumed he was another politico. Carpenters are supposed to look like Jesus or like Harrison Ford. But ours, a smooth-talker who knew everyone in the taverna, turned out to be more of a Dick Clark type. He said he could have the doors, windows and floors in place in six weeks. 'What about the ceilings?' I demanded. Now that I was twenty-eight, it was time to become a savvy negotiator.

'You can't put ceilings in until spring, because wood draws moisture and swells in winter,' he said, fixing his American Bandstand smile on me. 'Everyone knows that.'

Oh, right. Of course. We struck a deal; tomorrow he would measure the door and window frames. I wasn't sure I believed him about the ceilings, but I was just glad that I now had a new deadline to give Thomas and Vlad: the carpenter was coming on 26 November, so the interior walls and verandah would all have to be done by then. Mission accomplished, I raised a toast to Thitsa Kanta and Thio Angelo.

'I'm going to miss you guys,' I said. 'Thanks for staying with me.'

'Oh, we're gonna miss you too, honey, and everybody,' Thitsa Kanta said, becoming slightly tearful.

'When I get home, for a few months all I care about is what's happening in the village. Then I forget a little, and I'm OK until the next trip.'

Once the three of us were alone in the car on our way back up to Lia, Thitsa Kanta reported, 'Vangeli Panagiotou cried. He said, "Who knows if we'll ever see each other again?" and I tell him, "Vangeli Panagiotou, I'm not planning on dying anytime soon!" But he still cry.' She sniffed a bit herself, then added, 'I think he's a little drunk.'

Thitsa Kanta, Thio Angelo and all their assorted food-stuffs left the next day, with two pounds of feta in Thitsa Kanta's suitcase to replace the two pounds of American coffee she had transported here. I was sad that they were gone, but I didn't have time to wallow – the election was upon us. And I was surrounded by reminders that in Lia, the political is personal. The night before the election, I stopped by the *kafenion* to pick up Foti and Vangeli and drive them to the Xenona for dinner.

'Who was that woman?' I asked them in the car. 'I've never seen her before.'

'Which one?' Vangeli demanded. The *kafenion* was packed with Liotes in town to vote the next day.

'The tall, skinny one with dyed-black hair and the head wrap,' I said. 'The one who looks like death when it comes for ballerinas.'

'Oh, that's Laokratia,' Foti started to answer. 'She—'

'You can't call her that!' Vangeli shouted from the back seat. 'She'll scream at you. She wants to be called Katerina, she won't answer to Laokratia any more.'

'Laokratia?' I asked. 'As in, "Rule of the People"?'

'That's right,' Vangeli said. 'She was born when the Communists occupied the village, and her parents thought if they named her that, they might get preferential treatment – there's another Laokratia, and a Laokratis in the mountain range.'

'But they got taken away to Communist countries anyway, and changed their names when they returned,' Foti said, getting out of the car. 'Now it's Katerina, Sophia and Evangelos.'

It seemed fitting that Ms 'Rule of the People' had taken the bus all the way from Athens to exercise her right to vote, but I could also see why she'd chosen a new name; it would be awful to be named after a political statement, even if the word was kind of sexy, like 'Anarchy'.

The Xenona was packed. Election officials for nearby villages, mostly lawyers from Athens, were staying at the inn overnight.

'Too bad you had to travel so far,' I said to a middle-aged official sitting by the fire.

'Oh, no, this is a great gig – an inn, a fire, nice food,' he answered. 'One year I rode a donkey five hours in a downpour to get to a village in the Peloponnese. And in the end, it was all to collect twenty-eight votes!'

Compared to that, Lia was a metropolis. Especially now that everyone had stormed in to vote. Since voter registration is one way a village's population is counted and the amount of money distributed for public works is determined, many people feel obliged to return to their hometown for elections. Schools and businesses are closed on the Friday and Monday before and after Election Sunday to facilitate all the travel. 'Too bad there's not an election every few months,' Fanis the innkeeper whispered to me as he passed drinks around his booming establishment. But I wasn't sure the villagers could have handled all the excitement on a regular basis. Vangeli looked up from the list of voters that he and Foti were huddled over. 'Odds are even for tomorrow,' he reported.

On Election Sunday, all of Greece, every mountain and islet, woke up to torrential rain. Since the topography is so varied, it's rare that it rains all over the country. When I stopped in at Dina and Andreas's for a cup of tea and a look at their TV, the storm had made the national news. 'With rain keeping some voters from reaching the polls, the weather is going to play a decisive role in close elections,' the overly made-up news anchor chirped.

I sloshed through the downpour to church, but was so eager to vote that I couldn't sit through the whole liturgy. As Father Prokopi brought out the communion goblet, I burst out of Agia Triada and ran up the slick steps of the old schoolhouse, which now held the community offices. The polls had opened at seven a.m. and would close twelve hours later. 'You can vote from sunrise to sunset,' my old friends told me. Very Fiddler on the Roof.

Both Antonis and Cosmas were nervously milling about the hall of the old school, in front of an antique map of Ancient Greece. An old lady hobbled out of a classroom and a brisk young woman stepped forward to bleat, 'Next.' That was me! I flashed my new ID as the woman crossed my name off the list of registered voters. 'Here are both parties' ballots and the envelope — it's self-seal, so don't lick it,' she warned. 'Choose a ballot, mark it up, and when you're done with that, come out of the booth and slip it into this box.' It was all so official. I felt both intimidated and important as I stepped into the booth, drew the curtain behind me and studied the names for village president on the New Democracy ballot. Although I liked all four candidates, I had to vote for Foti — he would feel terrible if he only got his own vote, and hadn't he told me about the waterfalls in Babouri, taken me to see the skinning of the wild boar, and supplied me with fresh eggs? That made him a true patriot. I made a cross next to his name.

As I left, old men in three-piece suits and women in headscarves were hobbling out of church towards the schoolhouse. Voting is mandatory in Greece, although those who are over seventy-one are exempt from making the effort. But since the election was the most exciting thing to have happened in Lia since my father's near-death experience at the festival of the Prophet Elias, none of the old-timers would dream of missing it. Overstimulated by all the excitement, Costa, the eight-year-old son of the couple who owned the *kafenion*, kept running after old ladies on their way to vote, saying, 'Can I pull your headscarf?' 'No, don't pull it!' they'd yell, making shooing motions with their hands. He'd say, 'Just a little?' They'd screech, 'No!' and he'd pull anyway.

Back at the Haidis house, I dug in my bag for my keys only to realize that, in my rush to vote, I had locked them inside the house. My 83-year-old neighbour from Uptown Motsala took pity on me, hobbled down and tried to bash the door open by ramming into it with his bony, tweed-covered butt. It didn't work. Finally Andreas jimmied the lock with a plastic square cut from a soda bottle, and I was able to run in to get my camera. I was the only reporter covering this election, I realized, and it had to be documented. I dashed back out again.

'Can't you stay for lunch?' Dina called. I explained

that I couldn't as I had to get back to election HQ, the *kafenion*. 'Take some *patsavouropita* with you, then,' she said, shoving a snack of still-warm pie into my hands.

The *kafenion* was crackling with election excitement. Spiridoula was making the rounds in a purple-fringed miniskirt, and the older male candidates were treating everyone to coffee. All except Foti and Vangeli, who were still pursuing their no-campaigning campaign strategy, and whispering election gossip to each other. Everyone else was laughing, high on the free coffee and the pride of fulfilling important civic duties. Lia was an important entity in Greece and now we were busy nurturing the motherland that had produced us, joining together to choose our leader.

I wanted to linger, to herd with my fellow political animals, but Foti and Vangeli vetoed that, saying the *kafenion* was too crowded. We drove to the Xenona, ostensibly to watch the Athenian election on TV in quieter surroundings, but really, I suspected, because Foti didn't want to be around when Lia's new president was announced. Cosmas was Foti's brother-in-law, and he and Foti's sister were now sitting in the *kafenion* trying not to look nervous. No matter who won, whether it was his brother-in-law or himself, Foti would be disappointed.

At the Xenona, five border guards were engrossed in a serious game of cards. I thought they might be on riot-control duty in case the election got out of hand, but Fanis assured me that they were regulars. By eight, an hour after the polls closed, the mayoral race in Athens was officially narrowed to PASOK's Christos Papoutsis and New Democracy's Dora Bakoyiannis, since the many splinter-party candidates failed to get a significant percentage of the vote. Neither of the two main candidates achieved 51 per cent, the majority needed to win, so Athenians would be voting again in a run-off next Sunday, as in many urban mayoral races. If Dora won, she would be Athens's first female mayor in three thousand years. I was excited about the historic contest, but distracted by the race here at home, so I drove Foti and Vangeli to the school to check on our own results.

Outside the *kafenion*, Cosmas and Antonis were pacing nervously. Spiridoula rushed down from the schoolhouse in her knee-high boots. 'They've only counted 30 of the 103 votes,' she reported. (Apparently, 27 of the 130 registered voters had stayed away due to the weather.) 'They won't be done until ten at this rate!'

That was all Vangeli needed to hear. 'Let's go to Dina and Andreas's for dinner, and come back later,' he suggested. I agreed – a girl's gotta eat, even when she's the only election reporter in town. Everyone revealed their voting strategy over grilled chicken.

'What about you, Eleni?' Dina asked. 'Who did you vote for?'

I looked at Foti and Vangeli's expectant faces, and answered, 'It's a secret.'

A surge of laughter shook the table. 'How's the chicken, Eleni?' Vangeli asked. 'Or is that a secret?' Everyone dissolved into hysterics again. I suppose it was laughable to think that my vote could be anonymous in such a small community. But Vangeli said I might as well keep my secret – once the results were announced he would figure out exactly how every last Liotan had voted.

'How will you know for sure?' I asked.

He tapped his temple with his index finger. 'I have a masters in psychology from the University of the Street.'

Apparently, Vangeli was eager to get his Ph.D.,

because he kept calling the *kafenion* every five minutes for updates. During one call, at about nine forty-five, he jumped out of his seat, yelling, 'I don't believe it!' and knocking over his *tsipouro*. (Luckily, *tsipouro* is clear, albeit flammable.) He hung up and reported the news: the election had ended in a tie. ND and PASOK each got forty-seven votes; there were nine votes that the election officials had cancelled because the self-sealed envelopes had either been dropped in the wrong box, marked so they could be easily identified, or otherwise invalidated. Vangeli yanked on his coat.

'Where are you going?' Dina shouted.

'To the *kafenion*, to check things out,' he said. I grabbed my camera and followed.

Outside the schoolhouse, Cosmas barrelled towards us, electrical charges emitting from his wiry hair. 'It's forty-seven–forty-seven with nine invalid; eight for us and one for New Democracy,' he shouted, slapping his forehead. 'The *vavves* put their votes in the wrong box!' (A *vavvo* is an old lady, in village speak.) Voting is an intimidating process, old ladies tend to make up Greece's 5 per cent illiteracy rate, and the paperwork must have confused them. Cosmas was livid, having personally ferried several *vavves* into Lia from large cities to vote. He whirled to face me. 'Remember how you said in a few hours we'd know the results?' he spat. 'Well, you were wrong.'

I was tempted to take a photo of Cosmas, a portrait of tension. But I refrained; I worried he might smash my camera in a Sean-Penn-like rage.

The next day should have been a *panegyri* for the winning party. But there were no roasted lambs in sight. Instead, everyone was engaged in morning-after quarterbacking.

Having garnered only six votes, Vassili Deppis left town. Cosmas and Antonis Makos, the church council leader, had twenty-eight votes each and the rest trickled down from there. Foti had won four in the end, silencing speculation that he hadn't been going to vote for himself but for his brother-in-law. If he had done, Cosmas would be president today. Now Foti was moping around the *kafenion*, arguing with Cosmas's brother, who questioned his family loyalty. I had voted to prevent Foti getting his feelings hurt. But in the end, almost everyone's feelings were hurt, which really made it resemble a sixth-grade election. Even in Arta, Mayor Vaya had lost the race, despite his partying hearty at the gypsy wedding. The bride's parents had lost their voting privileges as punishment for stealing, and the groom's mother had demanded three thousand Euros in exchange for her family's eleven votes, Georgia Vayas told me. 'I told her, "*Koumbara*, that's not done," and she said, "Then unfortunately, *koumbara*, we aren't able to vote for you."'

I felt awful for my friends in Arta; after the mayor had danced so hard! And here in Lia, spirits were low, although the rain had stopped and the weather was now sunny and bright, mockingly gorgeous.

By afternoon, most of us had cheered up enough to start wondering what would happen next. 'Won't we just vote again this Sunday?' I asked as we sat in the *kafenion*.

'No,' said Vangeli. 'The people have spoken.' Well, we obviously weren't very good public speakers. 'In a case like this, there's a draw to find out which of the two leading candidates wins,' he continued. 'The municipality will schedule one for us after all the major elections are settled.'

'A draw?' I scoffed.

'That's right,' Vangeli continued, assuming I didn't know this unfamiliar Greek word. 'A judge will put Cosmas and Antonis's names in a bowl, and pull one out.'

But that was so undemocratic! Democracy had been invented here. Surely these people had a better Plan B than drawing a name out of a hat? Just then, Antonis strolled past the Xenona. 'Mr President!' Foti yelled.

'Not quite,' Antonis responded. 'The draw is scheduled for October 31st.'

With nothing else to do but wait, Vangeli put his degree from the University of the Street to work, divining who had voted for whom, and which two people had purposefully invalidated their votes by writing in the names of soccer teams instead of making the required cross next to a name. 'I'm in the *kafenion*, and Nassios comes up and says, "How about those invalid votes, huh?"' Vangeli reported. 'So I knew it was him.'

'But how can you be sure?' I asked.

He looked at me sadly, pitying my naivety. 'Because,' he said, 'only the person who did that would talk about it. A murderer always returns to the scene of the crime.'

By Day Two post-election, the soccer scam was small fry, eclipsed by a real scandal. Vangeli had uncovered a vote-buying ring. Apparently the PASOK candidates had visited several old people the day before the election, passing out cheques for ninety Euros. 'What did they write on the bottom?' I asked. 'Payment for vote?'

'No, the money was legal, from the government,' Vangeli explained. 'It's like Golf Air, like my brother says you have in the US.'

Golf Air?

'You know, money the state gives to poor people?'

Oh, welfare! Of course.

'Anyway, PASOK has had the cheques since August, but they gave them to their candidates to distribute the day before the election, so that the *vavves* think, "Oh, I'll vote for him, so I'll keep getting money,"' Vangeli continued.

'But if they really did that, that's corruption!' I protested. 'It's illegal!'

'I know,' said Vangeli. 'And they complain about our oily fingerprint!'

I thought this must be a folk saying I didn't know, a comment on how heavy campaigning left 'oily finger-prints' everywhere. 'What does that mean?' I asked.

'It means,' Vangeli said, 'that one of the ND ballots that the officials approved as valid had a big oily finger-print left on it – and PASOK somehow heard about it. Now they say that it's an identifying mark, so the ballot is invalid.'

I pitched forward in my chair. 'It's my fault!' I cried. 'Dina gave me pita on my way to the *kafenion*, and I gave Foti some before he voted – it must be his print.'

'Plug up your mouth,' Vangeli whispered urgently. 'Don't let anyone know it's our fault!'

Damn Dina with her delicious pitas, me with my generous ways and Foti with his ever-expanding gut!

'It wasn't us,' Foti laughed, pulling me out of a spiral of shame. 'It was the other Eleni Gatzoyiannis. She was seen eating fried dough on her way to the school.'

Phew! If we lost the election, it would be my doppelgänger's fault, not mine. But that didn't change the fact that the political climate in Lia was fraught, with no chance of calming down before 31 October. Luckily, we had Round Two of the Athenian election to distract us. On the second Sunday, Dora won the race for mayor by the largest margin in Athens's history, ushering in what the TV reporters called 'The Era of the Woman'. Dora was the first female mayor of any major European city, so I was thrilled. But not as thrilled as her family, who celebrated at her headquarters by Cretan line-dancing in a way I couldn't imagine the Bushes or Karenna Gore Schiff doing. Possibly Tipper. But here in Lia, no bouzouki would strum and no clarinet wail until Hallowe'en, which, since Greeks don't celebrate Hallowe'en, I now thought of as Draw Day.

In the meantime, we all tried to return to our regular pursuits, and to enjoy the lovely weather. The sky was a pure azure that Crayola has never quite managed to replicate, and the sun gave off the intense Greek light which overexposes the film of unsuspecting tourists every autumn. It was the phenomenon known as 'the little summer of St Demetrios', the last blast of gorgeous weather, which usually occurs around the feast day of St Demetrios on 26 October. It is also the season when sheep are led from mountain pastures to lowland winter fields, so I watched two distant cousins herd their seven hundred sheep down the mountain into the vast wilderness beneath the road to Babouri.

Foti taught me to placate their five possibly murderous sheepdogs by dropping down on my haunches and cooing, 'Ella, ella,' as my cousins led sheep of all sorts: woolly, shaggy, spotted. The sheep all somehow understood the shepherd's whistles and verbal cues to veer right or left. But they were discerning sheep; they wouldn't listen to just any human, and each time they sensed me walking towards them to stroke their fluffy fleeces, they would trot away, baaing, their bells ringing in a pastoral symphony.

Foti told me that, in their trek to a village near Filiates, the sheep would cover some of the same ground as my father and aunts had done when they had fled Lia, sneaking off at night, barefoot, down the mountain and up to the Great Ridge where the Nationalist troops were stationed. I decided I had to hike the escape route myself. I had come to Lia to recapture a bit of my family's life here; how could I leave without searching out the paths they had followed when they'd left the village behind? It was a trip Thitsa Kanta often referred to when she was annoyed with my father. 'NickGage shouldn't yell at me,' she'd complain. 'I'm older, and I carried him through the minefields!'

I turned to Foti. 'I know it's too late to start today,' I said. 'But could you maybe get someone to show me the escape route so I can hike it tomorrow?'

Foti frowned, leaning against a roadside shrine as a sea of woolly sheep trotted past. 'One of my friends hunts in those mountains,' he admitted. 'But I'm not sure it's a good idea.'

'Look, if the thitsas could do it . . .' I objected.

'I know,' Foti answered. 'But there were paths then that are all overgrown now.'

'They told me that they followed the streams so that they didn't step on any minefields,' I said. 'I could follow the rivers, too, wade a little if I have to. I'd really like to see the route for myself.' I looked at Foti evenly. 'If your friend can't show me, maybe you can describe the route to me and I'll try and hike it on my own.'

Foti sighed. 'OK, OK, I'll make sure he leads you,' he said. 'Just promise you won't tell Kanta about this. She'd kill me if she knew I'd let you hike off into the wild with only a middle-aged hunter with high blood pressure for protection.'

*

The next day, just after sunrise, Foti introduced me to Stavros Zafeiris. We met outside Panagia church, near the starting point for the escape that my father, his sisters and several other villagers embarked on in July 1948. Stavros, wearing head-to-toe camouflage, a red beard and a long-barrelled rifle, led me past a tree full of golden-red pomegranates on to the mountainside. We were above the tree-line; below us stood russet-coloured trees, and clouds as puffy as the departed sheep. With Stavros in the lead, we slid downhill, crouching under branches and stomping on brambles.

'This whole area used to be cultivated,' Stavros told me. The entire mountainside looked the same to me, but he could refer to patches of land by the names of the people who had owned them back when Lia was bustling. Shortly after passing a ruined home whose fireplace, carved with a fleur-de-lis, rose like a watchtower above the rubble, we reached the hilly grounds of the monastery of Agios Athanassios. A bush started shaking and I screamed – it could be a runaway Albanian, a ghost, or a disgruntled saint. Even if I survived the impending assault, Thitsa Kanta would kill me. Suddenly Father Prokopi emerged, wrestling with the branches; he was thinning them as part of his grand plans for the renovation of the monastery. 'Remind me, I have 150 Euros to donate from the hunters,' Stavros told him. 'Whenever we shoot a pig on the grounds of the monastery, we each put in five Euros for the church.'

I was jealous of Father Prokopi and Stavros, for whom this landscape was a familiar retreat. The streams, trees and hillsides belonged to them a little, but were new to me. We continued on, and after three hours approached the foot of the Great Ridge. 'Only one more hour now,'

Stavros said cheerfully. 'And it's straight up all the way.'
He whistled as we climbed, aided by walking sticks. But
once we reached the top, the old Nationalist camp, he
looked down and said soberly, 'There are corpses here
from everywhere – Greeks, Germans, Italians.' At least
they had an awe-inspiring resting place.

I thought of my grandmother, who was forced to stay
behind at the last minute to harvest wheat for the
guerrillas, missed the frightening, night-time hike, and
was executed for planning her family's escape. I hoped
that if Thitsa Kanta's dream was right, and my yia-yia
now watched over me, she had come along today to see
how her family had survived and how breathtaking their
passage to freedom remained.

October 28th was OXI Day, the anniversary of the date
during the Second World War when the Greek ruler
Metaxas had said 'No!' (or *C'est la guerre!*), he would not
cede the country to the Axis powers. I attended the
holiday service at church, and watched as veterans,
policemen and Nikolas Skevis, who was still president
until January, laid wreaths at the monument to Lia's
fallen soldiers. Later, at the Gatzoyiannis house, a minor
battle threatened to break out. Zervas, our ethereal
architect, had unexpectedly arrived to check on the
building. 'About the stairs from the verandah: the front
ones look good, but the ones leading from the door of
the *plistario* have to be done carefully,' he said, rolling
up the sleeves of his V-neck sweater. 'Vlad, let's do
them now.'

'No.' Vlad shook his head. 'First finish wall to the
stairs, then do the stairs.'

'But the stairs are important!' Zervas insisted. 'We
should handle them now, while I'm here, or else you'll

do them all wrong!' Since the hedgehog incident, when Zervas was convinced that Vlad had scared off his workers, there was no love lost between the two. And now Vlad was having a little 'OXI' day of his own.

'I no take down scaffolding in front of door until done with wall,' he insisted, shrugging. 'No can do stairs until scaffolding down.' With that, Vlad turned and resumed working on the upper wall of the courtyard. I glanced at Zervas, who looked as frustrated as I imagine Metaxas felt sixty-two years ago today. Zervas needed to be distracted, so I volunteered to treat him to lunch. When we arrived at the Xenona, I was delighted to see that Vassili Deppis, who had received a pitiful six votes after switching parties and had then disappeared, had returned. 'You're back!' I shouted, giving him a hug hello.

'Of course!' he boomed. 'I was just on Corfu, helping my sons close their hotel for the winter.'

'Oh good!' I said. 'I was worried you were feeling a little down.'

'Who, me?' Vassili laughed, raising his stick off the ground. 'About the election? I couldn't be president even if I had won; I travel too much! I have to be in Athens for the holidays, then Germany. Last year I visited a friend in Australia. This year, who knows?'

That's the spirit, I thought, driving home. Everyone's seeing reason. Zervas returned to Athens, and I didn't see Vassili again until Sunday, when most of us gathered in the *kafenion* after church. He was sitting opposite Nikolas Skevis, complaining that he couldn't make *tsipouro* from his grapes because the church-owned still had been locked by the customs office, which now required you to get a permit before making *tsipouro*.

'A traitor in our midst tipped them off!' he yelled.

Vangeli whispered to me that everyone knew he was referring to Cosmas, who was so mad when his own still got locked for the same reason that he informed the customs guy that the church had one too.

'As president, you should go and get permits for everyone,' Vassili scolded Nikolas.

But Nikolas was still fuming about having to give up the presidency in two short months. 'Get your own permits!' he shouted. 'And tell the traitor what you think of him to his face if you're a man!'

'I knew you wouldn't help us,' Vassili sneered. 'You won't do anything for the good of the village, just for your own profit!'

'No one cares about your opinion,' Nikolas spat. 'Hardly anyone voted for you! The village doesn't respect you! The village shits on you!'

Those were fighting words. And Vassili was ready to respond in kind. 'I wouldn't have cared if I didn't even get my own vote,' he blurted. 'Everyone knows I'm New Democracy! I just ran to keep you off the ticket! And I achieved my goal!' With that, Vassili stormed out, as much as a heavyset man with a stick can storm.

The next day, over lunch at Dina and Andreas's, I asked if they'd heard about the fight.

'Oh, that wasn't a real fight,' Dina said, rolling her eyes. 'Those two see arguing as a *panegyri*. This morning they went down together to Igoumenitsa and got the still unlocked. They're boiling their grapes for *tsipouro* today.'

I was shocked, but delighted. See, we can all get along! 'That's great,' I said. 'And tomorrow we'll know who won the election!'

'No,' said Andreas, tapping his fork in resignation. 'We won't know for weeks.'

'But tomorrow's Hallowe'en!' I said. 'I mean, October 31st. Draw Day.'

'Yes, but that was before the lawsuit,' Andreas explained. 'Now they're going to set a court date on Corfu, because the PASOK candidate who lost the mayoral race for the region says one of the ballots is invalid.'

The oily fingerprint! I knew my pita was at fault!

'If PASOK wins another village, they get one more city councillor,' Dina added. 'So they say a ballot was marked because the sign looks more like an X than a cross!'

I sighed, and helped myself to another glass of retsina. The lawsuit wasn't my fault, after all. Still, it seemed excessive to quibble over how some illiterate old lady draws a cross. But I was quickly realizing that politics is a rough game.

With the warm weather holding, I concentrated on the building site, where the Northern Epirote master stone-mason Yanni and his wife were giving the house a complete makeover, defining its features. Until now the verandah had been a skeleton frame, with two cement pillars rising to support the ground floor, and continuing on from the verandah to hold up the slate roof. Yanni had covered the pillars in front of the basement with flat, square stones and built elegant stone arches that curved underneath the concrete floor of the verandah. Now he was starting to cover with stone the pillars of the main floor. In the mid 1930s, my grandfather had closed in the verandah with corrugated tin to create another room, but I preferred to keep it open, so I could look out past the mulberry tree towards the bow-shaped mountain in the distance, the same view my grandmother gazed at over half a century ago. I was trying to imagine the house finished when Yanni stopped chipping and looked up.

'Good afternoon,' he said to someone behind me. I turned and saw the sparkling blue eyes and stark white moustache of Antonis Makos, my favoured presidential candidate, who lived in Perivoli.

'The pillars look great,' he said. 'Really make the house look like a home. Since I can't be here tomorrow, I wanted to come over and see how they turned out.'

'Where are you going?' I asked.

'To Corfu – for the court case,' he said. 'It's for the election. The judge will rule on whether the ballots are valid, or if, as the PASOK politician says, one is marked.'

'And if the judge decides they're valid?' I asked.

'If he says they're valid, I guess we'll have a draw,' he answered.

'Right then and there?'

He nodded, then shrugged. 'I guess so. It's been over a month since the election – we need to find out who the new president is before he has to take up office in January.' He was right. The suspense had to end. And I felt I had to watch the conclusion of this prolonged contest, almost as a monitor of justice.

'Can I come?' I called after him.

Antonis turned and smiled. 'The case is going to be heard at five at the old courthouse,' he said. 'If you take the two o'clock ferry you'll be there in time.'

The next day at four, I found Antonis standing outside the Corfu courthouse, dressed for battle in a navy suit, a leather waistcoat stretched over his slight paunch. He tried to smile, but his face kept collapsing into a network of nervous folds. I was glad I'd come, because without me, Antonis would have been a lone New Democracy wolf, and Cosmas appeared to be accompanied by the PASOK politician who was bringing the lawsuit.

Antonis and I decided to grab a coffee to pass the time. 'At the courthouse the guard said this is the only place open.' Antonis pointed to an elegant, colonnaded Venetian building with a sign reading 'Dirty Dick's Bar'. Dirty Dick's turned out to be the Algonquin Round Table of the Corfu courthouse, filled with politicians awaiting trial and poker-faced lawyers drinking ginger beer.

'Wasn't he on the ferry with you?' Antonis asked, agitated.

'Who?'

'Dr Doumazios; he's supposed to be here.' Doumazios was the New Democracy candidate who had won the mayoral race for our municipality of Filiates. We had elected him, he had promised to defend us, and now he was nowhere to be seen. Shades of agony passed over Antonis's face; it was like watching someone get stood up for the senior prom.

At ten to five, we filed into the courthouse, an imposing neoclassical job crawling with cops. We found the classroom-like hall marked 'Municipality of Filiates' and managed to get seats just in time — right next to Cosmas, who looked as nervous as Antonis. The opposing candidates from Lia sat together for mutual comfort. Even I felt nervous. A raised platform loomed opposite our lowly spectators' benches, and behind this dais were seven massive chairs. Above the chairs hung a painting of Jesus, but not the Greek Jesus we knew and loved, with a centre parting, ponytail, sunken cheeks and sorrowful eyes. This was a Western Jesus with cascading locks, doe eyes and a white robe, pointing to himself, just on his breastbone, with his left hand, and out at us with his right, as if to say, 'It's not me, it's you. I died for your sins.'

But He must have been blessing us after all, because just before the doors shut a grim lawyer waltzed in, followed by a sharp-dressed, slick-haired man who could only have been Dr Doumazios. Antonis sighed happily, and we were instructed to rise for the magistrates, who appeared behind the dais. It turned out that the judge was a smiling, twinkly-eyed brunette, flanked by two less attractive and less high-powered women. Lady Justice called our case, listened to our lawyers, then consulted with her gal pals behind her hot-pink dossier in a highly un-Ruth Ginsberg-like way. I was starting to think, 'Justice is fun!' when she turned to offer her decision. 'I'll take a look at the motions and get back to you in a few days,' she said, offering us a winning smile.

I turned to Antonis. 'That was it?' I demanded.

'Yes,' he said, breaking into a grin. I felt deflated, cheated, but he seemed relieved that our whole exercise in justice boiled down to a matter of five minutes. At least he didn't have to get up and defend himself, like they do on TV.

The local PASOK candidate giving moral support to Cosmas said goodbye and set off to meet a colleague for a drink. Now Cosmas was free to hang out with us — me, his opponent Antonis, Dr Doumazios and our lawyers. We settled in a maritime-themed bar opposite the harbour to await the seven o'clock ferry back to the mainland. Antonis and Cosmas sat next to each other and ordered orange sodas. Why was Antonis drinking with the enemy? I wondered. And what about Cosmas, who had been so enraged the night of the tied election?

Dr Doumazios leaned towards his lawyer. 'Cosmas here wants Antonis to be president, but he can't be seen to be withdrawing from the race,' he announced.

'I don't want to let the Party down, but I have to spend some time in America this year,' Cosmas said, nodding. 'And I live in Igoumenitsa. Antonis is in the village full time. He really should be president.'

'So,' Dr Doumazios continued, taking a sip of his Scotch, 'we know the judge is going to uphold the ballots; if they were at all suspicious, the election officials would have thrown them out the first night they counted them. Once she declares the ballot to be valid, is there any way we can make sure that Antonis wins the draw, since Cosmas doesn't want the job anyway?'

Stonefaced, the lawyer looked at Dr Doumazios. 'There's no way to control a draw,' he intoned. 'If someone doesn't want to be president, he should withdraw.' Cosmas shrugged and swigged his orange soda. He knew he couldn't withdraw at this point without alienating his fellow Party members.

If there was a solution, we couldn't figure it out tonight. Cosmas, Antonis and I had a ferry to catch. As we hurried to the boat, Cosmas asked, 'Any news from Worcester?' He always spoke to me in a mix of Greek and English. Cosmas had a facility for languages; when he and his siblings were taken across the border by the retreating Communists, he'd picked up Hungarian and Romanian, which came in handy when he moved to Germany and became a foreman at a car factory, overseeing Hungarian workers. There he learned German; then English in a Massachusetts pizza parlour. If he'd been a diplomat instead of a refugee, Cosmas might be an ambassador by now.

'No, nothing new,' I told him.

'I got something,' he said, grimacing. 'My son, he may be getting a divorce.'

'I'm so sorry,' I said.

'That's OK — they didn't have any kids, so not such a big deal.' He shrugged. 'His wife, she says she's not sure she wants to be married no more.'

As we boarded the ferry, I realized that this was the reason why Cosmas needed to spend time in America this year, to be near his son. A month ago, the election had seemed supremely important. But now everything was different, and he didn't really care about his political future. In the ferry lounge, we sat together and Antonis brought us coffees. As we sipped, the PASOK official who had brought the suit walked in and came over to say hello. 'I wanted to ask you a favour,' he said, handing me a piece of paper with a name on it. 'When you get to America, can you search for information about my grandmother's brother? He moved there in 1910, died in 1953 in San Bernardino, but that's all we know. Maybe he had kids. Anything you find out would be great.'

I said I'd try, and he left to get his bags. 'That's a good sign, that he asked you for help,' Antonis said. 'Maybe he thinks we're going to win, or he plans to drop the suit.'

But I felt that his request was apolitical. He wanted information about a relative he'd never known, and realized that in this battle we were on the same side, both trying to learn as much as possible about our families' pasts as they had played themselves out between the United States and the rocky coast where the ferry was now docking.

After we disembarked, I gave Antonis a lift to Lia. On the way he told me about the August day in 1948 when he saw my grandmother being led up the mountain to her execution with twelve other prisoners. 'I was thirteen, and had gone to collect water,' he recalled. 'One of the soldiers leading the prisoners asked for my canteen. I said, "No way — what will I collect water with?" He laughed and moved on. Now I can't believe I did that, talked back to a murderer. But I was young and thirsty, and I didn't know any better.'

Decades later, Antonis worked as a meat salesman, supplying bars and restaurants in Ioannina. In one bar, he recognized the decaying bartender as the once-brash young soldier who had demanded his canteen. When my father returned to Greece to learn the details of his mother's death, Antonis gave him the man's name, a key piece of information that got the investigation started.

Young boys grow up to run for president, sometimes of a country, and sometimes of a village as small as Lia. And children get older, and can't be protected from sorrow or heartbreak. I know that politics matter. Even in Lia, political differences resulted in the war which caused my grandmother's death and the abduction of children like Cosmas and Antonis. Today Lia is a tiny fragment of its former self, with only 15 per cent of the population it had before the war, no school, no businesses. But it has also turned into a place where a political fight is just a shouting match in the *kafenion*, not a death sentence, and where the man running against you for office is really just a friend in need.

I knew my aunts and my father thought I was naive not to see evil in the village. It existed there, and so did violence and hate, just as they do everywhere. I recognized that. But I was glad that friendship and community existed as well. Two weeks after the court date on Corfu, almost three months after Election Sunday, a cliffhanger that had dragged on for longer than some of my romantic relationships finally ended with an anti-climactic phone call from Dr Doumazios, informing Antonis that he was now Lia's newest representative. The first person to call and congratulate Mr President was Cosmas.

9

THE FUTURE IMPERFECT

«Άλλα σκαμπάζει ο γάϊδαρος, και άλλα ο
γαϊδουρολάτης.»
'The donkey has one set of plans, and the donkey
herder has another.'

5 November

I had a strange dream last night. I'm standing in the
door of the Gatzoyiannis house, watching Yanni build a
stone banquette between the corner of the verandah and
the wall of the house itself. I'm thinking about next
summer, when we'll set a table here and eat while gazing
down at the mountains to watch the shadows stretch along
their peaks, turning from gold to amber to purple.

'Watch out!' Yanni points at the stone steps leading
up to the verandah. There's now a slobbering, spotted dog
bounding up them. The dog trots right up to me and
opens his mouth so wide I can see past his yellow incisors
to his looming tonsils.

I wish I had brought some tooth-whitening paste with me from America.

'So what did the dog do then?' Kaity demanded when I told her the dream.

'I don't know,' I sighed. 'That's when I woke up. What does it mean?' In the village, at the Haidis house, I had stored the 2002 *Oneirokritos*, 'The interpreter of dreams', a booklet with horoscopes for the year, a list of saints' days, jokes and a handy glossary of frequent symbols seen in dreams, along with their corresponding meanings. But I couldn't find it that morning before driving to Ioannina, and I knew Kaity was such an expert at divination that she would never need to look up an answer.

'Well,' she said, putting down her coffee cup. 'What colour was the dog, black or white? Because white dogs are a good sign, but black dogs are bad.'

'The dog was black and white,' I fretted. 'It was Scrappy, one of the strays the soldiers abandoned when they left the border post. I feed him, and he's always jumping up and knocking things out of my hand, or winding in between my legs and tripping me.'

'It's your own fault for feeding him.' Kaity wrinkled her nose. 'You should know better. In any case, dogs in general are a sign of worry, complications, responsibilities. Maybe the dream was a warning about a problem with the house.'

I wanted a second opinion. What would Freud do? 'Maybe the dream doesn't mean anything about the future, it's just my subconscious reviewing things that happened that day,' I suggested.

'Oh, Eleni.' Kaity shook her head. 'All dreams tell us something about the future, whether we want to listen or not. Look at me; I had a prophetic dream the night before each of my parents died.'

'Really?' I asked. 'What happened?'

'The night before my mother's death, I dreamt I was walking on the beach, and I looked at the moon,' she recalled. 'The moon turned into my mother's face, with her hair undone, trailing into the night sky. Back then, women always had their hair up, so to me she looked scary, wild. The next day, I came home from school and she was dead.'

'That's amazing,' I said. 'Was it the same dream with your father?'

'No. I was married and living here by then, but I dreamt I was walking down a street in my hometown and saw my mother, running in her nightgown, her hair hanging down. I called, "*Mana!*" but she ignored me. Finally, I reached her and asked where she was going in such a hurry. She said, "To your father's funeral, of course."'

I was fascinated but terrified. If dreams are previews, are all coming attractions tearjerkers? 'I'm not going to try to remember my dreams any more,' I vowed.

'It's better to know,' Kaity insisted. 'So when a tragedy happens, along with sorrow you feel a tiny bit of relief, that you knew what was coming, it's now over, and you just have to get to the next surprise fate has in store – and to hope it's a good one.'

I nodded, but Kaity knew I wasn't convinced. 'Give me your cup, I'll read your coffee grounds,' she said to placate me. 'Then you should set off for Lia before dark.'

Over the past eight and a half months, Kaity had read my coffee grounds dozens of times. When Thitsa Kanta was around, I'd had her read my cup, too, so I could compare one reading to the other, my system of checks and balances. Thitsa Kanta's readings were delivered with as much advice as interpretation; she'd tell me that a cross, which signifies happiness, meant that I was about to meet a man, 'Because you gotta get married soon, while your thitsa is still strong enough to dance at your wedding!'

Perhaps because of Thitsa Kanta's less-than-subtle attempts at mind control, I didn't believe in coffee-cup readings any more than in horoscopes in the paper. Still, I liked to watch Kaity and Thitsa Kanta point out the patterns the grounds left when they oozed down the sides of the overturned cup, and describe what they symbolized. It was kind of like code-breaking. A snake, monkey or dog was an enemy. An E signified *eutuchia*, happiness. If the bottom of the cup was dark, coated in grounds, it indicated *stenachoria*, a word which translates as 'narrow places' but means the suffocating sensation of worry. Sometimes the signs were obvious – rings meant a wedding, a cradle signified a baby. But other symbols meant the opposite of what you'd expect: a pile of grounds on the lip of the cup looked like a big mess, but indicated a pile of money was about to come your way (just as dreaming of a pile of shit, pardon the expression, is a harbinger of riches).

In April, shortly after I'd arrived in Greece, Kaity had taught me a new symbol. 'Look, a tree,' she said. 'A tree is about planting something, then waiting to see it bloom. You're about to start a project that will bear fruit long into the future, offering shade and nourishment not just for yourself but for your descendants.'

Kaity knew I had taken a year out of my life to oversee the rebuilding of my grandparents' house. She could have made up the tree as encouragement. But when she pointed to the white trunk and branches spreading amid the dark coffee grounds, there it was — a tree as clear as in a drawing. I was stunned that something so inspiring could come out of mundane divination games, the grown-up, Greek equivalent of the Decision Ball.

Codified images like the tree had existed for ever, and I suspected that they didn't just tell Greek women what to expect, but also taught them how to think, shaping their emotions into culturally coded symbols, so that unbound hair indicates death, not a burning desire for a haircut. My own dreams had changed since I'd arrived in Lia. In New York, I dreamt about walking into my office in my pyjamas, or discovering extra rooms in my tiny apartment. But in Lia I'd see my beloved late uncle holding an eagle in his hands before it sailed off into the sky, and I knew that flying birds meant soaring spirits — somewhere my uncle was happy. In New York, my dreams were sitcoms; in Lia, they were haikus.

So I was starting to believe that my dreams could tip me off about future events that were preordained by fate. Luckily, at the same time that I was realizing that fate controlled me, I was also learning that I was able to influence it, to cheat fate, at least temporarily. When it comes to unlucky fate, it's better to be proactive than to react. So the villagers warned me to wear a blue-eye amulet for protection from the evil eye, the 'bad vibes' that a person who envies you, or who just adores you excessively, can cast over you with an admiring glance, sending a black fate your way.

By the time I returned to Lia from visiting Kaity, it was already too late; I had gone into the city amulet-less. Now I was caught in a storm, my computer wouldn't start, and I felt sick and headachey. Someone had it in for me — clearly I was *matiasmeni*, infected by the evil eye. So as soon as I arrived in Motsala, I headed to Dina's for aspirin and psychic relief. Her father had taught her an incantation to remove the evil eye when she had children, so she could cure them. But once he had given her the words, he lost the power to cure people himself, which happens when you share the secret knowledge. Before Dina could cure me, she had to confirm the diagnosis. She dropped a blob of oil into a shot glass of water. In a few seconds, the oil separated into four distinct, oily eyes.

'Yup, you're *matiasmeni*,' she announced. 'And by a man. When you have the *mati*, the oil rises to the top of the water and forms eyes. If a woman has given it, it becomes one big eye; if it's from a man, the blobs are spread out. Take three sips of this.'

I drank from the oil-and-water cocktail, sipping from three different sides of the shot glass as instructed. Then Dina dipped her hand in the water, made the sign of the cross over my head, and left the room to repeat the incantation. I felt better already.

That night, at dinner at the Xenona with Nikki, Fanis and our new president, Antonis Makos, I announced that I had been suffering from the evil eye. Thitsa Kanta once told me that my grandfather had a sixteen-year-old sister who died of the evil eye after a passing priest commented on how pretty she was. 'Priests are the worst for giving the evil eye,' she warned me. 'Priests and blue-eyed people like you. They don't mean to, but they give it anyway.' The pretty girl's mother took soil from the priest's footprint, put it in holy water and made the afflicted girl drink it, but it was too late, she died of the evil eye anyway.

Did they think it was genetic?

'Well, I hardly ever get the evil eye, but it's because of this,' Nikki said, pointing to a small scar on her temple. 'When I was born, parents used to burn a scar on their baby's forehead with a hot coal or poker.'

'But why?' I gasped, choking on my pita.

'So the babies would be imperfect and less likely to get the *mati*.' Nikki noticed my look of disgust. 'Of course, no one does it any more!'

'But you can understand why they did – the evil eye can be deadly. Just look what happened to your father,' Antonis Makos chimed in. 'Everyone noticed how quickly your grandparents' house is being built and they all talked about it, giving him the evil eye. So he drove off the road and crashed the car. But it was fate that he was unharmed; it wasn't his time to die.'

'I don't know,' I objected. 'It may have been fate, or the Saint himself, who saved him, but it was my father's own fault that the accident happened.'

Antonis slammed his glass of red wine down, sloshing some on to the tablecloth. 'Look, I know you're educated,' he blurted. 'But you may not know that we lose consciousness for three seconds every twenty-four hours – it's a fact, I saw it on TV. A total lack of consciousness. Now that's fine if you're just sitting in a chair, but if you have the misfortune of it happening to you while you're driving . . .'

Fanis, Nikki and I nodded. None of us could argue with an as-seen-on-TV fact. Antonis had called both science and media as witnesses for fate and convinced us. Liotes may have stopped burning babies in ritual scarification, but they still manage to clear a place for the evil eye in their modern lives.

The next morning, I was washing dishes when the doorbell rang. In the courtyard stood a handsome young man with a leather satchel, and a grinning woman in a long skirt. This could mean only one thing – Jehovah's Witnesses, known as Iahovades in Greek.

'We haven't seen you here before,' Handsome began. 'Are you from abroad?'

'Oh yes, me American,' I said. But what I meant was, 'My dear young people, don't waste your time trying to convert a non-native speaker like myself.'

'Do you read Greek?' asked Long-Skirt Widegrin.

'With great difficulty,' I answered, smiling sadly.

'We'll leave you literature in Greek and English,' said diplomatic Handsome. 'A lot of people find themselves wondering, "Why is there pain and suffering in the world?" We believe that the wars and poverty of this age are all foretold, part of a plan that is bringing us to a new world, a new life.'

As my dishes dried, I scanned their literature. The cover story of the Greek *Watchtower* asked, 'Do Superstitions Control Your Life?' and provided a list debunking popular ones. But I had news for Handsome and Long-Skirt; when the new world comes, there will still be superstitions in it. The belief in fate has survived all of the old worlds – no one is about to give up their small element of control over it.

The American side of me scoffed at superstitions, but the Greek side insisted on taking advantage of every chance at prognostication that came my way. Oh, I had some standards, guidelines I followed to keep me from sliding down into crackpotdom. I would never pay for my fortune, thus justifying my habit as a) being social and b) studying folklore, just like I did back in college! On my first foray into 'research', Kaity's friend, an Albanian Cher lookalike, flipped her long hair behind her chiffon-clad shoulder, picked up my coffee cup and predicted that this was the year I would get engaged. 'But I'm not even dating anyone,' I told her, hoping for a more realistic do-over.

'The cup doesn't lie,' she insisted. 'Within the year you will make a serious commitment to someone you already know but are not dating yet.'

I thanked her. But when she was gone, I complained to Kaity about her trite prediction. Cher was just saying what she thought I wanted to hear. This was a marriage-minded society; at every holiday, all the old ladies in my village automatically wished me, 'Next year, may you be here with a groom!'

'If I'm getting engaged this year, how come I'm not even dating my husband already?' I complained to Kaity. 'Because he doesn't exist!'

'Of course he does,' Kaity answered. 'You just need more information about him before you realize which one he is!' Luckily, she pointed out, 23 June was the eve of the festival of St John the Baptist, a night in which it is possible to see the face of your future husband, if you ask the saints nicely. 'Just before bed, put a red cloth in your lap, and a mirror on top of that. Looking in the mirror, comb your hair three times, repeating this verse each time,' Kaity instructed, handing me a slip of paper with a paragraph on it that asks John the Baptist and the Apostles Peter and Paul to reveal the identity of your intended. 'Then when you go to sleep you'll dream of your future husband.'

I was supposed to perform the ritual at midnight, but there was a *panegyri* in Glousta and it was three a.m. before I got around to it. Maybe because I was tardy, maybe because I used a brush instead of a comb, the religious wires got crossed. I didn't dream of anyone. Still, Kaity's fortune-telling friends kept dangling bachelors in front of me as if my life were a psychic game of Old Maid. 'Write this down,' Noula told me, slapping down worn, dirty playing cards, the reading of which was her speciality. 'Your husband will be Greek but educated abroad, and you will lead a happy, double life, between America and Greece.'

'And where will I meet this international jetsetter?' I thought. 'Out picking oregano?' But all I said was, 'How can you tell?'

'Just look,' Noula said. 'This card represents weddings, and this one your name, which is Eleni. That sounds like "Ellinas", a Greek, so your husband will be Greek.'

'From your mouth to God's ears,' Kaity said, in between puffs of her cigarette.

When I told Dina about the prediction, she insisted that I do my best to spur my husband's arrival. On 27 August, St Fanourios' day, she and Athina taught me how to bake a *Fanouropita*. 'Agios Fanourios is the saint who finds things,' Dina explained.

'Like luggage after the airline loses it?' I asked.

'Sure, like luggage, but also more important things, like health,' Athina clarified. 'Or, for example, you could ask him to find you your destiny.'

'My destiny?'

'Your husband!' Dina explained. 'All you have to do is pray for the soul of Agios Fanourios' mother while the cake is baking. She was a wicked woman, so she needs all the prayers she can get.'

'Wicked?' I asked, intrigued. 'Really? What did she do?'

'It doesn't say it in the book about the saint's life, but everyone knows she was a prostitute. Still, that doesn't matter,' Dina said, keeping her eyes on the prize. 'What matters is that you bake and pray for his mother, then distribute the cake to twelve people. The saint returns the favour by finding what's missing in your life. For you, that's a husband.'

Was that what was missing from my life? And if I had a husband, would he be as thrilled as I was to sit in Lia learning how to bake magic cakes? I wasn't convinced a spouse was what I needed. But I baked a delicious get-me-a-man cake anyway. And still my lover with a fancy foreign degree never appeared. Undoubtedly, while I was slaving over a hot stove, he was jumping off his yacht, hand in hand with his Eurotrash girlfriend.

By September, I was annoyed with divination. 'Good predictions never come true, or at least not fast enough,' I complained to a family friend at an art opening in Ioannina. 'And bad ones are depressing, even if they don't happen! It's a no-win situation.'

'Oh, you mustn't listen to any kind of fortune-telling,' she warned. 'Not only is it a sin in the eyes of the church, but it's also very dangerous. My mother-in-law read coffee grounds, and one day she told my brother-in-law that she saw an accident; he shouldn't go out on his motorcycle. He zoomed off, got hit by a truck and almost died. Later he told me that when he saw the truck coming, he didn't try to avoid it because he remembered his mother's advice. He made it a self-fulfilling prophecy.'

I saw her point — I didn't want to be a slave to divination. But on the other hand, maybe the moral of the story was that a boy should listen to his mother.

After that warning, I asked Kaity where she'd learned to read coffee cups. 'From my mother,' she answered. 'She was from Asia Minor; they're the best fortune-tellers.'

'And she learned from her mother?' I asked.

'I guess so,' Kaity responded. 'It's an inherited gift. But you can't read your own cup, or realize if you see yourself in someone else's. When I was fifteen and taking exams, my mother read my fortune every morning, to see how I'd do. One day she said, "I see a death in this cup!" By the time I returned home, she had died of an aneurysm.'

I almost choked on my own coffee. 'Aren't you afraid you'll see something horrible one day?' I asked.

'What is there to be afraid of?' Kaity shrugged. 'It's all in God's plan.' She stood up, giggling, and disappeared into the kitchen. In a minute she was back, holding a yogurt container. 'You have to promise not to tell anyone,' she said, handing it to me.

I flipped off the top, extricated a bundle swaddled in tissue and bubble wrap and began undoing it. Underneath all the neat layers was a coffee cup, covered in lacy-looking grounds that were now hard and crumbly.

'My daughter sent it to me,' she laughed. 'From grad school. I got a notice that I had a package at the post office and it turned out to be this. She wants advice on her break-up.'

'But she's an engineer, a mathematician,' I sputtered. 'Isn't she too logical for this?'

'Please,' Kaity scoffed, collecting the well-travelled cup. 'Even engineers break up with their boyfriends.'

I decided that Mr Right, Ph.D. could stay on his yacht. It was time to stop looking for Mr Goodbarrister and start concentrating on aspects of my future that I could control, such as rebuilding the house. Back in Lia, I stood watching Vlad and Xalime lay flagstones on the verandah of the Gatzoyiannis house, in between the stone banquettes that Yanni had finished the week before. There were still no doors or windows, but the front of the house was really starting to look polished, I thought, glancing over the flat, irregularly shaped stones. Suddenly I realized that something was missing: the *plistario*, the little kitchen, had no stairs leading from the ground to its outside door. You would have to jump from the verandah to the ledge in front of that door, risking possible death and certain ankle-twisting. The dog in the dream had tried to warn me that there was a problem with steps! This was exactly what Zervas had been worried about, what he had wanted to work on when Vlad refused. If I didn't think of a solution before he arrived next week, my architect was liable to pass out when he noticed the oversight.

'Eleni!' A voice called from below the property. A sickeningly familiar voice. I moved to the edge of the wall. There was Zervas, standing below, waving up at me.

'You're a week early!' I trilled.

'Yes, to make up for all the times I was two weeks late,' he answered, walking towards me. 'No, I was checking on another job in a village near by and I thought I might as well come now and save myself a trip. I'm glad I did. How beautiful this all is — the benches, the columns. I was worried that they were going to be too thick, but they look even better! The flaw turned out to be an improvement!'

At least he was in a good mood. 'Yeah, the place looks amazing,' I said. 'It's getting close to done now. Just a few details, the doors, windows, and, um, the stai—'

'And you look wonderful!' Zervas continued. 'I must

look different too. Because when you take unshapen rock and turn it into a piece of art, something changes, both in the rock and in you. We are both forever changed because of this house.'

I stared at him, then at the house, a grey stone cottage that looked as if it should always have a puff of smoke rising from the chimney. I had been so concerned with the steps that I had forgotten about the complete transformation of the place, from ruins to a thing of beauty.

'When Solzhenitsyn was sent to Siberia, the convicts were forced to work non-stop, building stone walls,' Zervas continued. 'Everyone was exhausted and miserable, but occasionally he would step back and say, "Look what a beautiful wall we're making!" He knew it was art, and he was glad to be creating something.'

Zervas seemed so happy. I couldn't deceive him any longer. 'But look at the door to the *plistario*!' I moaned. 'There are no steps to get to it.'

'Oh, that's nothing,' Zervas said, beaming at the rock. 'Vlad, if you cut into that wall, three steps curving up from the courtyard, that would look perfect. Very organic.'

'Sure,' said Vlad. 'Good idea.'

They were agreeing with each other for the first time since the hedgehog incident. I couldn't believe my luck – maybe my dream Scrappy had had more white fur than black after all.

'Eleni, let's go,' Zervas said. 'The man whose house I came to check on, he's driving up to meet us at the Xenona in an hour and I promised him fish.'

We drove through golden autumn sunlight that intensified the rust-coloured trees and azure sky, to the trout farm just before Kefalovriso, a tree-lined spring that resembled an enchanted grove so much that I expected naiads and dryads to pop out from behind the branches.

'Barba Lambro!' Zervas called. A white-haired hunchback scuttled across wooden grids sticking up through his trout pond. Using a net, he pulled up twelve long, shimmering grey trout, dropped them into two blue plastic bags, and tied the handles together tightly. I heard the fish flapping in the double-bag and felt a twinge of guilt.

'These trout are lucky,' I told Zervas as we drove towards the Xenona with the bagged trout thrashing in the back. 'Now they won't have to survive the cold winter.'

Zervas looked at me. 'You're an optimist,' he said. 'Just like Solzhenitsyn.'

At the Xenona, Nikki cooked the trout as we drank wine with Zervas's friend, who turned out to be a master carpenter – this was a business lunch, hence all the effort to secure the fish. 'I just came from your house,' the carpenter said, pumping my hand. 'It's so beautiful, I want to contribute something to it. I know you have someone doing the doors and windows already, but I'd like to build the wooden door for the outer gate. Zervas told me about your grandmother; I want to leave my mark on her monument.'

Zervas had called this man the best carpenter in Greece, but said he was way out of my price range. And now he was offering a gift, a tribute to the house and the people who had loved it. Maybe this was the news Scrappy had been trying to tell me as he ran through the empty outer gate frame and up the steps towards me in my dream. I couldn't be sure. That's the great thing about divination – you hear some shadowy hint of your fate, but when the predicted event actually happens, it still manages to surprise you.

After lunch, our guest drove off to measure the pagoda-like frame of the *exoporta*. As he walked out, he passed a young monk in a black robe with a long, red ponytail. 'Father Gerasimos is the abbot of the monastery of Giromeri, outside Filiates,' Nikki said, introducing us. 'He's here to pick up the slate tiles we took off when we fixed the roof, because the monks are doing some renovations.'

'It is so important to refurbish the monasteries of Epiros in their traditional style,' Zervas said, shaking the monk's hand. 'They deserve to be showplaces. After all, we have so many significant local saints.'

'We do?' I'd been to church here hundreds of times and this was news to me.

'Of course,' Father Gerasimos replied. 'Agios Donatos is the most beloved. He worked miracles, killed a dragon. But the scholar Agios Deodochos is more important in the history of monasticism.'

'Isn't that always the way?' I asked. 'The flashy dragon-killing saint gets all the kids named after him, and the ascetic gets no love.'

'Oh, but Agios Deodochos is very inspiring,' Zervas said. 'It was after reading his work on poverty and celibacy that my wife left me to join a convent.'

My jaw dropped. I knew Zervas didn't have a wife, although he wore a wedding ring. But I'd assumed she had died or run off with another man — and I didn't mean Jesus.

'The thing is, Father,' Zervas was saying to the monk, 'when you get so wrapped up in something, there comes a point when you have to decide if you're going to move forward or stay where you are. If you move forward, you know you can't go back again, but if you stay where you are, you feel as if you're drowning.'

I couldn't believe it! Zervas sympathized with his wife's internal struggle, even as he was hurt by her desertion. This struck me as being even more generous of spirit than Solzhenitsyn. I didn't know how to respond. I looked at the red-headed abbot expectantly. Wasn't counselling people about this sort of thing his job?

'Well, in true Christianity, nothing is irreversible,' Father Gerasimos said finally. 'Because nothing is unforgiven.' Then he went into the kitchen to strike a deal for the roof slates, leaving us to our coffee.

'What was your wife like?' I asked Zervas, who seemed still tangled in the complicated knot of his feelings towards her.

'She was beautiful,' he smiled. 'She looked just like Jackie Kennedy, so elegant. That's why she left – it was the evil eye. Everyone coveted her and drove her away.'

'Do you really think that's why?' I asked gently, not wanting to suggest that the cause might be less paranormal – she'd simply wanted out of her old life.

'Why else?' he sighed. 'She regrets leaving. I know she's ready to come back.'

'Oh?' I was startled again. 'So you talk?'

'No, never,' Zervas answered. 'But she told people she was ready to return, and they told me. I could go and get her today, when I leave Lia.'

'So will you?' I asked. Maybe fate would morph this tragedy into a love story.

'Probably not.' Zervas sighed. 'Not today, maybe never. It may be better this way – she's peaceful where she is, I'm calm as I am.' He put down his drained cup. I longed to be able to turn it over and see his future, and his wife's, in it.

'I could try to read your cup,' I said, to lift his mood. 'Or do you think it's a sin?'

Zervas thought for a moment. 'Most religions teach us that we shouldn't try to learn the future, that we should leave that to God, and be satisfied,' he said. 'But if we stop yearning to know how our lives will unfold, it's a little like not yearning to live. It's such an ancient desire. Look at Dodona.' He glanced at me sceptically.

'The oracle, right?'

'The oldest oracle in Greece, right here in Epiros,' he clarified. 'It's just outside Ioannina. Surely you've been there.'

A few days later, Zervas left after approving Vlad's undulating stone steps which now curved towards the *plistario*. Vlad began laying flagstones on the floor of the tiny bathroom. And I drove to Dodona on a spiritual field trip. This didn't count as divination, I reasoned. It was sightseeing. Ruins. A perfectly wholesome, purely academic exercise.

I sped through Ioannina and turned off at the exit for Dodona, a seventeen-kilometre drive that took me right in front of the University Hospital, where I was expected for a sonogram the following day. I had successfully ignored my ovarian cysts for four months, and thought it in poor taste of the oracle to drag me past the scene of my impending medical tests.

But all was forgiven when I arrived at Dodona, a field surrounded by solid-green hills, silent witnesses to aeons of earnest pleas. I bought a guidebook and walked past the chainlink gate. To my left an amphitheatre from the third century BC stood in a smug semi-circle, embracing the stage with its perfect acoustics and illustrious history. I wished I had taken the time to see a performance here over the summer, to have the breeze rush past me at a particularly dramatic point in the play, functioning like the scary music in a made-for-TV movie about a woman in jeopardy. How had I let time rush by as quickly as the Kalamas River? It was mid November, I had a little over a month left here and I hadn't even made it to a performance at Dodona, although in nine months in New York I could manage to fit in several mindless made-for-TV movies about women in much less jeopardy than, say, Medea. Was I making the most of my life or just marking time here? I whirled away from the theatre, angry that I had turned into a cliché. Here I was at a sacred oracle, having a little existential crisis. That was old hat even in antiquity.

On his way home from Troy, Odysseus had come to ask this oracle if he should return to Ithaka in secret or out loud and proud; Jason built the prow of the *Argo* from a branch of Dodona's sacred oak tree, and Achilles prayed to the oracle during the Trojan War. Built around 2,500 BC, Dodona was already a top tourist attraction by the second century AD, when Pausanias described it as 'worth seeing'. According to my guidebook, the high point of a visit to ancient Dodona wasn't the dramatic offerings of the amphitheatre, but an audience with the oak tree in which Zeus and the local incarnation of his wife, Dione, were said to live. There supplicants asked a question and the Selli, the oracle's priests, interpreted the answer from the rustling of the sacred oak.

That oak tree was uprooted in the fourth century by either proselytizing Christians or anti-environmentalist souvenir-seekers. But a stately oak had been replanted in its place long ago, so I hurried over. There were no Selli to interpret, but that was just as well. I wasn't sure what to ask. I was anxious about my sonogram tomorrow, but 'Will the tests go well?' seemed like a wasted opportunity; I'd know soon enough. What I really wanted to know was whether or not I was healthy, whether I would have children who would one day visit their great-grandparents' house, which I had spent so much time rebuilding. But that was too important a question to ask; I didn't want to risk a negative answer. Besides, I knew that any answer I'd interpret would be too vague to satisfy my New York scepticism. I wanted an oracle that not only knew the future, but also spoke its mind in pithy soundbites, that might answer the question, 'Will I meet the man of my dreams?' with 'Not in that outfit, honey.'

The wind blew and a white card fluttered on one of the massive stone blocks surrounding the oracular oak. I stepped over the rope meant to keep tourists out and picked it up. There, in English, was written the query, 'Will the Hearts win the cup?'

Sports? Someone trekked to the oldest oracle in Greece and wasted his question on sports? I stared at the oak, which looked strangely familiar, like the white image of the tree that Kaity had discerned among the brown residue in my coffee cup. Maybe the tree I was planting to bloom for future generations was an oak. I didn't need Selli; I had interpreted an answer on my own. Of course, it was the answer I wanted to hear, and I could have been reading my own hopes into the leaves' rustling. But making people feel better is what has kept Dodona in business for over four thousand years.

I still felt confident the next day as I entered the ultrasound room at Ioannina University Hospital. But during the test I found myself missing the paper gown you get at hospitals in America, wishing that the male med student would leave, and that the pelvic ultrasound wasn't so painful. 'The cysts haven't got bigger,' the radiologist said. 'But they're still there. If you're staying another month you should consult a gynaecologist here. If I were you, I wouldn't wait until you return to the US.'

Kaity pulled some strings and got me an appointment with Ioannina's best gynaecologist for the following week. I was grateful for the referral. At least, I knew I should be. But really I was annoyed that I would have to submit to more humiliating tests. That evening, back in Lia, I was anticipating a quiet night at home when the phone rang.

'Lenitsa, where you been?' a familiar voice shrieked forth from the receiver.

'Hi, Thitsa Kanta,' I said. 'I was at the hospital, checking up on my cysts.'

'But I thought you were through with that after the operation in March?'

'I thought so too,' I said. 'But since it turned out that the tumour they took out was a low-malignant potential, you know, this really weak form of cancer . . .'

'I don't want to hear that word!' she shrieked. 'You're healthy! I read your cup and I didn't see nothing, so don't worry about it — and don't tell anyone in Greece or they'll think you can't have babies!'

I knew Thitsa Kanta meant well, but this was not exactly the kind of moral support I needed. So I called my mother, Joanie, and vented.

'I know, it's annoying that you have to keep doing all of this,' she consoled me. 'But at least the test results were good — the cysts haven't gotten any bigger!'

Joanie's upbeat chirping was somehow as annoying as Thitsa Kanta's wild shrieking. I explained that the results weren't good; the cysts were still there. OK, they weren't growing wildly, and I wasn't going to die, but at twenty-eight, 'not dying' isn't a great diagnosis. I hung up and went over to Dina's, where I listed my troubles: I hated doctors, had nagging cysts, and no one I talked to realized that this was a big deal, at least to me.

'Your mother just said the test results were good because she wants that to be true so badly,' Dina said. 'You can't do anything until after you see the gynaecologist, so you might as well stop thinking about it. Self-pity is like a loose tooth — you can keep worrying it to make sure it's still there or just ignore it so you don't make things worse.'

She had a point. I would try to move on, starting by setting her table for dinner. Then Vangeli Panagiotou showed up. I told him I'd visited Dodona, and he said that when he was a travelling salesman after the war, villagers near Dodona kept digging up ancient coins. 'So I show up in town, and kids run up, yelling, "Hey, Pedlar, what do you buy?"' he recalled. 'I say, "Old bronzes, silver, coins," and they take me to this geezer who shows me five ancient coins. Ancient, I mean older than Jesus, older than Jesus's grandparents! I offer to buy all five, thinking I'm really putting one over on poor grandpa. But on the way out of town, three policemen are blocking the road, doing random checks for the Department of Archaeology.'

'They knew the town was full of old coins?' I asked.

'A farmer couldn't plough a field without digging up ten, fifteen old coins that he'd throw out, or make a hole in for his daughters to wear on necklaces. Anyway, the cops say, "We're looking for old coins, turn out your pockets." I had to give up the coins, but I

convinced them I had no idea they were antiques.'
Vangeli smiled. 'I pretended to be a stupid hick. Of
course I was a stupid hick – I should have hidden the
coins in my shoe. Then I could have taken them to
Athens and made a nice profit.'

I laughed; I hadn't realized I'd been hanging out with
scam artists. Having dealt in antiques before dowry
linens, Dina and Andreas shared their own stories about
outrunning the law. 'But one thing we never did was
take icons,' Dina said definitely.

'You mean from a church?' I gasped. 'People do
that?'

'Not from a church, but from an old lady, say,'
Andreas explained. 'Plenty of pedlars would go and say,
"I want to make a copy of this beautiful icon – I'll leave
you a deposit, then when I return the original you'll give
me half back." And then they'd take off, and no one in
the village would ever see them again.'

'That's terrible!' I said.

'And dangerous,' Dina added. 'You don't want to risk
the wrath of the saint.'

She was right, of course. I had visited a monastery
outside Konitsa which contained a buckled Byzantine
icon of the Panagia; it had been stolen by a man who
had removed its gold covering to melt down, then
thrown the icon into the Aoos River. One day a
shepherd heard screaming, followed the sound to the
river, and retrieved the sunken icon. The icon-stealer,
consumed by his own guilt and grief at having been
found out, drowned himself in the same spot where he
had thrown the icon.

Listening to them, I realized that there was a major
power source that I hadn't tapped in my attempt to
control fate – divine intervention. As a tourist, I had

visited icons, churches and monasteries all over Greece, from island chapels to the compounds of Meteora, which perch miraculously on top of freestanding cliffs. In every church, I'd lit a candle and prayed for my family or dead relatives. But now I had a more specific request. I decided to visit Father Gerasimos's monastery at Giromeri as a pilgrim, to light a candle for my health.

The next day, I set out with Foti, who had promised Thitsa Kanta he'd accompany me wherever I wanted to go, as long as it wasn't on a hunting day. I drove us along the Kalamas River, and as we approached a steep cliff Foti pointed to a hole high up on the right, a cave where a hermit had once lived. A door and window were carved into the whitewashed cliffside; even a metal balcony from which the hermit could have surveyed the river view and the valley far below him. Next to that loomed another door, with a fresco of a gold-haloed Virgin Mary above it.

'Agios Neilos lived in that cave in the first half of the fourth century, and built the church in the cave above it,' Foti explained. 'One night he saw a strange light in the trees on the cliff across the river. He climbed down, went to investigate, found an icon of the Panagia, and built the monastery over there.'

We followed the winding road uphill to see the monastery of Giromeri, which turned out to be an impressive brick castle. Father Gerasimos, the present-day successor to Agios Neilos, served us coffee in the flower-filled piazza, then led us to the old church, which was covered with wall frescoes and ornate wood-carvings. In the centre, in a two-sided glass case, stood the miracle-working icon of the Panagia, which was reversible, with Peter and Paul on the back. I lit a candle and prayed, 'Panagia, Peter and Paul, I ask that you safeguard my health and one day bless me with children, and I promise to bring them back here to visit you.'

A week later, I arrived at the hospital early. It turned out that my doctor wasn't in the gynaecology wing, as I'd assumed he would be, but in the *maieutiko*, a word which I had never encountered but which turned out to mean 'obstetrics'. By the time my manhunt/impromptu vocabulary lesson was over, I had run up and down four floors, avoiding old men with sticks, patients in gurneys and breastfeeding gypsies, before arriving ten minutes late.

The doctor performed an ultrasound, then sent me for blood tests to check for the presence of cancer hormones in my bloodstream. 'If the tests come back negative tomorrow, you can wait until you return to the US to discuss the cysts with a doctor there,' he explained.

Lighting candles and saying prayers had felt good at the time – at least I was taking some sort of action. But now I felt paralysed until the next morning.

The following day, just after the hospital opened, I arrived at the blood centre and waited my turn. 'Your results aren't ready,' the nurse said. 'Come back in an hour, and go straight to the lab to ask in case they haven't notified us yet.'

Hot tears of frustration filled my eyes, but I nodded and walked blinking towards the car park.

'Excuse me, miss,' a shrill voice called behind me. I turned around. 'Are you going into Ioannina?' A wrinkled, grey-haired old woman in a wrinkled, grey cardigan was tugging on my arm.

'Yes,' I said, not able to lie to a direct question.

'Well, can you take me into town?' she demanded, the thin moustache on her upper lip twitching.

'Yes,' I said again, not able to think of a reason why I couldn't.

As we drove towards the clock tower in the centre of town, she explained that she had left her wallet at home, and had used the last bus ticket in her cardigan pocket that morning. She had been worrying that she might have to walk back into town, when she saw me, may God bless me and grant me good health and good luck in the future. I was grateful for her chatter and her blessing. I knew I wasn't doing anything heroic. But it felt good to be able to provide an answer to a question, even one as simple as 'How am I going to get home?'

I dropped off my elderly hitchhiker, then returned to the hospital. This time I pushed past the geezers, gurneys and gypsies and went straight to the lab, drumming my nails on the counter until the technicians dug slowly through their files to extract my results. I stared at the computer print-out: five test results, which consisted of a number on the left and a range of normal responses on the right. At the bottom, a summary was printed in block letters: WITHIN NORMAL RANGE.

I had been granted a reprieve. I might need surgery some day, but not yet, certainly not before I returned to the US. I called Kaity and told her the good news, and that I would be heading straight back to Lia. I wanted to stop in at Agios Demetrios, to light a candle in gratitude for the test results being good, but also for the old lady. Because glad as I was about the results, I was also grateful to have had someone with me who cared enough to bless my future, even if it was an old woman with no wallet.

In Lia, after visiting St Demetrios I walked up to the Gatzoyiannis house to check on the building site. It was mid November, but the weather was turning the corner slowly, ambling from the bright light of autumn to the muted grey glow of winter. It would be cold and rainy soon enough. The interior of the house needed to be finished, the bathroom installed, and doors and windows put in place and locked up tight before I could abandon the house to the isolation and rains of late December. I would have to be firm with Thomas, to insist that the interior get finished fast.

As I strode into the house, rehearsing my opening line ('Everything looks exactly the same!'), I heard a noise in the room to the right, which was once the *mageirio* and would become a bedroom in the house's new incarnation. There was Thomas, leaning against the wall. He turned towards me and suddenly, behind him, I saw it. A beautifully formed fireplace with a carved grey decorative stone just below the mantel, etched with a diamond and the date 1914.

'It's perfect,' I whispered.

'It is,' Thomas grinned. 'I was just trying it out.' The charred remains of crumpled paper glowed in the fireplace as smoke rose up the chimney. 'Come into the main room,' he added, halfway there already. I ran in and found Vlad standing next to another even larger fireplace, whose decorative stone was painted a patriotic Greek blue, with a white compass rose design in the middle and the date 1922 above that.

'It's so beautiful!' I said.

'Fireplace in other room from your great-aunt Nitsa's house,' Vlad informed me. Apparently, they had slipped into the crumbling ruins of Yia-yia Nitsa's house and removed her fireplace stone for use by her descendants. She was no longer around to approve the permanent loan, but then again, there was no way she would miss it.

'Where is this other fireplace stone from?' I asked, staring at the compass rose.

'I was hoping you wouldn't ask me that,' Thomas answered. 'I can't tell.'

'Oh come on – it's my house!' I insisted. 'I have to know!'

'Let's just say it's from the village,' Thomas answered. 'A gift . . . from an anonymous donor who is happy to see this house rise again.'

I went on a mental stroll through town, futilely trying to locate a house where I might have seen a stone with a white compass rose on it.

'Can you tell me some day?' I started to negotiate. But when I tore my eyes away from the fireplace, Thomas was no longer standing there. I ran out to the verandah in time to see him pull away and zoom off in his pick-up truck.

I had watched this house grow from the beginning, and still it held secrets I might never learn. And I had spent nine months in Lia, but there was still so much I didn't know about the village. Soon I'd return to New York, my old home, but a city that would have changed in my absence. Friends would have moved, my editors at magazines would have found other writers to work for them, and the city itself would have continued morphing at its non-stop pace. Part of me was tempted to stay in my cosy village for ever, but I knew I couldn't live here indefinitely. That is a privilege reserved for the elderly, who have already successfully completed the difficult tasks of creating families and careers, and have returned to claim their reward. By the time I reached the Haidis house I was desperate for more divination – I needed reassurance that my time here had been worthwhile and that when I returned to the US I would be as happy as I had been here. I was ashamed to realize it, but I was craving a coffee-ground reading.

I went home to call Kaity, but as soon as I got back to the Haidis house, the phone rang.

'Where you been?' It was Thitsa Kanta, calling about the tests. I told her that the results were good, and she said, 'Didn't your thitsa tell you?' She paused – an uncharacteristic silence emanated from the receiver. 'I got bad news,' she said finally.

'What?' I asked. 'Thitsa Olga and Thitsa Lilia didn't like the house?' I knew that a Thitsa Caucus had been scheduled to view Thio Angelo's documentary on Lia.

'They don't know,' Thitsa Kanta cried. 'Ange's tapes were all blank. Your thitsas couldn't see the house, the Babouriotes couldn't see Panagia church, and Jimmy Bazooka, he no see his village in Albania.'

'But that can't be true!' I insisted. 'I saw some of those scenes on playback!'

'It was the metal detector in the airport, erased all of it,' Thitsa Kanta replied. 'They stronger now for the goddamn terrorists.'

Some people coerce fate into blessing their futures. I couldn't even protect the images of my past. I hung up, depressed, and went to sleep, but my dreams held no messages for me.

The next morning, I woke to the jubilant peals of church bells, although it was just a regular Thursday. I quickly dressed and ran to the church of Agia Triada. After the service, on my way out of church, Ekavi, a widow with high cheekbones and short white hair, tapped my arm. 'Come over for coffee,' she insisted. 'You know why I like you?' she added as we walked towards her house. 'Because you go to church. I was just saying to my neighbour, "Eleni Gatzoyiannis is a young person who loves the church."'

'Well, I go more here than in New York,' I admitted, worried I might not live up to this pious image. 'I don't even know why there was church today — is it a holiday?'

'St Philip's day,' she said, leading me inside to a chair at her oilcloth-covered table. 'Forty days before Christmas, the last chance to eat meat before the fast.'

Wait a minute — there's a Christmas fast? I was proud of myself for kind of keeping the Lent fast. I chewed my lip, confused.

'You know St Philip?' Ekavi prompted, boiling our coffee in a shiny metal *briki*. 'He was a farmer in a poor village, and had only one ox to plough his field. One year, no one had meat to feast on before the fast. So he killed his ox, and distributed the meat to his neighbours.' She set a steaming cup in front of me, then sat down. 'The next day, he went to yoke himself to the plough, and his ox was there! The Lord returned it to him.'

Aha! Here was the religious expert I was looking for, having been too embarrassed to bring my latest question to Father Prokopi. 'That's fascinating,' I said, before glancing down at my cup. 'So, do you think reading coffee grounds is a sin?'

'That's what they say,' she nodded. 'So I don't have my grounds read.'

I shrugged as if to indicate, 'Oh yeah, me neither.'

'Why sin when you can just read the egg?' Ekavi continued. 'That's all right, because eggs come from God.'

So do coffee beans, I thought, before realizing that I had no idea what she was talking about. 'What do you mean, "read the egg"?' I asked.

'Oh, it's like coffee grounds, but you pour the white of an egg into a cup of water and go from there – then you can use the yolk for baking,' she explained. Economical and ecclesiastically approved! 'Do you want me to read yours?'

'You know how?' I asked. Maybe fate was starting to smile on me, however shyly, after all – one simple trip to church and I had a fortune-teller right in front of me.

'Sure,' Ekavi replied. 'When I was fifteen in my hometown, I worked for a dressmaker. A client, a beautiful girl a few years older than I was, said to me, "Will you do me a favour? Bring this egg to Kyria Maria and tell me what she says." She wanted to know who she would marry, because she loved a gypsy, but her parents opposed the match.'

'Kyria Maria was an egg-reader?' I asked, trying to keep us on topic.

'Oh yes,' Ekavi continued. 'She was a widow who lived in the shell of a bombed house – this was just after the war. Her daughter died during World War Two in a bombing, and her son, in his sorrow, threw himself off the bridge. Kyria Maria was left to make a living reading eggs by candlelight, because there was no electricity. So I went, and she must have liked me, because she told me to come back and she'd teach me to read the egg.'

'What about the heiress?' I asked.

'Oh, I had to tell her that Kyria Maria said she'd marry the boy her parents had in mind. And she did. But ten years later I bumped into her, and she told me that her husband had died and she had remarried – her gypsy boyfriend.' Ekavi raised an eyebrow.

'Kyria Maria hadn't seen that coming,' I said, taking a last sip of coffee.

'Oh no,' said Ekavi. 'Only God knows everything that is going to happen. But I could tell you a few things if you'd like.'

She shuffled out to the chicken coop and returned with a smile on her face and an egg in her pocket. 'This is yours,' she said, pulling it out. 'Five letters in Eleni, right?'

She filled a glass with tap water, then tapped the egg on the rim of the glass in four different spots, making the sign of the cross. Reserving the yolk, she dumped the egg white on to a plate, splashed her fingers in it five times, then poured the egg white into the glass. A ginger-ale-coloured layer settled at the bottom, then white stalagmites slowly rose through the water, some hitting the top of the liquid and turning to drip down into it again. An air bubble was trapped in the middle of the glass, shining like a silver ball. 'That's you,' she said, pointing to it. 'See, it's a full face.' I looked, but only saw an orb – this was trickier than a coffee cup. 'You recently passed through a serious worry,' Ekavi whispered. I nodded. 'You worry a lot,' she continued. 'But you shouldn't. Everything in life will open up before you. See those shoes on the floor?' she asked, pointing across the room. 'Let's say they seem out of place. Don't worry, just say, "Shoes, I am going to put you right where you belong!"'

She continued, making predictions about my family from the floating white swirls. But it was the shoe advice that stayed with me. Regardless of what fate had in store, it was up to me to put my angst in its proper place, under the bureau. I thanked her and strolled home, eager to tell Kaity about this new method of divination.

I dialled her number, but didn't recognize Kaity's voice at first, because she was sobbing. 'You heard?' she said, when I identified myself. I hadn't, and so she told me. Her favourite brother had died unexpectedly of an aneurysm, and in a few hours she would be driving across the country to attend his funeral.

'And the worst part is that it's such a shock,' she said. 'I had no warning.'

'You didn't have a dream, like with your parents?' I asked.

'No, nothing at all,' she whispered. 'It's the strangest thing.'

'There was nothing you could have done,' I said. 'Even if you'd been warned.'

'No,' she answered. 'It might have helped me, but it wouldn't have helped him; this was his fate. The end of our lives is written at the beginning of them.'

'Do you really think so?' I asked.

'Oh, I know it's all pre-destined, because when I was fourteen my mother read my coffee cup and told me that I'd have three children and take many trips abroad,' Kaity said. 'How could she have known that then if it wasn't already programmed for me?'

'I guess you're right,' I answered. It seemed to comfort her to know that her brother's death was meant to be, even if it was a tragic event.

'No one really knows their fate,' she continued. 'None of us knows when we'll die. All we can do is make sure we spend time with people we love while we're alive.'

I offered my condolences and hung up. Dina called to me and I stepped on to the verandah. She wanted to make sure I'd come for dinner; Vangeli would be there, too. She went inside, but I stayed, watching the swathes of pink that still stained the sky, long after the sun had disappeared behind the mountain. I was in a place I loved, and it kept handing me gifts and inheritances, from friends to fireplaces. People die and even video-tapes get erased, but memory persists, and the places in which we met and lived and loved remain. No matter where I went, Lia would always be here, a place to which I could return, as it had been all along, even before I realized it. It must have been pre-destined.

10

THE STONE POMEGRANATE

«Σπίτι μου, σπιτάκι μου, φτωχοκαλυβάκι μου.»
'My house, my little home, my poor little shack.'

20 November

I'm staring at the loveliest toilet bowl in the world. It's smaller than the average bowl in circumference — a little squat, but in a cute, 'I'm a little teapot, short and stout' kind of way. It's not a working toilet yet; it's currently lying on its side on the flagstone floor of the plistario. But the plumber has just arrived to install it, and other chic little fixtures, in the tiny bathroom we added on to the back of the Gatzoyiannis house. Since a bathroom didn't exist in the original house, we're keeping the new one small — only five feet, four inches square. It will be basic but beautiful, with a corner shower set apart by two clear doors, a white porcelain sink, and, of course, this lovely toilet.

'It's the wrong toilet,' a voice behind me announces. I

turn to see the plumber, who removes his cigarette from his mouth, the better to shake his head grimly.

'What do you mean?' I demand. 'The guy at the store said that Ideal Standard is the best, and he just drove all this stuff up the mountain.'

'The toilet itself is fine,' the plumber responds, taking another puff. 'It just doesn't work with the pipes I laid. This toilet has a receptacle for a wall pipe. In that little room, we've got a floor pipe. You should have consulted with me on the fixtures.'

What I should have done is realized that, like all the other steps of construction, the bathroom was going to be a huge migraine. I look around. Yanni is gone, finished with the stonework, and Thomas is off hunting. We are down to a skeleton crew of Vlad and Xalime. I have to handle this myself, and I refuse to panic in front of the plumber.

'I don't know the first thing about construction,' I sigh. 'What do you suggest?'

The plumber smiles. 'Well, I have to go to Ioannina next Monday to pick up supplies. I could get the right version of this toilet, and install the bathroom after that.'

'Perfect!' I actually clap my hands, in an effort to massage the artist's ego. 'I'm so lucky to have an expert like you on the job! Thank you so much!'

I think the plumber is blushing, but with his beard, it's hard to tell. 'May you be well,' he says as he walks to his pick-up truck, stubbing his cigarette out on the road.

High on Thitsa Kanta's extensive list of reasons why Greece is inferior to America was her complaint that 'No one in Greece says "Have a nice day!"' It's true that shopgirls often acted as if I was dragging them away from their real job of non-stop gossiping in order to force them to sell me something, but other Greeks I'd met more than made up for the missing 'Have a nice day' with continuous blessings. Instead of 'You're welcome,' people respond to 'thank you' with 'May you be well.' On the first of every month, people wish, 'Have a good month!' And when I set off for a trip, everyone would say, 'God be with you.' If I actually did anyone a favour – say, gave them photos I had taken or bought them a coffee – then a shower of blessings would rain on me, along the lines of 'May you live happily for a thousand years, as strong as the tall mountains, and with a good husband.' Aware that fate is tempted by the request for so much luck, I'd respond, 'Good health and joy for all of us,' so that the blesser would rein in her expectations and say, 'Yes, health is everything. Let us be healthy.' Now I worried about returning to New York. With no one to bless me there, was I less likely to have health, luck, love and a thousand years of happy life? Because I would much rather have all that than a nice day.

In the meantime, I had my more immediate future to worry about. My parents were arriving in two days to spend Thanksgiving with me, and to celebrate the expected completion of the house on my father's name-day, St Nicholas's Day, on 6 December. I had invited everyone in town months ago, eager to return their hospitality and sure that by December the project would be completed. But now, just a few weeks before D-Day, there was no bathroom, and the electricity had not been activated. The carpenter was supposed to have come today to start installing the floors, doors and windows, but Vlad had been working alone, buffing the grout between the flagstones on the kitchen floor. I was upset about the setbacks. But I was also grateful for the distraction. If I had too much time to sit around thinking about leaving Lia, I would just get depressed. Tomorrow I would harass the carpenter, hassle the electrician, and start packing up a year's worth of clothes and books. But right now, I decided, I would take a walk through my village. The last walk I could take alone, without tourists like my parents hanging around.

It was the kind of clear, sharp day that makes early winter beautiful, when the hint of frost is presented as a cool, silver glow, illuminating everything. I decided to dress up for the occasion, changing out of my jeans into a black shirtdress and paisley shawl. Shutting the gate to the Haidis house, I looked up at the walnut tree, ready to cover my head if irate squirrels started lobbing nuts my way, their second-favourite pastime after walnut-bowling tournaments in my roof. But they were busy in the upper branches, so I stood under the tree, where my grandmother was working in her father's garden when my grandfather walked by and saw her for the first time, her hair shining in the sun. My grandfather had once told me that walnut trees can steal your brain and turn it into a walnut; he had a brother who slept under one and went crazy. But that afternoon, when he first saw Eleni Haidis, he didn't even notice the tree, and in that glance was the beginning of my family.

A car zoomed down the asphalted path. It was Vangeli Panagiotou, the only man who ever dared drive off the road and down the steep incline.

'Eleni, how come you're dressed like a *vavvo*?' he asked.

I looked at my chic ensemble – black dress, large shawl – and realized I was the height of Lia widow fashion. 'Oh, you know, it's cold,' I mumbled. 'And I'm going for a walk.'

'Well, I came by to give you a present,' he announced. He opened the trunk and pulled out a faded blue wooden cradle with pink roses painted on its round headboard.

'It's a *sarmanitsa*!' he beamed. 'See these holes on the side? Women used to pull swaddling cloth through those and tie the *sarmanitsa* to their backs. Then when they got home, they could put it on the ground and rock the baby. We were all rocked in these things – me, your father. You can't get them any more.'

'Thank you!' I said. 'It's amazing! Where did you find it?'

'Oh, I stole it,' Vangeli smiled, carrying the *sarmanitsa* to the verandah. I thought he was joking, but I couldn't tell.

'Well, at least you didn't steal the baby along with it,' I remarked.

'Don't worry about how I got it,' he insisted. 'It's a going-away present.'

'But I'm not leaving for three weeks!' I protested.

'I know, but I'm leaving tomorrow,' Vangeli replied. 'It's the Christmas season, and I have to help my son with the store in Athens.'

'Do you have to go so soon?' I cried. Vangelis's dramatic stories had us laughing so hard every night that we could barely manage to eat Dina's delicious dinners.

'It's not soon,' Vangeli responded. 'All the summer people are gone already, and most other folks will leave before Christmas, to spend the holidays with their kids. Soon only Dina, Andreas and a few others will be left.'

I thought I was doing a good job of disguising how much this thought depressed me. But I'd forgotten about Vangelis's degree in psychology from the University of the Street. 'Don't be so sad,' he consoled me. 'We'll all be back in a few months. Give me a hug goodbye.'

I trudged up the path. I was sad to lose my eloquent dinner companion, but I also worried about Vangeli, who had once confided that since his wife died, he couldn't fall asleep if he hadn't had enough to drink. How would he fare without our company? And if one goodbye depressed me this much, how could I handle three weeks of farewells? At least Vangeli would return in a few months. I didn't know when I'd be back, and I worried that the people I now loved would forget I had ever lived in Lia.

I forced myself to try to remember the things I hated about living in Greece. Having to run through the rain in my pyjamas at eight a.m. to move my car for a honking bus to pass. Visiting the IKA office in Filiates every month to pay social security for the workers. And that certain breed of young man I'd bump into in Ioannina, known as a *Mangas*, a Blowhard, who wears his anti-Americanism as proudly as his Armani manbag.

I tried to drum up righteous indignation that would make me glad to leave, but I softened when I passed a cluster of lacelike spider webs, wet with dew, framing the bushes like embroidered collars. And I had to laugh at the House Divided Against Itself, whose roof was split in half – one side was orange tile, the other grey slate – because the brothers who inherited it can't agree on anything, not even repairs to the ancestral home they seldom visit.

By the time I made it to the *kafenion*, I needed a drink. I ordered retsina and looked at the grim faces of the men, and the happier expression of Laokratia. Costa was busy doing his second-grade homework, filling a regulation blue notebook with neat facsimiles of the letter Π that his teacher had drawn at the top.

'Why's everyone so glum?' I asked Costa, after checking his penmanship.

'This morning the pretty doctor said it was her last week,' Costa reported. 'We get a new man doctor now.'

Even the doctor was abandoning Lia. An era was coming to an end. My neighbours seemed to like me, as they did the female doctor, and to appreciate our young, blond non-local presence. But as I prepared to leave, I began to wonder if I had really become part of the village, or if I was just another occupier, more welcome than the Germans, of course, but no less foreign.

I drove to Ioannina to pick up two more outsiders, NickGage and Joanie. They were tired, so I suggested we stay in the city overnight. But I had a hidden agenda.

'Tomorrow, on the way home, we can stop at the supermarket and stock up for Thanksgiving,' I said over dessert in a tiny old *kafenion* inside Ioannina's *kastro*.

'We don't need that much stuff,' Joanie responded. 'There's only three of us.'

'Actually,' I said, attempting a winning smile, 'I've invited a few friends to join us.'

'How many?' my father asked.

I did a mental count. 'Oh, eleven.'

'Eleven!' Joanie screeched, causing the owner behind the bar and two weathered blondes at the next table to snap their heads towards us. 'But your father only smuggled in one package of cranberries! And I can't cook for expert chefs like Dina!'

'No one is going to judge the food!' I insisted, at a slightly lower decibel. 'These people fed me all year; I think we can prepare one little meal for them.'

'What do you mean, "we"?' Joanie sneered. 'How many turkeys have you roasted?'

'Greeks don't like turkey anyway,' my father added. 'Or sweet sauces with meat – they have really specific ideas about food. Remember the ice-cream store?'

That summer NickGage had been outraged when he'd tried to order plain ice cream – no sauces, whipped cream or nuts – from a waiter who clearly felt that ice cream cries out for embellishment the way village ladies feel flat surfaces beg for a doily.

'There won't be any ice cream at Thanksgiving,' I promised. 'Everyone will love it. We could serve these people peanut-butter-and-jelly sandwiches and say, "This is our tradition," and they'd all tell us how delicious it was. You forget how friendly people are here. Whenever I travelled, strangers would stop me to say, "Are you visiting? Come to our village next – just go to the main square and ask for Lambros; you can stay with us."'

'You never took them up on that offer, did you?' my father demanded.

Joanie was still stuck in her own personal hell, muttering, 'Fourteen people . . .'

The bartender, feeling my pain, slipped out from behind his wooden cage and walked over to us. 'I'm sorry, I couldn't help but listen – it's a small café,' he said in his excellent university English. 'Your daughter is right; villagers tend to be very friendly. Perhaps you haven't been to Epiros before.'

I laughed; this was the wrong thing to say to NickGage, Son of Epiros, who liked to refer to himself as 'the Fred Astaire of the Balkans'. My father opened his mouth, but before he could educate the waiter as to his heritage, one of the middle-aged blondes at the next table leaned over. 'I'm Danish, but I live in Parga and lead Danish tour groups around Epiros – it's such an interesting cultural area, this, especially for foreigners.'

'I'm not a for—' NickGage sputtered, but was cut off by the other woman.

'Most Danes just go to the islands,' she said. 'But for me, Epiros is Greece.'

'I was just explaining that to my parents, but they're tired after their trip, so we have to go,' I insisted, hoping to get out of there before NickGage began a lecture on the pre-Christian history of Epiros, which the Danish lady might find helpful for her tours.

But it was true; so much of what made Greece unique existed in our obscure province. On her last visit, I had taken Joanie to the Ambracian Gulf, the largest wetlands in Europe. At a state-of-the-art wildlife centre we'd watched live video footage of silver pelicans and herons frolicking on one of the twenty-two coastal lagoons while tiny, tubelike cameras spied on them. Driving along the coast, Joanie had chatted with a little boy watching his father spearing an eel with a trident, while I'd ducked into a chapel covered in frescoes which used the Byzantine cobalt that modern paints seem unable to equal. 'That's what's so amazing,' I'd told my parents. 'You can be in a seaside chapel where monks still draw water from the well out front, and ten minutes later, spy on pelicans using the latest technology.'

'So where are we going on this visit?' Joanie chirped.

'Well, nowhere,' I answered, flustered. 'I've only got two and a half weeks left in the village. Not only do we have Thanksgiving, but then there's the nameday.'

'The nameday!' NickGage yelled. 'We're having two parties?'

'It's the least we can do!' I insisted.

'I certainly didn't expect to spend this whole trip

cooking,' Joanie huffed. 'I'm not making Thanksgiving unless you take me on at least one field trip.'

I summoned the negotiating skills I had honed over ten months of haggling with the workers on the house. 'How about a day trip to someplace really good?'

'It's a deal,' Joanie agreed as we unloaded their luggage from the car.

'I can't believe you had me smuggle cranberries,' NickGage said, lifting his bag.

The next morning, back in Lia, we unpacked the groceries as Scrappy trampled us to see what was in our bags. I then suggested we drive to the house to check on the carpenter.

'I can't leave – Thanksgiving is in two days!' Joanie cried. She boiled potatoes to mash as I drove my father up the mountain. I was eager to produce NickGage because, after watching construction stagnate, I had been forced to admit something: the workers thought of me as a nice girl who really cared about the house, but they never forgot that NickGage was actually paying for the production. NickGage was a man and he had been born here, so they were more inclined to listen to him anyway. Now that he was in town, I expected the house to be finished at lightning speed. The crew was probably working away right now.

But when we arrived, the house looked deserted. I panicked silently. Then I heard the hollow thwack of a hammer hitting wood. 'The carpenter's here!' I cheered. 'Let's go.' My father marvelled at the roof, the stone-covered columns, the flagstone verandah and, when we went inside, the 1922 fireplace. A lot had been done since his last visit; I just hadn't realized it, because I'd watched, like a parent, as the house grew inch by inch, while he, visiting it months apart, was shocked at how much it had matured. In the 1914 room, as I now called the *mageirio* with Yia-yia Nitsa's dated fireplace stone, a bald man dressed entirely in camouflage stopped hammering and grinned, revealing a few missing teeth. He had set up frames of four by fours on the concrete and was nailing narrow planks together on top to form smooth wooden floors. 'These look great,' I said.

'But what about the doors and windows?' NickGage demanded, slipping comfortably into his Bad Cop role. 'I thought the carpenter said he'd install them today.'

'He's coming tomorrow,' the floor man assured us. 'He was delayed on another job, but just for a day.'

With things in order at the house, I drove my father to the *kafenion* so he could catch up with old friends and give Foti the jeans, Tylenol and stack of social security cheques Thitsa Kanta had sent him. I joined Costa by the potbellied stove and admired the stars his teacher had drawn on the page of perfect Πs.

'What's new?' I asked.

'At the Xenona Fanis and Nikki are treating everyone to sweets because they have a new grandson,' he reported. 'You can hear music coming from there every night – Christmas songs. Even the Chipmunks.'

'The Chipmunks?' I asked. 'Singing in Greek?'

'Of course.' Costa eyed me suspiciously. 'That's what they speak.'

Over dinner at the Xenona, I explained to Nikki and Fanis that this Thursday was Thanksgiving, an annual American holiday commemorating how the settlers gave thanks to God for surviving their first year in the new land, and invited the Indians to join them in a feast. 'I love traditional customs like that!' Nikki exclaimed, as if I'd just described a tradition as bizarre and ancient as sacrificing a rooster to bury its severed head in your new home. But I realized that both rituals involve killing poultry for the greater good, so I just continued my pitch. 'We'd like to have the ceremonial dinner here at the inn, with you as guests. Our house isn't big enough to hold everyone, so we want to use this dining room. If you provide wine and salad, we'll bring the food, including two turkeys.'

'You have turkeys in America?' Nikki asked.

'Turkeys are a Thanksgiving symbol,' I explained. 'They're native to America.'

'I thought they were French,' Fanis said. 'We call them *gallopoules*, French birds, because they go "glou, glou, glou", which sounds like French people talking.'

The man had a point. 'In America, turkeys say "gobble, gobble",' I informed him. Fanis and Nikki laughed uproariously at this ridiculous idea.

I soon realized that I had misinformed everyone about the true meaning of Thanksgiving. I'd told them it was about pilgrims, Indians and turkey, but it seemed really to be all about Joanie, who was still convinced no one would like her food. At least she was trying to get into the Thanksgiving spirit. NickGage had turned into a conscientious objector, chiming in with phrases like, 'Greeks don't eat boiled green beans!' as we rushed around the kitchen. I knew he was more excited about the house than the holiday, so I tried to be understanding. Then he went too far. We had forgotten to buy ready-made pastry for the pumpkin pie, so Joanie needed a recipe to make it from scratch. 'Don't worry,' I called to the kitchen. 'I'll email Mrs Kalber – she taught home economics.'

My father looked up from his book. 'No one's going to eat pumpkin pie; these people have never even heard of pumpkin pie. Why go to all this trouble to make it?'

'Because, NickGage, Thanksgiving without pumpkin pie is un-American,' I shouted, leaping up out of the taverna chair I had set in front of the first computer in the Mourgana mountains. 'This is going to be a traditional Thanksgiving and you can love it or leave it, mister!' He lay low for the rest of the afternoon.

Eventually I forgave my father for his culinary critique and drove him up to the Gatzoyiannis house. The carpenter had come and gone, installing a wooden front door with a wrought-iron handle, and small wooden shutters in the basement. On the verandah lay the other shutters, unfinished wood with diamond-shaped peep-holes covered by sliding wooden diamonds. Resting there, the shutters seemed to have magical powers; they were the ingredient that would transform the house into a cosy home.

Thanksgiving dawned bright and sunny. Up in Perivoli, the Dick Clark-like carpenter, his two handsome sons and his dentally challenged employee were installing windows, doors and three built-in cabinets in the walls, just like those in the original house. Even the plumber had arrived – three days ahead of schedule – bearing the platonic Ideal Standard of a toilet. He had gone to Ioannina early and decided to drive up today, since it was such nice weather. I knew it was a Thanksgiving miracle, but I kept this to myself; I wasn't about to explain about the turkey all over again.

At the Xenona, Joanie and I helped Nikki push enough tables together to seat fourteen. Joanie created a centrepiece starring a pineapple surrounded by a chorus of plums, grapes, apples and pears, and I set the table, using paper napkins which showed a cornucopia pouring out Thanksgiving treats, including a cooked bird. 'So it really is all about the turkey,' Nikki muttered as she passed by.

At eight p.m. people started trickling in, dressed in their best – after all, it was the first Thanksgiving for everyone except Foti, who had spent years in the US. On his first November in America, when Thitsa Kanta had told him she was going to roast a 'Turko' instead of a 'French bird', he'd thought she planned on doing something nasty to a Turk. 'I wouldn't put it past her,' he laughed.

Finally Dina and Andreas arrived bearing a second turkey, which Dina had prepared her own way, in traditional Greek style, with pepper and lemon juice, and had cooked until its skin was blackened. 'Mine looks more tender!' Dina trilled when she saw our pale bird. Joanie was right; these were competitive chefs! 'Who made these?' Dina asked, fondling a warm brown 'n' serve Pillsbury roll.

'I did,' I jumped in, not wanting to let on that half of the meal, from Uncle Ben's wild rice to the biscuits, came out of a box. An imported box, but a box nonetheless.

'Did you hear, Atheena?' Dina beamed. 'Eleni made these with her little hands!'

Just as I was about to confess, my father tapped on his glass, and we took our seats. 'Thanksgiving is about giving thanks, being grateful that God has blessed you with such good friends,' he began. 'Which is why we're so glad you're here to celebrate with us. These are the same dishes the settlers in America shared with the Indians. The Indians taught them how to cook the local turkeys; to turn cranberries into a sweet sauce for the meat; and to harvest wild rice, which grows along riverbanks. Even today only Indians harvest it, in canoes along the river.'

Was NickGage for real? I thought Uncle Ben, in his infinite wisdom, had invented wild rice. But our guests were eating this stuff up – literally.

'The black rice is delicious!' Athena said, passing it to her husband, Spiro.

'But I don't like the cranberry sauce with the turkey,' Dina announced as an evil grin of triumph spread across my father's face. 'It's so tasty, I'm eating it on its own!'

'Everything on this table has such meaning behind it,' Antonis Makos whispered.

I wanted to tell them that every meal they had served me had just as much meaning, was the product of as many years of history and had been cooked with as much care as my carved-orange-rind sauce baskets and Joanie's home-economics-approved piecrust. But I didn't, because I felt it was better if they realized themselves that sharing your customs, food and lives is what Thanksgiving is about. Because nobody's really in it for the lima beans.

Sure, there were a few glitches: Dina kept telling people on our side of the table that there was 'spicy turkey' down at the other end, because 'They don't cook theirs like we do.' And I still felt guilty about stealing the Pillsbury Dough Boy's intellectual property. But over all it was a resounding success, judging by the reactions of our guests, who pocketed their placecards and napkins as souvenirs. I knew the napkins with overflowing cornucopias would appeal to them. Atheena had told me that when she was starving in Hungary, a friend of hers had found an unattended orchard and stolen as many cherries as she could stuff into her bag. 'She dumped them into a tin basin until it overflowed. It was so beautiful,' Athena recalled. 'Since then, I've always liked large displays of fruit.' But more than the abundance of Thanksgiving food, our guests seemed to enjoy the wealth of lore – the noble Indians canoeing up-river, searching for black rice; the noble Joanie, standing at Dina's food processor to make potato soufflé. The event was exotic to them and familiar to us, a photo negative of my experience all year.

Two days later, we were invited to lunch at Athena and Spiro's house. As I sat under a family portrait, Athena pointed out her great-grandfather, an imposing, seated man in baggy Cretan breeches, and her mother, a slim, serious young woman in a long embroidered tunic.

'Do you have any other old photos?' I asked.

Athena brought out boxes of pictures, including an army photo of picnicking young soldiers, one of whom was a young, handsome Vangeli Panagiotou.

'Where's this?' Joanie asked, handing Spiro a photo of a ceiling fresco of Jesus with outstretched arms.

'Oh, that's Makrialexi, the monastery two villages over,' he explained. 'A monk lived there until the war, but now it's deserted.'

'But the monastery is beautiful,' Athena insisted. 'And old, from 1004.'

'We have to go!' Joanie exclaimed. 'That can be my field trip.'

'You'll have to get someone with a four-wheel drive to take you,' Spiro advised. 'The road doesn't go all the way there. And bring a flashlight; there's no electricity.'

A few days later, NickGage went to Athens for some meetings, and Joanie and I showed up at Foti's, where one of his hunting buddies, swathed in a symphony of camouflage, waited along with his jeep. The truck was tiny and filled with guns and ammunition, but Joanie jumped eagerly into the front seat, I sat on her lap for the first time in decades, and Foti perched on a stool in the back, next to a long-barrelled rifle. From my high vantage point it seemed as if we were veering dangerously close to the edge of a dirt road, which also happened to be the edge of a cliff. Soon the road, such as it was, disappeared, and we careened over rocks and through shallow rivers. As one rock sent us flying, Joanie screamed and the hunters giggled nervously.

'Just don't look,' I hissed at Joanie, who responded, 'Is it too late to turn back?'

'You wanted adventure, and now you've got it,' I grunted.

But when we got stuck in a muddy rut, I started to think Joanie had a point. The driver got out, adjusted the tyres, and soon the jeep jerked out of the valley of mud and veered straight to the edge of the road. I yelped, making Foti laugh even harder.

'What's wrong?' he asked.

'I fear death,' I answered.

Finally we pulled into a grassy square shaded by willows. Inside a stone wall stood Makrialexi, all ruddy Byzantine brick, dominated by a round bell tower. Above the door loomed a faded, scratched icon of the Mother and Child — the monastery was dedicated to the Panagia, but called Makrialexi after the first monk who lived there, a tall man named Alex. Inside, all the way up to the vast dome above, Foti's flashlight illuminated familiar saints and fantastic animals: dragons, griffins, all the signs of the zodiac. Four circular columns had supported the dome for almost a thousand years, but the saints' yellow haloes remained as bright as egg yolks. A window high in the wall was broken, letting rain drizzle in, but the building where the monks' cells once stood had recently been renovated.

'Vangeli and his brothers spent the night here during the war,' Foti said.

'Really?' I asked. 'Why?'

'When the Communist army took the kids away from Lia, they walked them over here, set up camp, and stayed two nights before crossing the border into Albania,' he explained. 'Now Albanians crossing the border illegally hide out here at night.'

I walked into the two recently whitewashed cells. In one room, a nameless guest had left the remains of a fire in the hearth. I looked out of the window, and there, on the sill, was another souvenir – a burgundy plastic booklet embossed with 'Letternjoftim'. It was clearly an Albanian passport, but the name sounded like 'Letters of Transit', or something equally *Casablanca* to me. It had been issued in 1992 and last stamped in 1996, so it was probably useless. 'Do you think someone's going to come back for this?' I asked Foti. He laughed, which I took to mean no, so I slipped it into my pocket as an illicit keepsake, feeling very Ilsa Lund.

When we made it back to Lia, we visited the Gatzoyiannis house. The bathroom was installed and shutters rested in the windows. Vlad was overseeing the carpenter's son install the final door.

'Look what I found,' I said, handing him my souvenir.

'Forgery,' he announced, flipping through the pages. 'To make Northern Epirote, not Albanian, for visa and work papers. Somebody pay much for this.'

'But it's old!' I insisted, suffused with guilt that I might be putting a fellow immigrant to Epiros at risk. 'Do they still need it?'

Vlad peered at the badly pasted-in photo of so-called 'Niko Graboka', born 1956. 'I know this man,' he said. 'He works in Keramnitsa.'

'Does Niko want this back?' I pressed Vlad, imagining life-and-death scenarios that depended on this forged passport. But he just laughed. He had more important things on his mind. 'Dorina and fiancé want move to New York,' he said, putting his hand on my shoulder. 'You find them jobs when you go back,' he instructed me.

'That's really hard to do,' I warned him. 'I can't just forge papers for them.'

As Joanie and I walked down to the Haidis house, she advised, 'You'd better help out Vlad. What if he tells that guy you have his passport, and he hunts you down?'

'You're right!' I joked. 'When we get home, border guards might be there to tell us that elderly Eleni Gatzoyiannis was found dead, murdered in a fatal case of mistaken identity, a note pinned to her tattered cardigan reading, "Where are my letters of transit?"'

I felt like the star of a film noir. But when we arrived at the Haidis house, the only suspicious-looking character lying in wait for us was Scrappy, who had been moping around for days and was now whimpering in front of our gate. I worried that the turkey leftovers had done him in, but on closer inspection I saw that he was missing half a toe; a ring of red flesh circled the lower half of his claw. 'That looks infected,' I said to Joanie. 'We can't leave him here to die on the doorstep.'

We stared at each other for a moment before agreeing to follow the course we always chose in times of crisis, such as power outages or locking ourselves out: call on Dina and Andreas.

Armed with rubber gloves, sterile wipes and

Bacitracin from our First Aid kit, Dina swabbed Scrappy's toe as Andreas held and petted him, and Joanie and I looked on helplessly. 'Don't worry, we're not going to hurt you,' Andreas cooed. 'That's a good dog.' After the procedure, Scrappy limped off to his left-overs, much improved already.

'It's good that they bonded,' Joanie mused as Dina and Andreas returned home. 'Now they can look after Scrappy and he can look after them once you're gone.'

These people had been looking after me all year. Now they would have each other and I would be back in New York, without Dina's advice, Andreas's tender heart and Scrappy's leaping enthusiasm. When I thought about leaving, I felt a knot of controlled panic. So I concentrated on my to-do list: packing, checking on the house and, of course, getting ready for the nameday/house-warming party.

The next day, en route to Ioannina, Joanie and I stopped in Leptokaria to see the electrician. 'You're all set,' he said, handing me a receipt and some forms. 'You just need to get this signed by the contractor, that signed by the plumber and workers, have them all stamped in Filiates by the IKA office, and then in Ioannina by the prefect who gave you the building permit.'

'Is that all?' I joked lamely.

'Well, once that's all done, then you drop it off at the Electric Company in Igoumenitsa, and when they've approved it all, they come and power up the house.'

I looked at the electrician. 'There's no way I'll be able to get that all done in the next two days, before my father's nameday, is there?'

He laughed so hard that I could see the pointy tips of his canines. 'Not a chance.'

'But then I leave for America,' I sighed.

'I could take care of this for you, for a small fee,' he said. 'If you leave it with me, the electricity will be working by spring. You will be coming back then, won't you?'

'Of course I will,' I said, deciding that the house-warming/nameday party would be even lovelier in the glow of candlelight. I left the papers in his hands and continued on to Ioannina, where Joanie and I picked up foil-wrapped chocolates, boxes of pastries, and the main ingredient for the nameday party: the celebrant. After getting NickGage at the airport, we had one more stop, a frame shop with a small sign that read 'Icon Factory'.

'I need to see the iconographer,' I told a tall redhead about my age.

'That's me,' she answered, pointing to an icon on an easel of St Philip.

'We'd like to order an icon of Prophet Elias ascending to heaven, for a chapel,' I explained to the foxy iconographer. 'The saint saved his life.' I pointed to NickGage.

'Then you definitely need to offer an icon in gratitude,' she agreed.

After we'd paid our deposit, NickGage turned to me. 'How did you know we should offer an icon?'

'It's common knowledge. You have to be thankful for your blessings,' I replied, as we drove away from Ioannina towards Lia for the last time that year. I kept imbuing every event with significance: my last church service at Agios Demetrios, final chance to watch the news at the *kafenion*, ultimate sighting of a wild-boar carcass tied to the back of a truck. But on this last drive, Joanie drowned out my sighs with her more powerful whining. 'What if we got the wrong liqueurs?' she moaned. 'What if cognac is just for memorial services? I'm not a Greek, I can't be expected to know these things!'

'Take comfort in being a honky, Joanie!' I encouraged her. 'If someone says we're doing it wrong, just shrug and say, "What do we know – we're Americans!"'

All year I'd enjoyed the leeway afforded to guests who are forgiven for serving, wearing or doing the wrong thing. But this party was my debut as a home-owner in Lia, a fellow villager, and I was suddenly worried. The stakes were now higher for me, and I didn't want to blow it.

The next day was devoted to the one aspect of restor-ation I felt I could handle on my own: decorating. The house wasn't actually ready; there still was no electricity, no furniture, and the cement ceilings still had to be covered in wood. Although the toilet flushed, Thomas hadn't dug the septic tank, so it emptied out in the back yard. I knew the house wasn't perfect, but I still wanted it to be as pretty as possible. I scattered candles on the windowsills, in the glass-fronted cabinets and wall niches, arranged bottles of booze and platters of foil-wrapped sweets, then rested an elaborate icon of the Virgin Mary above the 1922 fireplace and set a table in front of it. Just before I locked the doors using my shiny, new gold keys, I placed my grandparents' wedding photo on the mantel, so that they could enjoy tomorrow's ceremony, the blessing of their new old home.

St Nicholas is the patron of unmarried girls, so he blessed me with clear weather for my housewarming and his nameday. While Joanie arranged orange and burgundy chrysanthemums from Dina's garden and pale-green hydrangeas from Athena's, NickGage and I heeded the church bells for the St Nicholas day's service. We were nearing the end when Stella ran in and whispered in Athina Ganas's ear. Athina and Grigoris were up from Athens for the weekend; his health was improving and the weather was good, so they had come to celebrate. But now Athina's face fell, and her smile crumpled into tears. I watched whispers pass in a chain throughout the church. Dina, standing next to me, called Stella over to learn the news.

'Aspasia Daflakis died of a heart attack in Athens last night,' Stella reported. 'Her daughter called. They're on their way here with the body; the funeral is tomorrow.' An image of the white-haired woman appeared in my mind; Aspasia used to walk past the Haidis house every evening in summer, taking the air with some of her girl-friends. I didn't know her well, although she had kissed and blessed me on several occasions.

'If her daughter calls again, tell her we're going to ring the death bell this afternoon, after the celebration at the house,' decreed our village president, Antonis Makos, who was passing round the offering basket. Tomorrow, another Liote would be buried behind the Panagia church. But today was for the resurrection of a house. Antonis had made an executive decision; sorrow could wait a few hours.

By the end of the service, the whispering had stopped, as had Atheena's tears. Having lived long, eventful lives, the villagers were used to this continuous cycle of end-ings and beginnings. 'Happy St Nicholas day and many years to all of you,' Father Prokopi announced. 'We're all invited to the home of our co-villager Nikos Gatzoyiannis up in Perivoli at eleven, with lunch at the Xenona to follow.'

As we streamed into the churchyard, people descended on me, wishing that I be overjoyed in my father on his nameday, and that I return next year with a husband – the villagers were clearly eager for more beginnings to celebrate. But I couldn't listen to people who had just remembered a nephew in Athens I must meet, or a godson in Thessaloniki. I had forgotten a key ingredient to the party's success: the oranges.

I left my father basking in blessings, and drove home to collect three oranges and the three blue-bordered handkerchiefs I'd bought in Ioannina. Up at the house, Thomas and Foti had already dropped off a four-foot-tall wooden cross. I knotted a twenty-Euro bill into each handkerchief, tied them on to the arms and top of the cross, and, after much struggling, secured the oranges to the cross with wire. Thomas climbed on the roof and rested the cross against the chimney. Months ago we'd buried a rooster head into the house. Now we were setting up the ritual that indicates a house is finished, when the cross is placed on the roof and the workers climb up to collect their handkerchiefs, oranges and accolades. The oranges glowed against the Greek blue of the sky, and the handkerchiefs blew in the wind. This ritual was definitely prettier than the decapitated rooster.

But what if the villagers were offended by the house's resurrection? I knew well that it had the power to bring sorrow as well as joy. I was re-creating a building that was new to me but remembered fearfully by my neighbours for the tortures and killings that had gone on there. What if their pain and anger returned when they entered the gate? In trying to do something good for me and my family, to change our feelings about the past, perhaps I was doing wrong to the villagers, digging up memories that they'd rather let lie.

A black-clad, white-haired old widow floated in, told me that she had many memories here, and touched my cheek, smiling through tears. Then she wandered off, crossing herself as she entered each room. Soon more villagers started filing in, many bearing gifts for the house – a decorative plate, a set of glasses, a bottle of Vassili Deppis's homemade *tsipouro*. 'It looks just like the old house,' Grigoris Ganas marvelled. 'I remember it from when I was a boy.'

Through the open front door I spotted Father Prokopi's long black frame striding towards us. He pushed through the crowd, arranged a bowl and censer on the table in front of the blue and white fireplace, and stood there facing east towards Jerusalem. 'Ready, Spiro?' he asked the cantor. 'The service should take an hour.'

'Are you trying to starve us?' Foti was indignant, his admirable gut growling.

But the priest would not be dissuaded. 'This is an important event – a nameday and a blessing for the house,' he insisted. 'I looked up chants in two different books!'

The table was set with three offering breads, an icon of the Panagia leaning against them, and a bunch of basil resting in a bowl of holy water, which Father Prokopi would soon sprinkle on the faithful. Fifty people were crowded into every corner of the room as Father Prokopi chanted, intoning the names of everyone who would live in the house. A sweet trail of incense rose in front of my grandparents' wedding photo. I had never met my grandmother, nor known my grandfather when he was young. But their faces seemed as familiar as those of the people I had come to love, who were now in this room, watching raptly as Father Prokopi turned a construction site into hallowed ground.

These people had seen me once a year for decades, watching as I grew up. Now that we had lived together for a year, I realized that I knew almost as much about them as they did about me. There was Grigoris, who had just finished chemotherapy but said the scariest experience of his life was when, as a boy, he'd walked past a priest who had been buried up to his neck by the invading guerrillas and left to die. And Athina, whom he'd courted in Hungary, where they'd lived next to each other in refugee council flats, both mourning the same lost home. They made it back home together, and were now standing next to Andreas and Dina, who had lost two sons in traffic accidents, and spent their lives nurturing other people, from a hungry American neighbour to a stray dog with a sore foot. Next to them was Foti, who had shown me both wild boars and unexpected waterfalls, and who had been so in love with Thio Angelo's sister when he was a young shepherd that, Thitsa Kanta told me, 'He almost killed his mule trying to get down from the flocks faster so he could see her.' Now his beloved was dead, their sons lived in America, and he had returned home to the village where he had once been a lovesick shepherd.

An elbow in my back knocked me out of my reverie. 'Go over to that corner too,' Athena whispered in my ear. 'So you can take a picture of us.' I scuttled across the room, cutting through a wafting cloud of incense, to photograph Athena and the other ladies and record their participation in this significant event. I stopped remembering stories of the villagers' past and noticed how absorbed they were in the present, how attentively everyone watched and prayed. It wasn't enough simply to attend the event; they wanted to be a part of the house's transformation, to see it in a new way.

Soon Father Prokopi dipped a silver cross into the Holy Water and offered it to me, Joanie and NickGage to kiss. 'May you live many years to enjoy the house,' he said. 'Have a safe trip, and may we meet again in health and happiness, soon.'

The cluster of celebrants broke into smaller groups, some heading into the 1914 room to try Vassili's *tsipouro*, others veering towards the sweets table, where Stella pocketed several gold-wrapped chocolates for Costa before kissing me and running back to the *kafenion*.

Looking at the photograph of my grandparents on the mantelpiece, I realized that the ceremony couldn't be over yet. I went up to Father Prokopi, who was sipping a glass of Vassili's homemade wine. 'Would you mind blessing the basement?' I asked.

'Not at all,' he smiled.

Father Prokopi, Joanie, NickGage and I walked through the crowd of well-wishers on the verandah and down to the small, dark basement, where thirty-one prisoners once huddled in fear. He began chanting, then dipped the basil into the Holy Water and flicked it around the dark room. A drop splashed my forehead, and relief washed over me. As I stood in this space, for the first time the constriction I felt in my chest when thinking of the basement failed to appear. I still shuddered at the thought of my grandmother's pain, but no longer felt it was trapped here within these walls.

Father Prokopi finished and stepped outside, now inspired to bless the bathroom, kitchen, even the mulberry tree, in a fit of overconscientious beatitude. Dina walked up behind me, her footsteps echoing on the flagstones. 'This is nice,' she said, indicating the basement, which was originally meant to stable the family's animals. 'You could use it as a room, too.'

I nodded, but knew I would never do that. I wasn't afraid any more, but because it was the last room my grandmother and so many others had lived in, it could never be a regular basement, a place to store suitcases and ironing boards. The house might be a home now, with fireplaces to lie in front of and cabinets that already had glasses in them, but the basement would remain a monument to those who had lived and died in it. It was here that I planned to display the treasures Vlad had unearthed, the physical artifacts of my grandmother's life — the rusted spoons and broken plates, the tools, mangled headboard and used hand grenade.

'Eleni — I'm about to climb up on the roof myself!' Foti yelled from the verandah. So I scrambled up and called everyone outside. Thomas, Vlad and Xalime climbed a ladder on to the roof of the *plistario*, then the men strode over to the cross resting against the chimney, and Xalime, in a smart navy trousersuit and heels, followed shakily. Thomas untied each kerchief and held it up as the crowd clapped and yelled 'Bravo!' and 'Long life to your hands, which created such a beautiful home!'

Once they'd descended back to the verandah, Spiridoula grabbed Thomas's arm and asked, 'Eleni, will you take a picture of us?' I agreed. 'And now one of the three of us,' she added, pulling Net into the photo. 'I'm going to baptize Net, you know, so now he's part of the family.' As I snapped photos of Thomas, Spiridoula and Net, a childless couple and their already beloved surrogate son, I asked the boy how school was.

'Good,' he answered.

'Great,' Thomas clarified. 'Next year Net is going into the vocational class, specializing in plumbing.'

'One day he can take over your business, Thomas,' I joked.

'That's the idea,' Thomas smiled. I felt proud to have employed Net and Thomas on their first joint job; the house had already brought one family closer together.

The Net shoot led to other photo requests: Athina and Grigoris wanted one, then Vlad and Xalime. All of Lia was ready for their close-up, and had been all year, ever since I'd passed out the photos I snapped at the *panegyri*. From toothless old crones to three-year-old toddlers, everyone wanted their Kodak moment. A stranger at a *panegyri* once asked me, pointing to a three-foot-tall kerchiefed lady, 'See that yia-yia? She raised me. Would you take her picture and send it to me?'

I had been shocked to find everyone so camera-ready. In New York, my unwrinkled young friends seldom let me photograph them. 'I hate being in pictures,' they'd whine, offended that I wanted to remember them as they were rather than as they looked in their minds, artfully made up and illuminated with flattering lighting. In Lia, everyone just wanted to be remembered.

Foti tugged on my arm. 'Here,' he said, handing me a small bundle. 'I had a guy in Babouri join these together.' I unwrapped the paper and saw two curved tusks from a wild boar, joined into a crescent by a filigreed silver band. 'It's to hang from the rear-view mirror in your car for good luck,' Foti said, blushing.

'In the car – no way! I'm going to wear this,' I said, stringing it on to my necklace. I felt instantly empowered by my barbaric-looking pendant.

Foti walked away laughing, as Ekavi, the old woman who had read my future in egg whites, pulled me aside conspiratorially. 'I don't know if you noticed,' she whispered, looking around to see if anyone could overhear us. 'But on Holy Thursday, while the priest read the Gospels, I was kneeling on the floor, praying and knitting. Then during the year, I cut up that piece of knitting and sew it into little bundles for good luck and divine protection.' She pressed something about the size of a piece of bubblegum into my hand. 'This is to bring you good luck – and a husband! Wear it in your bra.'

For now my pocket would have to do, because Vlad was tapping on my back. 'I bring you things from our yard in Albania that we find last month when we go to visit, see Dorina, and fix up house,' he said, handing me a blue plastic bag stuffed with dented tin cups, caved-in canteens, and the metal bases of lanterns – antiques which he had unearthed and lugged across the border into Greece for me. 'I know you like the old things.'

I thanked Vlad, promised I would take the artifacts to a tinker in Ioannina to have them shined so I could display them in the house, and hugged him, causing the bag of tin to rattle. He blushed and scurried towards Xalime as Athena walked over to me.

'I have something ancient,' she said. 'I don't know if you're interested in having it, but I wanted to give it to you.' She pulled out the long tunic I remembered seeing in her old family photograph. 'This was my mother's,' she said. It was a black wool sleeveless garment called a *sengouni*, heavily embroidered in scarlet and gold curlicues.

'I love it! But are you sure?' I asked, holding it up.

'Of course,' she replied. 'Who else but you would care about it?'

I hugged her and didn't speak. I loved the gift, but more than that I loved her reason for giving it to me – she knew I would appreciate it, and that this piece of her past would be treasured in the future.

'I'll hang it in the house as a decoration, when I'm not wearing it,' I finally said.

Spiridoula interrupted. 'I'm making something for the house, too,' she said. 'A crocheted wall-hanging like the ones I have in our home. It's a pair of swans; they stand for fidelity. I'd love to have something of mine up in your grandmother's house.'

Dina looked pained. 'Don't leave our neighbourhood to move here,' she pleaded.

I told her not to worry; I couldn't stay in the Gatzoyiannis house until it was furnished, anyway. Even then, I'd go back and forth between my grandparents' house and my great-grandparents', hiking from generation to generation. The important thing was that the house had risen from a pile of stones, and would always call me back to Lia — and it would be filled with the specially chosen gifts of the villagers, who didn't hold its tragic past against the house, but welcomed it as they had me, and wanted to embellish the interior with pieces of their own past.

Of course, Zervas had made the trip to see his architectural drawing realized in stone and wood. He approached me with tears in his eyes. 'It's even better than what I saw in my imagination,' he said, holding my hand. 'Your father must be so happy.' NickGage was almost too happy to speak — except to say that it was the first time he had celebrated his nameday in the village in fifty-four years. But when we arrived at the Xenona, I suspected that the villagers were happier than any of us.

First there was the amazing spread of food: Nikki and Fanis had set up a lavish buffet, complete with a whole roast piglet whose eyes they'd covered with orange slices to prevent him from seeing the lusty looks he inspired. There were the usual salads, pitas and rice, along with two platters of lamb. Within fifteen minutes the buffet was cleaned out by fifty Liotes who took two plates at once, in case the delicacies should have gone when they came back for seconds. Apparently, it is unwise to put a table groaning with food in front of people who survived a decade of starvation.

Most of all, the villagers seemed to enjoy celebrating a new beginning in a place where memorial services and funerals are all too common. This event was surprisingly free of the discussion that had taken place at every *panegyri* all summer: the Death of Lia dirge. An old person looks around and says, 'In the old days, the *panegyri* would draw a thousand people. Tonight there are only four hundred.' Sigh. 'Take a good look around, because when this generation dies, that will be the end of Lia.'

In 1945, Lia had 1,200 inhabitants, my neighbour Barba Prokopi had told me. Now it's 300 in summer and 50 in winter, with 600 Liotes in Athens and 3,000 the world over. But I had watched Thitsa Kanta and other Liotes engage in enough suffer-offs, where each maligns their own fate, trying to win the coveted position of most downtrodden, to suspect that the oldsters exaggerated the death of Lia in order to feel irreplaceable themselves. After all, sixty years ago Lia had plenty of people but no electricity, roads or toilets. Now it has an inn, streetlights and indoor plumbing; I'd say things are looking up. Over the next half-century, Lia will change, but maybe it will improve. Perhaps those three thousand people across the world will also return to restore their family's homes.

The next morning we went to Panagia church to say the one goodbye we knew would be final. Aspasia's husband, children, grandchildren and siblings stood behind her coffin, where she lay surrounded by so many bouquets that I could barely see the white top of her head. Father Prokopi led us in chanting to her everlasting memory, then held an icon of the Resurrected Christ for us to kiss as we circled the coffin, kissing the dead woman goodbye. When the service ended, Aspasia's husband stepped forward. 'I just want to thank all of you, my fellow villagers, for being so nice to Aspasia,' he said, then collapsed, weeping, into the arms of his children, who led him out of the church.

As we sat in the *kafenion* afterwards, I thought about what Aspasia's husband had said. It had been his wife's last chance to let everyone know how much she had enjoyed sharing her life with them.

Father Prokopi leaned over, interrupting my thoughts. 'Eleni,' he said, 'you'll come back for Easter, won't you? It's April 27th next year.' I nodded. 'I hope you'll stay until May 20th, the other day we celebrate St Nicholas, when we hike to the chapel near where your grandmother was killed. I'd like you to take a photo of me there, so that I can have one to remember it by.'

That night, at our final dinner at Dina's, Joanie told Dina how wonderful her meals always were. 'But it's company we want,' Dina answered, smiling sadly. 'You can't enjoy your food unless you have someone to share it with.'

'Now you're leaving,' Andreas sighed. 'And we got used to having you here.'

'Don't worry,' I promised. 'I'll be back at Easter to turn the spit for the lamb.'

The next morning, Joanie, NickGage and I frantically loaded the car. We still had so much to do: pay IKA in Filiates, then drive to Ioannina to bid farewell to George and Kaity, drop off the car and catch the plane to Athens, then to the US. I was grateful that my emotions were swallowed up by the chaos as we locked the house, left the key with Dina and Andreas and kissed them; that the sorrow of the goodbye was mitigated by millions of last-minute concerns.

As we packed up the car, a light snow began to fall, the dusty, powdered-sugar-like flakes that make you think you're inside a snow globe.

'Where are you going?' Joanie demanded as I set off, turning up the mountain.

'I want to see the house in the snow,' I answered.

I had a set of keys, so I unlocked the door. The house was still glowing, filled with the *kefi* – party spirit – of the people who had celebrated there a few days ago. I walked over to the fireplace, where the photo of my grandparents stared back at me. I had overseen the rebuilding of their house, and in return the house had stopped time for me, allowing me to live in a village full of grandparents, a place where people treated me like a beloved daughter. As I looked at the photo of my grandparents, who died oceans apart, I realized that every happy family is a tragedy, because it exists for a limited time only. Children grow up to form their own families, parents die, and the original family is lost for ever. Every family is a civilization and all of them decline too quickly. Immersing myself in the village allowed me to extend my family a little longer, and to expand its sphere to include many people who had been there at its beginning.

In Lia, people who didn't recognize me never asked, 'Who are you?' but 'Whose are you?' because they suspected they would know my family, and therefore understand why I was there. After almost a year here, I had begun to feel I belonged to Lia itself. I watched snow fall on my grandmother's mulberry tree and smiled, because although I was leaving, I knew I'd return. I had lambs to roast and photos to take. My card reader had been right, at least partly. I didn't need a bicultural husband to have the lucky fate she had predicted. I could live my own transatlantic life, between two happy homes.

After my ten months in Lia, I suspected that Persephone knew exactly what she was doing when she ate the seven seeds of the juicy red pomegranate. She hadn't asked to be sucked into the Underworld, but once fate had brought her to a kingdom she feared, maybe she began to feel that she belonged there. By consuming the seeds, Persephone ended up blessed with two homes and the ability to travel between two very different worlds. The pomegranate was the pawn, the excuse she created so that she would always have to return.

I discovered Persephone's secret because fate had given me a second home, too, a place that I once saw as a sinister, dark side of my personal history, but that I had come to love and found myself unwilling to leave for long. This house which I had rebuilt was a stone pomegranate, my reason to keep returning.

APPENDIX: RECIPES

Spiridoula's Winey Rooster

As a contractor, Thomas may do the heavy lifting in the family, but I have to hand it to Spiridoula for turning a skinny old fowl into a nutritious, delicious, celebratory meal. This dish is worth eating even if you haven't watched the rooster being beheaded yourself (although that certainly added to my enjoyment of it).

One rooster, plucked, cleaned and cut into pieces
One large onion, finely chopped
Oil
Butter
Salt to taste
Pepper to taste
One glass red wine
½ can diced tomatoes or 2 large tomatoes, finely chopped
Water

Stirring continuously, sauté rooster and onion in oil, butter, salt and pepper, until onion is softened and rooster is browned. Now throw in the red wine and turn down the heat to simmer. Add a can of diced tomatoes or fresh, chopped tomatoes, whichever you have handy – Spiridoula does not judge. Add enough water so that the rooster is covered, and simmer over a low flame until most of the water is absorbed by the rooster, with just a little rooster juice remaining.

Serve over macaroni and you'll find that the occasional rooster sacrifice is good for the body and the soul.

Marcia's Kosher-for-Passover Spanakopita

Romaniote Jews traditionally prepare this dish for the Pessach holiday, but it's delicious at any time of the year. Spinach and matzah – two great tastes that taste great together. Who knew?

Well, I'll tell you who knew. Marcia Ikonomopoulos, the president of the Association for Friends of Greek Jewry. Along with Isaac, she led the tour group I spent time with in Ioannina. Marcia gave me this recipe and very kindly allowed me to reproduce it. Thanks for sharing, Marcia!

3 lbs fresh spinach
½ lb fresh dill
4 onions
4 fl oz olive oil
3 lbs matzah meal
15 eggs

Juice of 2 lemons
Salt and pepper
Additional matzah broken into small pieces

Preheat oven to 350 degrees Fahrenheit. Chop onions. Clean spinach and dill well and chop very fine. Heat oil in heavy frying pan. Fry onions until soft, then add spinach mixture and stir until wilted and well mixed with the onions. Stir in matzah meal. Add salt and pepper to taste. Remove from heat and put in large bowl. Beat eggs with lemon juice and add to spinach. Stir in well. Oil bottom of large baking dish (10 × 14 inches). Line bottom with broken matzah pieces and sprinkle with oil. Pour in spinach-egg mixture. Bake for 45 minutes until brown on top. Serves 6–8.

Mmm-mmm, matzahlicious!

Kollyva in Memory of Dina and Andreas's Sons

I hope you never have to make kollyva, *because it is served by people who are hosting a funeral or memorial service. But if the time comes, here's what you need to know: the wheat berries symbolize the resurrection of the soul. With all the advice about reaping what you've sown, wheat is a common image in the Bible. But it has symbolized resurrection since pre-Christian times, as Demeter would only let the wheat grow in the spring, once Persephone had re-emerged from the Underworld. Similarly, the pomegranate seeds represent Persephone's time spent in the Underworld, and therefore life after death.*

All the other trimmings are there to make the kollyva sweet and encourage people to eat it, as accepting the treat indicates that you've forgiven the dead for any trespasses he may have committed against you in life. I wish I could give you a recipe for garnering forgiveness while you're still alive, but I'm still looking for that one.

At the service, you and/or several sympathetic ladies should spoon the kollyva into a cup and pass it out along with plastic spoons. When Dina made kollyva for the one-year memorial service of Andreas's son, this recipe easily served forty Liotes.

If you're on the receiving end of kollyva, and it's handed out by a family member of the deceased, say, 'Long life to you,' or 'May you live to remember him.'

2 lbs boiled wheat berries
8 oz sliced almonds
8 oz chopped walnuts
8 oz raisins
8 oz sultanas
8 oz sugar
8 oz finely chopped parsley
8 oz pomegranate seeds
1 lb toasted breadcrumbs
2 lbs icing sugar
White or silver Jordan almonds, and assorted spun-sugar decorations for trim

Cook the wheat berries by bringing water to boil in a large pot, then adding the wheat berries, reducing the heat and simmering for about two hours.

Drain the wheat berries and mix in a large bowl with all the other ingredients EXCEPT the breadcrumbs and the icing sugar. Once it has cooled, arrange the mixture on a silver tray, so that it rises into a slight hill in the centre like an ancient burial mound.

Shortly before the service, cover this mound with a thin layer of toast crumbs, then a thick, smooth layer of the icing sugar (the crumbs prevent moisture from seeping through the powdered sugar in ugly wet splotches).

You can decorate the mound with the Jordan almonds (usually placed around the border and in the shape of a cross in the centre) or with a cross or leaves made of spun sugar, and sold at pastry shops for this purpose.

Long life to you.

Patsavouropita – 'Dina's Dishrag Pie'

This recipe is easy and fun – it is to pita as Rice Krispie Squares are to dessert. It's called 'dishrag pie' because it involves scrunching store-bought filo up into balls that resemble dishrags. You want to be careful when tossing around the term 'dishrag', however; it can also be used to refer to a lady who is not so skilled at the domestic arts, but has other more salacious talents. Another word of caution: this pita can't be made with homemade filo pastry (it's too thick), so don't get all ambitious and start rolling out your own. And it's rather oily – don't eat it if you don't want to leave tell-tale fingerprints anywhere.

500 grammes of shop-bought filo pastry
500 grammes feta cheese (in the US I have been known to
use half regular feta, half low-fat – not that Dina would
approve)
5 eggs
200 grammes melted butter
1 can soda water
Oil (to grease pan)

Preheat oven to 400 degrees Fahrenheit. Take one sheet
of filo pastry and grate a scattered, thin layer of feta
over it. (If you run out of feta, you can use other salted
cheeses instead – go crazy!) Fold the feta'd sheet in half
and then scrunch it up so it resembles a discarded
dishrag. Repeat with the other sheets of filo.

Place the scrunched-up pastry in an oiled casserole
dish, and pour the melted butter over, making sure it
gets stuck in all the crannies.

In a bowl, beat five eggs. Beat in one can of soda
water. (This will make the final product fluffy, more
like a soufflé than a pita. It is Dina's secret ingredient
– when people ask her for this recipe, she gives it to
them but leaves out the club soda. But I couldn't do
that to you, Dear Reader. My apologies to Dina.)

Pour this mixture on top, again so that it oozes into
all the folds of the dishrag blobs. Bake for an hour.
When it starts to brown slightly, lay a sheet of tinfoil
on top of the dish so that it won't burn – you can
remove it for the last five minutes or so to watch the
dish turn into golden brown goodness. When it is
brown and fluffy, remove from heat and serve.
Dishraglicious!

Fanouropita — *Get-Me-A-Man Cake*

Dina taught me how to make this cake in the hope that Agios Fanourios would find me a mate. It hasn't worked for me — yet — but my friend Anna has made the cake several times, then brought it to church to be blessed and left a piece of paper with the names of all her unmarried friends on it for the priest to read during the ceremony. And all the people on Anna's list have since got married. (Don't worry, the priest just reads the names and doesn't say what the supplicants are seeking — for all the church-goers know, you might be hunting for lost jewellery or asking for good health. Of course, churchgoing old Greek ladies are not stupid, so if you're young and single and they hear your name, they might suspect.)

You have to drop off the cake at a Greek church for this to work — if you bring it to the Unitarians they'll be very polite but have no idea what to do with it, besides serving it during the coffee hour. If you want to sidestep church altogether, you can simply distribute the cake to friends and family — but make sure that twelve different people eat it (twelve being a very important number, I'm guessing because of the Apostles).

Not to go too Kabbala on you, but speaking of numbers, this cake must have nine ingredients to work (nine being, like twelve, a multiple of three, the most important number of them all thanks to the Father, Son and Holy Ghost). So if you remove one, add a substitute (like, say, almonds instead of sultanas, which I've never liked anyway).

8 oz sugar
16 fl oz orange juice
2 lbs sifted self-raising flour (not plain flour or it won't
rise)
1 tsp vanilla extract
1 shot of cognac (like Metaxa)
8 fl oz oil
6 oz sultanas
6 oz chopped walnuts
1 tsp baking soda

Preheat oven to 350 degrees Fahrenheit. Beat sugar and oil together until creamy in texture and yellow in colour. Dissolve the baking soda into the orange juice and pour it into the sugar mixture (this is what makes the cake rise – it's science. Science, magic and religion in one tasty cake!). Mix in the vanilla extract, cognac and flour. Stir in the walnuts and sultanas. Bake for an hour, and while it's cooking, say a prayer for Agios Fanourios' mother, along the lines of, 'Dear Lord, please forgive the mother of Agios Fanourios for her wicked deeds and grant her peace.' Let the cake cool, then distribute or bring to church, but don't reveal what you're hoping to find (as if I didn't know!).

Because it contains no dairy products, *fanouropita* is also good for fasting during Lent (except on days when you can't have oil) and for the lactose-intolerant. Something to keep in mind if the man the saint nabs for you suffers from dairy issues. Happy hunting!

Greek Coffee Recipe

Any fool can make Greek Coffee (no, we don't call it Turkish coffee in this house). All you need are the right ingredients:

GREEK COFFEE: This is finely ground so that it is powdery as opposed to granular. It is to American coffee as icing sugar is to granulated sugar. The thitsas favour either Loumidis' Papagallo brand or Bravo, both of which you can get at Greek grocery shops, or online at sites such as www.greekgrocers.com.

ONE METAL BRIKI: This looks something like a beaker with a long handle, which lends a mad-scientist air to making coffee. Again, try a Greek shop or website.

SUGAR, if desired. NO MILK EVER.

FLITJANIS (cups) for serving. The thick plain white ones they use in *kafenions* look less sissy than the traditional French demi tasse, if you're worried about that sort of thing.

To make one cup of Greek coffee, fill one *flitjani* with water and dump it into the *briki*. For two cups, dump two *flitjanis* in – you see where I am going with this. You've probably thought of this already, but if you start with hot water, the coffee will be ready faster.

Add heaped teaspoons of coffee, one for each cup you're making.

Add sugar as desired. No sugar leaves your coffee *sketo*, plain. A scant teaspoon makes it *metrio*, medium. And a heaped teaspoon makes it *glyko*, sweet. If people get fancy on you and ask for it *me oligi*, they just want a little bit of sugar, like a pinch. Yes, this endeavour is full of subtleties. Do not try this at Starbucks.

Mix everything together with a spoon.

Place *briki* on a hot burner. Boil until the coffee rises and is about to overflow (but doesn't, because that would be a huge mess). Now remove the *briki* from the burner and pour the coffee into the waiting *flitjani*. Serve with a tall, cold glass of water.

For the advanced coffee-maker: once the coffee boils up, take the *briki* off the burner for a few seconds until it subsides, then put it back on until it starts to boil up again and you snatch it back off just in time. Repeat a couple of times. This will make for more *kamaki*, foam, on top of your cup, which is a good thing. And if there are bubbles in the foam, those represent eyes that are admiring you, which is even better.

Drink down to the mud at the bottom of the cup, but don't drink the mud, even in an attempt to look tough — no one does.

If you have the connections, secure a *flitjanou* to read your fortune in the grounds. She'll turn your cup over, make the sign of the cross on top of it (although this act is in no way sanctioned by the church, so don't be thinking it is), and let it dry as you all chat. Then she'll flip it back up and all your secrets will be revealed in the lacy patterns inside the cup. Good luck!

BIBLIOGRAPHY

Antoniades, Anne Gault. *The Anastenaria Thracian Firewalking Festival*. Athens: Thracian Archives, Society of Thracian Studies, No. 36, 1954.

Baker, D. S. comp., *Αρχαίες Ελληνικές Παροιμίες, Greek Proverbs*, Ελληνίκες Παροιμίες. Belfast: Appletree Press, 1998.

Dakaris, Sotirios. *The Nekyomanteion of the Acheron*. Athens: Ministry of Culture Archaeological Receipts Fund Direction of Publications, 2000.

Dalvin, Rae. *The Jews of Ioannina*. Philadelphia: Cadmus Press, 1990.

Danforth, Loring M. *Firewalking and Religious Healing: The Anastenaria of Greece and the American Firewalking Movement*. Princeton: Princeton University Press, 1989.

Δημητρίου, Σωτήρης. *Τους τα Λέει ο Θεός*. Athens: Εκδόσεις ΜΕΤΑΙΧΜΙΟ, 2002.

Economou, Steven G. *Greek Proverbs*, Volumes 1 and 2. Copyright: Steven G. Economou, 1976, 1978.

Gage, Nicholas. *A Place For Us*. Boston: Houghton Mifflin Company, 1989.

Gage, Nicholas. *Eleni*. New York: Ballantine, 1983.

Graves, Robert. *The Greek Myths*, Volume 1. London: Penguin Books, 1955, 1960.

Leigh Fermor, Patrick. *Roumeli: Travels in Northern Greece*. London: Penguin Books, 1983.

Megas, George. *Calendar Customs of Greece*. Athens: B. and M. Rhodis, 1963.

Παυλή–Κορρέ, Μαρία, και Σπανούλη, Ρίτα. *Τσιγγάνες: Μύθοι, Έθιμα, Παραδόσεις*. Athens: Εκδόσεις ΟΛΚΟΣ, 1991.

Plutarch, *The Age of Alexander: Nine Greek Lives*. Translated by Ian Scott-Kilver. London: Penguin Books, 1973.

Sakellariou, M. B., ed. *Greek Lands in History: Epirus, 4000 Years of Greek History and Civilization*. Athens: Ekdotike Athenon S.A., The Demetrius and Egle Botzaris Foundation, 1997.

Stoneman, Richard, ed. *A Literary Companion to Travel in Greece*. Malibu: The J. Paul Getty Museum, 1994.

INDEX